Words, Thoughts, and Theories

Alison Gopnik and Andrew N. Meltzoff

A Bradford Book
The MIT Press
Cambridge, Massachusetts
London, England

This book was set in Bembo by Asco Trade Typesetting Ltd., Hong Kong, and was printed and bound in the United States of America.

First printing, 1997.

Library of Congress Cataloging-in-Publication Data

Gopnik, Alison.
  Words, thoughts, and theories / Alison Gopnik and Andrew N. Meltzoff.
      p.   cm. — (Learning, development, and conceptual change)
  "A Bradford book."
  Includes bibliographical references and index.
  ISBN 0-262-07175-4 (hc : alk. paper)
  1. Cognition. 2. Cognition in children. 3. Psycholinguistics. 4. Philosophy and cognitive science. I. Meltzoff, Andrew N. II. Title. III. Series.
BF311.G63   1996
153—dc20   96-11804
                                                                          CIP

To the children, Alexei, Nicholas, Andres, and Kate, who inspired and created the theories, and to George and Pat, who inspired and created the children

Contents

8   The Darwinian Conclusion   211

Series Foreword

This series in learning, development, and conceptual change will include state-of-the-art reference works, seminal book-length monographs, and texts on the development of concepts and mental structures. It will span learning in all domains of knowledge, from syntax to geometry to the social world, and will be concerned with all phases of development, from infancy through adulthood.

The series intends to engage such fundamental questions as the following:

The nature and limits of learning and maturation The influence of the environment, of initial structures, and of maturational changes in the nervous system on human development; learnability theory; the problem of induction; domain-specific constraints on development

The nature of conceptual change Conceptual organization and conceptual change in child development, in the acquisition of expertise, and in the history of science

Lila Gleitman
Susan Carey
Elissa Newport
Elizabeth Spelke

Preface and Acknowledgments

Almost exactly twenty years ago, two extremely young and rather arrogant graduate students had their first lunch together in an Oxford dining hall. They remember very little about the food, though it was almost certainly terrible, or the surroundings, though they were almost certainly beautiful. They do both vividly remember the conversation, though. The younger (and somewhat more arrogant) of the two, who in those days was an evangelical Chomskyan, said she didn't think there was much point in reading Piaget, and the older (and somewhat wiser) replied that he thought actually Piaget was pretty interesting. The argument went on until dinnertime. The conversation they began that day has gone on ever since, across five cities, three countries, and two continents; by letter, phone, e-mail, and fax; to the successive accompaniment of babies cooing, toddlers pretending, schoolchildren multiplying, and teenagers playing hallway roller hockey. They are a bit grayer and more lined, and some of the sharp edges have been knocked off, but their youthful pleasure in just talking about this stuff has never diminished. This book is the latest installment of the talk, and we hope it will give other readers and talkers some of the same pleasure.

As we have grown older the conversation has widened to include colleagues, friends, teachers, and students around the globe, and we want to thank all these common and individual interlocutors. Our first Oxford conversation would never have taken place without Jerome Bruner. In fact, for fifty years or more he has been stimulating this kind of talk, and our lives, as well as the whole large conversation that is cognitive science, would not have been the same without him. This particular turn in the talk has also depended on Harry and Betty Stanton, who invited us to write for the MIT Press, and to Amy Pierce, our editor there. A number of our colleagues and friends read and commented on various drafts of the manuscript, and we are very grateful for their attention and time. They include Dan Slobin, John Heil, Carolyn Mervis, Simon Baron-Cohen, and Daniel Povinelli. Susan Gelman, John Campbell, and Liz Spelke also served as exceptionally acute, sensitive, and generous reviewers for the MIT Press—all authors should have such reviewers.

At this point we need to acknowledge our individual debts too, so Alison is now speaking rather than the authorial we. (Managing the first person has been an interesting challenge throughout this book.) I am exceptionally fortunate to spend my days in the psychology department at Berkeley. The exciting talk wafting through the corridors of Tolman Hall is the product of all its individual minds, but I particularly want to acknowledge my conversations with Dan Slobin, John Watson, Steve Palmer, Lucy Jacobs, and the late Irvin Rock, who have all contributed specifically to this book. Like many others, I also owe a special moral debt to Irv Rock for demonstrating how goodness and intelligence can be combined. My students here, I am happy to say, are just as great talkers as we were at Oxford, and the book has benefited from conversations with all of them, particularly Virginia Slaughter, Betty Repacholi, Therese Baumberger, Jennifer Esterly, Reyna Proman, Andrea Rosati, and Eric Schwitzgebel. The support of the National Science Foundation, grant no. DBS9213959, has been crucial.

Henry Wellman suggested that we write a chapter on the theory theory together, and that joint work was the source of much of the theoretical material in chapter 2. Rarely has writing a chapter been so fruitful! His comments and discussion have always been illuminating. I have tried to move back and forth between psychology and philosophy. Two philosophical mentors have helped enormously in allaying the anxieties of that amphibious project (I leave it to the reader to decide which is ocean and which dry land). John Campbell has constantly been a thoughtful and imaginative reader and correspondent, with an inimitable knack for coming up with precisely the point I was trying to get at myself and then coming up with brand new points I would never have gotten myself but that seem exactly right. Clark Glymour discussed almost everything in this book at one time or another by e-mail. He also read the sections on philosophy and science and gave me a terribly hard time about them. This is a much better book as a result and comes much closer to emulating his own intellectual seriousness and rigor, and I am grateful.

I spent my own childhood in constant conversation in the best setting for intellectual research I have ever known. My warmest gratitude and love goes to the directors of the Gopnik Academy, Irwin and Myrna, and to my colleagues there, Adam, Morgan, Hilary, Blake, and Melissa. It's conventional at this point to apologize to your children for neglecting them while you got your book written and to express your gratitude for the fact that they absented themselves during the process. The apology is in order, but for this particular book and these particular children, Alexei, Nicholas, and Andres Gopnik-Lewinski, the acknowledgement has to be a bit different. Without their constant presence, their conversation and company, without the example of their insatiable curiosity about the world and their genius in figuring it all out, this book could not have been written at all. Their father, George Lewinski, more than once changed his work so that I could pursue mine. Without him, I certainly could never have managed to produce such splendid children and at least a passably good book too. I am deeply grateful.

Andy thinks he won the argument that began in Oxford (this is Andy speaking now), but it's difficult to know. Alison's first child was born just when I was about to tell her the results of a critical test of theory and that trumped my words. In truth, it was the babies who changed our minds more than we've changed each others'. At the University of Washington I have been extremely fortunate to collaborate with Keith Moore, who himself has studied infants since the 1970s. His creative insights have deeply shaped my thinking about cognitive development. Keith and I have spent hours together in front of newborns, nose to nose with the only people who really *can* answer the question of what's innate. It's difficult to match the excitement we've shared in doing psychology with people whose eyes blinked open only a few hours previously. Also at the University of Washington was an extremely alluring speech scientist, Pat Kuhl, who became my wife in about the middle of this protracted conversation. Pat has regularly contributed terrific ideas, and she's kept me honest about perception, or has tried to anyway. Our daughter, Kate, is a magical child. She effortlessly and joyously does what this book struggles to explain. For the guidance of Julian Meltzoff, who first revealed to me the beauty of a good experiment, and Judith Meltzoff, who loved to read and talk, I am grateful.

We didn't need telescopes to study infants, but there were things to buy. The National Institute of Health (HD22514) provided generous support, as did the Center for Human Development and Disabilities and the Virginia Merrill Bloedel Hearing Center. I thank Craig Harris and Calle Fisher, who have helped in innumerable ways, from infant testing to reference checking. Finally, to a generation of scientists who taught us that babies could see, believe, desire, and intend, that they were good minds to consider when considering philosophical matters, I feel profoundly indebted. Without such work by others, this book would not have been written.

Words, Thoughts, and Theories

1

The Other Socratic Method

Socrates' Problem

About 2,400 years ago Socrates had a problem. The problem was how we could learn about something like virtue from our sensory experience. Socrates' problem is still unsolved. The difficulty is that we typically seem to have highly abstract and complex representations of the world. These range from mathematical to logical to causal knowledge, from our basic understanding of space, time, and objects to our equally basic understanding of our own minds and those of others. No one has ever been able to explain how we could derive these representations from the concrete and simple information of our senses. Rationalists from Socrates himself to Kant to Chomsky resolve this problem by claiming that the abstract structures are there all along. Empiricists from Aristotle to Hume to the connectionists either insist that we can get there from here if we just keep trying or, more skeptically, that there is no there to get to. That is, they end up denying that these abstract and complex representations really exist.

While the significance of Socrates' question has always been recognized, his method of answering it has not been. Socrates' method was to be a developmental psychologist. In Plato's *Meno* Socrates does not just use theoretical or conceptual arguments to bolster his view of knowledge as recollection. Instead, he conducts a developmental experiment. The anonymous slave boy plays as crucial a role in the argument as any of the aristocrats. Socrates poses a series of questions to the boy, questions intended to reveal his underlying knowledge. He asks the boy whether he believes a number of geometrical facts. When the boy answers "yes" to each question, Socrates concludes that the boy has the abstract representations in question, independent of education and experience. It is this empirical fact that anchors Socrates' arguments.

After 2,400 years of philosophical speculation Piaget tried Socrates' method again. Like Socrates, and for the same philosophical reasons, Piaget wanted to ask children whether they had the same knowledge as adults. But where Socrates' child always said "Yes, O Socrates," Piaget's children always said "Non, M. Piaget." Piaget's empirical work, like Socrates', was an attempt to find out whether children's abstract conceptual structures—their understandings of objects, minds, space, time, and numbers—were indeed the same as those of adults. But where Socrates saw only similarities, Piaget charted consistent differences. And Piaget drew the opposite conclusion. Most of the child's knowledge was radically different from adult knowledge, and that knowledge changed as the child interacted with the world. Therefore the changes in that knowledge must be due to the child's interaction with the world. Piaget attempted to construct a theoretical account of how these changes took place.

Of course, it is difficult to read the *Meno* without a sense that Socrates' questions are not as probing or accurate as we might wish; the "yes"es, we suspect, are imposed as much as they are detected (to be fair, this is, after all, Socrates' general technique with grown-ups too). More recently, Piaget's own ways of asking the questions have also been subject to criticism and revision. Recent empirical work in infancy and early childhood has led us to a very different view of when children say "yes" and when they say "no."

Moreover, this empirical work has led to the rejection of the central tenets of Piaget's theory: cognitive development does not depend on action, there are complex representations at birth, there are no far-reaching domain-general stage changes, young children are not always egocentric, and so on. This is not an indictment of Piaget. Fifty years is an impressive run for any theory, any really good substantive theory ought to be testable, and most really good substantive theories will eventually be overthrown by new empirical work.

One very prevalent reaction to the overthrow of the Piagetian picture has been a return to Socrates' own position. The many early "yes"es seem to indicate that Socrates was right after all, that powerful abstract representations are not derived from experience but are there all along. This reaction is not limited to developmental psychology but rather is part of the broader contemporary zeitgeist in philosophy and cognitive science. Piaget's theory was, after all, one of the more succesful attempts to explain how concrete sensory experience could lead to the development of abstract complex representations. If Piaget eventually failed to answer Socrates' question, the failure of accounts like classical learning theory or associationism was far more profound.

While this rush toward rationalism has been taking place, an alternative view has gradually been emerging in the developmental literature. The developmental picture is not, after all, simply that we now think children say "yes" when we used to think they said "no." The empirical research also confirms many of Piaget's examples of genuine conceptual change in children and has generated important new instances of such change. Children are still telling us that their knowledge of the world is radically different from our own (Flavell, 1982).

The theoretical position that is emerging to deal with these empirical facts is what we will call "the theory theory." The central idea of this theory is that the processes of cognitive development in children are similar to, indeed perhaps even identical with, the processes of cognitive development in scientists. Scientific theory change is, after all, one of the clearest examples we know of the derivation of genuinely new abstract and complex representations of the world from experience. The model of scientific change might begin to lead to answers to the developmental questions and, more broadly, might begin to answer Socrates' philosophical question.

This theoretical position has been advanced in a number of very different areas of cognitive development, including children's categorizations, their naive understanding of biology and physics, and their understanding of the mind (Carey, 1985, 1988; Karmiloff-Smith, 1988; Karmiloff-Smith & Inhelder, 1974; Gelman & Wellman, 1991; Gopnik & Wellman, 1992, 1994; Gopnik, 1984b, 1988a; Keil, 1989; Perner, 1991; Wellman, 1985, 1990; Wellman & Gelman, 1992). In each of these fields the theory theory has guided experimentation and provided explanations. Often, however, the invocation of the theory theory has seemed like little more than a helpful metaphor. It has not been clear exactly what the theory is supposed to claim or how it could be differentiated from other accounts. Our first aim in this book is to articulate this alternative theoretical position with as much detail and precision as we can and to show how it can generate specific predictions, predictions that are not made by other theories.

Almost all of the applications of the theory theory have involved older children, and sometimes older children who are explicitly learning scientific concepts. If the theory is supposed to answer Socrates' question, that is, to account for our general capacity to develop new knowledge, it should apply more generally and be true from the beginnings of life. In addition, infancy and early childhood are the periods in which there has been the greatest explosion of new research. So a second aim of this book is to apply the theory theory to explain what we know about infancy and very early childhood.

Augustine's Problem

About 1,700 years ago Augustine had another problem. How did we learn our first words? The philosophical difficulties behind this question parallel Socrates' difficulty. Given the highly arbitrary connections between words and the world, how could we settle so quickly on the right meanings? Like Socrates, Augustine thought the method for answering this question was to be a developmental psychologist. Also like Socrates, his experimental techniques were a bit shaky. He embarked on a retrospective analysis of his own childhood experience. His answer to the question is famous. Augustine reported that adults around him had pointed to objects and said their names and that he had therefore concluded that the names referred to the objects.

After 1,700 years of speculation, serious empirical investigation of this problem began only 20 years ago, with the rise of developmental psycholinguistics. A group of psycholinguists began looking at children's very early words in the mid 1970s (Bloom, 1973; Bowerman, 1978; Nelson, 1973). A landmark in this field was Lois Bloom's book *One word at a time* (1973). Bloom's book, a diary of her child's first words, was significant because it looked at those words with strikingly few theoretical preconceptions. To a remarkable degree Bloom let Allison, her daughter, speak for herself, charting the contexts in which various words appeared and inferring the child's meanings.

Looking at Allison Bloom's first words would have been a shock for Augustine and ought to be similarly shocking for various linguistic and psychological theories of meaning since then. None of the prevailing linguistic or psychological theories could predict the set of concepts that Allison chose to encode. Allison said things like "allgone," "there," "uh-oh," and "more," and she used these words in ways that were quite different from adult uses. She began using "more," for example, not as a comparative but as an expression of recurrence, a kind of déjà vu. She used the word "allgone" in a dizzying array of contexts: watching a bubble disappear, finishing a bottle of juice, searching for a nonexistent toy cow, encoding generalizations not encoded by any lexical form (including "gone") in the adult language. Allison did use names, as Augustine had predicted, but her uses of those names altered in interesting ways as she grew. At one point in her development she became "name crazy," not simply, as Augustine suggested, associating adult names with words but seeking out names for even the most obscure objects.

Allison Bloom's early words were not simply labels pasted on to convenient objects. Instead, they reflected a universe organized in sharply different ways than the universe of the adults around her. This was a universe in which the temporary disappearance of objects from sight, or the recurrence of an event, was deserving of a word all to itself, out of a linguistic repertoire that included a total of only about 15 words. Allison's early words could not have been learned as Augustine proposed. Allison's language said "no" to Augustine as loudly as the behavior of Piaget's children said "no" to Socrates.

Unlike Piaget's results, however, the divergent results about early language were not accompanied by any clear theoretical alternative. For 20 years the theoretical accounts of early word learning have made assumptions very similar to Augustine's, even if the details of the theory differed. Almost all of the many accounts of early meanings assumed that the child's first words were object names. Moreover, the rush toward rationalism has, of course, been more pervasive in developmental psycholinguistics than even in cognitive development. A mix of Chomsky and Augustine has become the prevailing account of very early language. On this view, even before they have any experience of language, children assume that the first words refer to objects, in the same way that adult names refer to objects (see, for example, Gentner, 1982; Markman, 1989). This is part of a more general view that assumes strong continuities between the semantic structures of adults and children and that provides a rationalist account of semantic development. On this view, there are strong constraints on the possible thoughts we can think and the possible meanings we can express (Pinker, 1989). Allison Bloom's early "relational words" remained as a sort of needling anomaly to this theoretical consensus. Allison's early words were not all object names, and they were very unlike the meanings encoded in the adult language.

A third purpose of this book is to show that the answer we will propose to Socrates' question is also an answer to Augustine's question, and an answer that can explain the empirical facts about early meanings that were discovered by developmental psycholinguists. Thinking of cognitive development as theory change also gives us a new and better way of thinking about semantic development. The shock, for us ordinary adults, of trying to understand Allison's universe and the language she used to describe it should be a familiar sensation. It is, we will suggest, similar to the shock of trying to understand developments in science. Like Allison's thought and language, scientific thought and language force us to rethink what appear to be fundamental, commonsense, conceptual distinctions. Conceptions of the world, theories, that violate these fundamental conceptual structures, that mix space and time, matter and energy, turn out to be not only possible but true. Given this fact, philosophical and psychological views of meaning that rest on assumptions about fundamental limitations on possible conceptual structures ought to seem suspect.

One way of putting this is to say that Allison's early linguistic development depended on and reflected her cognitive development. This is an old, indeed hoary, claim. But the claim we will make is much more focused and specific than this general position. It is not that every linguistic development, or even every semantic development, reflects some general change in cognitive stage. Rather specific semantic developments are intimately related to the development of particular conceptual understandings, and these understandings can be construed as theories. As in the scientific case, the specific words that Allison and her fellow children choose to use are deeply related to the children's particular developing theories of the world. The child's conceptual structures help determine the child's early meanings. We will argue that the evidence of early language supports the theory theory and that the theory theory can help to explain the nature of early language.

The fourth purpose of the book is to suggest that there may, in fact, be an even stronger relation between language and cognition than this. Allison was born into a community that had already developed a theory of the physical and social world, a theory reflected in their own language and semantic structure. As in science, much of the motivation for theory formation is internal: it is an attempt to explain counterevidence, make good predictions, and so on. In addition, however, language itself may play a major role in theory change, as it does in science.

One way of putting this is to say that cognitive development depends on language development, an almost equally hoary claim. In particular, many versions of the claim that language influences thought imply that conceptual and semantic structures are somehow merely conventional. That is, children internalize the linguistic structures given in their community independently of the role of those structures in organizing or explaining experience.

We will argue that language influences cognition in quite a different way. We will suggest that the adult language is another source of information, admittedly a particularly important one, that the child uses in theory construction. On this view, the child treats the adult language as another source of information about the structure of the world, along with her own experience. While the child is inferring the structure of the outside world, she is also untangling the structure of language itself, and she may use solutions in one area as clues to solutions in the other.

A Road Map

So here is the overall picture. Very young children just beginning to talk are engaged in profound restructurings of several domains of their knowledge. These restructurings are analogous to theory changes. The children's early semantic development is closely tied to these theory changes. This relation goes in both directions. The child's cognitive concerns shape and motivate her use of early words. At the same time her attention to the linguistic system itself may reshape her cognition.

In the first part of this book we will try to flesh out the theory theory. We will demonstrate that this is a coherent and even plausible idea conceptually, and we will differentiate it from other current theories of cognitive development. Much of this part will be quite philosophical.

In the second part of the book we will apply the theory theory to the specific case of cognitive and semantic development in infants and very young children. We will sketch a tentative account of the succession of theories and theory changes in three important domains—the understanding of appearances, the understanding of actions, and the understanding of kinds—from birth to about age three. We will focus on the changes in children's problem solving and language that occur at about 18 months. We will argue that these changes can be fruitfully considered to be theory changes, and we will present both linguistic and behavioral evidence to support this view.

In the third part of the book we will consider the implications of the theory theory for broader questions about language and thought. In chapter 7 we will present evidence suggesting that children's early words consistently encode concepts that reflect theory changes and that may be quite different from the concepts encoded in the adult language. Our strongest evidence comes from empirical relationships between specific emerging problem-solving abilities and specific related semantic developments. All this evidence suggests that children's very particular conceptual discoveries play an important role in shaping their early language.

Another line of evidence and argument is relevant to our claim that linguistic input may itself structure conceptual change and discovery. The primary evidence for this claim comes from cross-linguistic studies and studies of individual differences in input. These findings suggest that there is a bidirectional interaction between semantic and conceptual development. Children's early meanings are a joint product of their own cognitive concerns and the cognitive structures already developed by adults.

Finally, in the last chapter we will concentrate on some of the consequences of these views for more general accounts of cognition and meaning in cognitive science and philosophy. We suggest that this evidence supports a version of what is sometimes called semantic holism. More generally, we argue that if the theory theory is correct, we should revise some of the basic asumptions of cognitive science. Cognitive science has focused on an attempt to give a general account of the representations and rules that constitute our adult knowledge of the world. We suggest instead that cognitive science should focus on the dynamic processes by which these rules and representations can be transformed. This chapter too will be quite philosophical.

We have every hope and expectation that this book will leave the reader with the impression that we are simply fascinated by infants and toddlers. When we see small children in the room, even at a dinner party like Meno's, we are unable to resist talking to them. However, the motivation for our research goes beyond this fascination. Ultimately, our reason for watching and talking to children is the same as Socrates'. The most central questions in cognitive science are questions that only they can answer.

I

The Theory Theory

In this book we will argue that children's conceptual structures, like scientists', are theories, that their conceptual development is theory formation and change, and that their semantic development is theory-dependent. In the next two chapters we will elaborate and defend this claim in general terms, and then we will consider specific cases in succeeding chapters. The best argument for any empirical claim is, of course, the data. However, in the case of the theory theory, a number of prima facie objections to the idea might be made. So we will begin by dealing with some of these objections, clarifying just what the theory theory is claiming, and differentiating it from other theories. We first want to show what the idea is, and that the idea is at least plausible, before we try to show that it is true.

2

The Scientist as Child

But Surely It Can't Really Be a Theory?

The claim that children construct theories is often greeted by scientists, philosophers, and psychologists with shocked incredulity. Surely, they cry, you can't really mean that mere children construct theories, not real theories, the kind of theories that we—that is, we serious, grown-up scientists, philosophers, and psychologists—construct with so much sweat and tears. Injured *amour propre* aside, these foes of the theory theory point to a number of differences between children and scientists. Scientists are supposed to be consciously, in fact, self-consciously, reflective about their theory-forming and theory-confirming activities. They talk about them, and they are part of the scientific stream of consciousness. Only a few adult humans become scientists (there is a division of labor), and they only do science part of the time. They do so in a structured institutional setting in which there is much formal interaction with other scientists. Scientific theory change takes place within the scientific community, and a single change may take many years to be completed.

Obviously, none of these things is true of children. For example, 18-month-olds don't talk about the fact that they are formulating or evaluating theories, and they certainly don't publish journal articles, present conference papers, attend seminars, or attempt to torpedo the reputations of those who disagree with them. All children develop theories. Conceptual change in children takes place within a single individual and takes place relatively quickly: children may develop and replace many theories in the space of a few months or years. Insofar as these particular types of phenomenology and sociology are an important part of theory formation and change in science, whatever the children are doing is not science. Given these plain differences, we might ask whether the idea that children form theories is anything more than a vague metaphor. For the theory theory to be more than just a metaphor, there has to be some interesting, substantive *cognitive* characterization of science, independent of phenomenology and sociology. Is it plausible that science has this kind of cognitive foundation and that it is similar to the cognitive processes we see in children?

We might imagine that we could turn to the philosophy of science for a simple answer to this question. But philosophers of science have really only begun to consider the question themselves. Historically, the philosophy of science has been riven by conflicts between two very different traditions. One tradition has seen philosophy of science as a normative enterprise. Its job is to prescribe ways in which scientists can do things that will lead to the truth. Classically, many philosophers of science identified the actual practice of scientists with this normative project: they assumed that at least most scientists most of the time did what they self-consciously calculated as most likely to lead to the truth. (Philip Kitcher [1993] has recently called this view "Legend.") Moreover, for many philosophers of science in this tradition, the normative project was seen as an essentially logical or mathematical one. Just as formal, deductive logic gave us a way of guaranteeing the truth of certain types of inferences, so we might be able to construct a logic that would guarantee the truth of scientific inferences. (Some of the classic references in this tradition include Hempel, 1965; Nagel, 1961; and Popper, 1965.)

This tradition was notoriously challenged by an alternative view, starting with Thomas Kuhn (1962). Philosophers of science who looked in some historical detail at the actual practices of scientists found a rather different picture than the picture of Legend. The actual practice of science was often characterized by deep divides between proponents of different theories and was highly influenced by apparently accidental sociological facts, such as the professional power of proponents of particular ideas. This view led, in some circles, to the position that there was little relation between the actual practice of science and the normative project of finding the truth. In its most extreme form (e.g., Feyerabend, 1975), this school suggested that sociology was all there was to science, that there was, in fact, no truth to find.

These historical facts led to a standard view in the philosophy of science in which cognitive and psychological factors played little role.

The view is still prevalent. It emphasizes the sociological institutions of science, on the one hand, and on the other hand, the logical structure of explicit, self-conscious scientific reasoning, or rather, of scientific reasoning as normatively reconstructed by philosophers of science.

A Cognitive View of Science

What might an alternative cognitive view of science be like? Science is cognitive almost by definition, insofar as cognition is about how minds arrive at veridical conceptions of the world. In one sense, scientists *must* be using some cognitive abilities to produce new scientific theories and to recognize their truth when they are produced by others. Scientists have the same brains as other human beings, and they use those brains, however assisted by culture, to develop knowledge about the world. Ultimately, the sociology of science must consist of a set of individual decisions by individual humans to produce or accept theories. Scientists converge, however painfully and slowly, on a single set of decisions. The view that is the consequence of these decisions converges on the truth about the world. Scientists must be using human cognitive capacities to do this. What else could they be using?

The assumption of cognitive science is that human beings are endowed by evolution with a wide variety of devices—some quite substantive and domain-specific, others much more general and multipurpose—that enable us to arrive at a roughly veridical view of the world. Usually in cognitive science we think of these devices in terms of representations of the world and rules that operate on those representations. At any given time people have some set of representations and rules that operate on these representations. Over time, there are other cognitive processes that transform both representations and rules. Representations and rules may not have any special phenomenological mark; we may not know that we have them, though sometimes we do. They may be, and often are, deeply influenced by information that comes from other people, and they allow us to communicate with others who have similar representations and rules. Nevertheless, they are not merely conventional, and they could function outside of any social community.

We might think of science in terms of such an abstract system of representations and rules. The question that we would ask, then, is whether there are any generalizations to be made about the kinds of

representations and rules that underlie scientific knowledge and the kinds
of processes that transform those representations and rules over time. Is
there anything distinctive or special about scientific representations and
rules, anything that differentiates them from other possible cognitive
structures? Moreover, does the epistemological force of science, its ability to get things right, come from the nature of these representations
and rules or from some feature of reflective phenomenology or social
institutionalization?

A further question, then, would be whether these representations
and rules are similar, or indeed identical, to those we observe in children,
and whether changes in these rules and representations are like the
changes we see in cognitive development. This might be true even if
the phenomenology and social organization of knowledge in children
and scientists are quite different. And it might be particularly likely to be
true if, in fact, the specific phenomenology and sociology of science are
not a necessary condition for its epistemological force.

These seem to us like straightforward and important questions. It
might, of course, turn out that there is, in fact, no distinctive or interesting characterization of the representations and rules that underlie
scientific knowledge. The formation and confirmation of scientific representations might be completely unconstrained, the result of some
whimsical process of "genius" or "insight." It might be that the phenomenology and sociology of science really do the interesting work. It
might turn out that there is little relationship between the representations and rules of scientists and those of children. Is it worth trying to
find out if there is such a relationship? The detailed empirical work is
what we will ultimately have to turn to, but the project is, we think,
more plausible and promising than it might seem on the standard view.
A cognitive view of science, and in particular, a view that identifies cognitive change in science and childhood, might provide at least a partial
explanation of the most important thing about science, namely that it
gets things right. In contrast, it is difficult to see how the phenomenological and sociological features of science could explain its epistemological potency.

Recent work in the philosophy of science presents a dilemna.
Science is an activity that is performed by human beings in a social context and that proceeds in various and haphazard ways. But it nevertheless manifests a kind of logic and converges on a truthful account of

the world. The sociologists of science typically say to the logicians, "But how does this abstract structure for finding truth relate to what real scientists actually do?" and the logicians reply, "But how could the mess of what scientists really do ever lead to the truth?"

A cognitive view of science might provide a useful middle ground, even a bridge, between logical and sociological views of science. It might indeed be true that particular kinds of abstract logical structures characterized the important cognitive achievements of science. And it might also be true that in looking at the practice of actual science, the real maelstrom of human beings, we see rather little of that abstract logical structure. But this is quite similar to other cases of cognitive science, from perception to decision making to parsing to problem solving. Human beings quite typically acquire knowledge in a way that leads at least approximately to the truth but that also may produce errors or incoherencies, that is grounded in a social life but not socially arbitrary. Quite typically, underlying any human cognitive activity is an abstract structure that is not at all apparent in superficial phenomenology or practice.

A cognitive scientist would say that evolution constructed truth-finding cognitive processes. On this view, science and our ordinary practices of explanation, inference, prediction, and causal attribution, in which science is grounded, reflect a particularly powerful set of these cognitive abilities. Science uses a set of representations and rules particularly well suited to uncovering facts about the world. Science gets it right because it uses psychological devices that were designed by evolution precisely to get things right.

As well as providing a new way of thinking about the descriptive questions, cognitive science might also contribute a new way of thinking about the normative project. Cognitive science might ask what sort of device could be constructed, with what rules and representations, that could find out about the world in the way that science does (see, for example, Langley et al., 1987). Such a device need not, of course, work in exactly the same way that human scientists do. Maybe many human cognitive procedures are inefficient or misleading. It seems plausible, though, that developing a cognitive view of science would interact with this normative project in interesting ways, just as artificial intelligence has interacted with cognitive psychology in cognitive science. If we want to build a device that can do science, or if we want to understand how doing science is logically possible, it would seem sensible to look at how humans do it, since they are the only successful scientific creatures we know of. On the other hand, knowing something about how it could be done is likely to inform our guesses about how evolution actually did it.

Naturalistic Epistemology and Development: An Evolutionary Speculation

The idea that science is related to our ordinary cognition and that both science and ordinary cognition work for evolutionary reasons is not, of course, new. It is the basic idea behind the "naturalistic epistemology" of Quine and others (Quine & Ullian, 1970; Goldman, 1986; Kornblith, 1985). We want to propose, however, a specific version of the naturalistic-epistemology story. This view also might be a reason for supposing that the structures of science are particularly likely to be similar to those involved in cognitive development. On this view, there might actually be a closer link between science and childhood cognition than between science and our usual adult cognitive endeavors.

Let's go back for a minute to the basic idea of cognitive science. We are endowed by evolution with devices for constructing and manipulating rules and representations, and these devices give us a veridical view of the world. Here is an interesting evolutionary puzzle: Where did the particularly powerful and flexible cognitive devices of science come from? After all, we have only been doing science in an organized way for the last 500 years or so; presumably they didn't evolve so that we could do that. We suggest that many of these cognitive devices are involved in the staggering amount of learning that goes on in infancy and childhood. Indeed, we might tell the evolutionary story that these devices evolved to allow human children, in particular, to learn.

A number of writers have recently suggested proposals for an evolutionary account of cognition (Barkow, Cosmides & Tooby, 1992). The view that cognition evolved has been associated with a particular strongly modular and nativist account of cognition. There is, however, no reason to identify the general claim that evolution is responsible for cognitive structure with a modular view. Moreover, the evolutionary arguments for these claims are typically extremely weak. They simply consist of the speculation that a particular trait might have been helpful to an organism in an environment, in fact, in a hypothetical past environment for which we have almost no evidence. None of the kinds of evidence typically required to support evolutionary arguments are advanced. For example, there are no comparisons of closely related species in different environmental niches or of distantly related species in similar niches, no studies of differential reproduction or survival with or without the trait, no hard empirical evidence of the heritability of the trait.

Ironically, moreover, these accounts actually contradict one of the most firmly established findings in other areas of evolutionary psychology, a finding supported by such comparative studies. Several distinctive traits are found to correlate with large relative cortical size across a wide range of species, including birds and mammals. Moreover, they are also correlated within variants of closely related species. The traits include variation of diet, polygamy, small clutch size, and, most significant for our case, the relative lack of precocious specialized abilities in the young, that is, a period of long immaturity (see, e.g., Bennett & Harvey, 1985).

Passing quickly over polygamy, we find that human beings are at the extreme end of the distributions of all these other traits, and also of relative cortical size. A serious evolutionary hypothesis about human beings would oppose the idea that human babies have highly specialized innate cognitive structures and instead favor the idea that they have more multipurpose and flexible learning capacities, which they employ during the period of protected immaturity.

From an evolutionary point of view, three of the most distinctive features of human beings are their long, protected immaturity, the plasticity of their behavior, and their ability to adapt to an extremely wide variety of environments. Equipping human children with particularly powerful and flexible cognitive devices might be an important part of this picture. Indeed, we might think of childhood as a period when many of the requirements for survival are suspended so that children can concentrate on acquiring a veridical picture of the particular physical and social world in which they find themselves (Bruner, 1974). Once they know where they are, as it were, they can figure out what to do. These devices operate in, and indeed, may often assume, a social context. We are social animals in general, and children, in particular, depend on a social world both for their survival and for much of the information they will use in theory construction. On this view, we might think of infancy as a sort of extended stay in a center for advanced studies, with even better food-delivery systems.

Science as Horticulture

It is an interesting empirical question as to how much of this epistemological activity survives in ordinary adult life. Perhaps not much. Once, as children, we have engaged in the theorizing necessary to specify the features of our world, most of us most of the time may simply go on to the central evolutionary business of feeding and reproducing. But, we suggest, these powerful theorizing abilities continue to allow all of us some of the time and some of us, namely professional scientists, much of the time to continue to discover more and more about the world around us.

On this view, we could think of organized science as a special cultural practice that puts these cognitive capacities to use to solve new kinds of problems, problems that go beyond the fundamental problems we all solve in the first 10 years or so of life. This very fact almost certainly means that scientists will face problems and find solutions that we will not see in childhood. For example, it is characteristic of the child's problems that the evidence necessary to solve them is very easily and widely available, within crawling distance anyway. It is characteristic of scientific problems that the evidence necessary to solve them is rather difficult to obtain. Formal science quite characteristically applies cognitive processes to things that are too big or too small, too rare or too distant, for normal perception to provide rich evidence. Children, in contrast, typically make up theories about objects that are perceptible, middle-sized, common, and close (including, of course, people). This fact about science raises special problems and leads to special solutions. Often these solutions involve particular social institutions.

Moreover, scientists may themselves add to or even revise their theory forming and testing procedures in the light of further experience (though most likely at least older children do the same). For example, evolution may not have given us very good techniques for dealing with probabilistic information (see Kahneman, Slovic & Tversky, 1982) and we may have to invent cognitive prostheses like statistics to do so. Our hypothesis, however, is that the most central parts of the scientific enterprise, the basic apparatus of explanation, prediction, causal attribution, theory formation and testing, and so forth, is not a relatively late cultural invention but is instead a basic part of our evolutionary endowment.

We might think of formal science as a sort of cognitive horticulture. Horticulturalists take basic natural processes of species change—mutation, inheritance, and selection—and put them to work to serve very particular cultural and social ends in a very particular cultural and social setting. In the sixteenth century horticulturalists bred roses to look like sixteenth century women (like the alba rose Cuisse d'une Nymphe Emue), in the mid twentieth century horticulturalists bred roses to look like mid twentieth century cars (like the hybrid tea rose Chrysler Imperial), and in the late twentieth century horticulturalists bred roses to look like pictures of sixteenth-century roses (like the English rose Portia). In one sense, an explanation of the genesis of these flowers will involve extraordinarily complex and contingent cultural facts. But in another sense, the basic facts of mutation, inheritance, and selection are the same in all these cases, and at a deeper level, it is these facts that explain why the flowers have the traits they do.

In the same way, we can think of organized science as taking natural mechanisms of conceptual change, designed to facilitate learning in childhood, and putting them to use in a culturally organized way. To explain scientific theory change, we may need to talk about culture and society, but we will miss something important if we fail to see the link to natural learning mechanisms.

There is an additional point to this metaphor. Clearly, horticulture was for a long time the most vivid and immediate example of species change around. And yet precisely because it was so deeply embedded in cultural and social practices, it seemed irrelevant to the scientific project of explaining the origin of species naturalistically. It was only when Darwin and then Mendel pointed out the underlying similarities between "artificial" and natural species change that these common natural mechanisms became apparent. Similarly, science has been the most vivid and immediate example of conceptual change around (particularly since most philosophers hang out with scientists more than with children). Its cultural and social features have distracted us from looking at it in naturalistic terms. Looking at the similarities between conceptual change in children and conceptual change in science may similarly yield common natural mechanisms.

Objections: Phenomenology

With this cognitive perspective in mind, we can turn back to the real differences between scientists and children. Do these differences undermine the idea that there are deep cognitive similarities between the two groups?

Take the question of phenomenological differences first. Scientists appear to be more consciously reflective about their theorizing than children. But it is difficult to see, on the face of it, why conscious phenomenology of a particular kind would play an essential role in finding things out about the world. A characteristic lesson of the cognitive revolution is that human beings (or for that matter, machines) can perform extremely complex feats of information processing without any phenomenology at all. It is rather characteristic of human cognition that it is largely inaccessible to conscious reflection. There are various speculations we might offer about the role of consciousness in cognition. At the moment, however, we must be more impressed by how little relation there seems to be between cognition and consciousness, rather than by how much. Why should this be different in the case of scientific knowledge?

Moreover, the actual degree of conscious reflection in real science is very unclear. When asked about the stream of consciousness that accompanied his work, Jerry Fodor is alleged to have replied that it mostly said, "Come on, Jerry. That's it, Jerry. You can do it," and this seems reasonably true of much scientific experience. Certainly if we accept, say, Kepler's (1992) writings as a sample of his stream of consciousness, it seems unlikely that we would want to take such a stream as a direct representation of the cognitive processes involved in Kepler's theory construction. Indeed, scientists' own accounts of their theorizing activities are often met with indignant dismay by philosophers of science.

It is true that scientists articulate their beliefs about the world or about their fields of scientific endeavor. So do children, as we will see. But scientists do not typically articulate the processes that generate those beliefs or that lead them to accept them, nor are they very reliable when they do. The reflective processes are really the result of after-the-fact reconstructions by philosophers of science. If it's not very likely that scientists' phenomenology is a prerequisite for scientific success, it is far less likely that philosophers' phenomenology is.

Of course, scientists may sometimes do philosophy of science. They may, from time to time, be reflective about their own activities and try to work out the structure of the largely unconscious processes that actually lead them to form or accept theories. When scientists engage in this work, they seem to us more like (rather narcissistic) developmental psychologists than children themselves. Moreover, there may be circumstances in which this kind of deliberative self-reflection on their own theorizing practices is a real advantage to scientists, given the particular kinds of problems they face. However, it seems, at least, much too strong to say that such self-reflection is a necessary condition for theory formation and change in science. It seems unlikely that the reflective phenomenology itself is what gives scientists their theorizing capacities or gives the theories their epistemological force.

Finally, it is also not clear that children's phenomenology is radically different from that of adult scientists. The conventional wisdom, or if you prefer, the conventional rhetoric, is to say that children's theories and theory construction must be "implicit" rather than explicit. It is true that young children have a much more limited ability to report their phenomenology than scientists do. But all this means is that we simply don't know very well what their phenomenology is like. We work with very young, barely linguistic infants, and we can't help but be struck by how similar their expressive behavior is to the behavior we normally associate with scientists. Developmentalists are familiar with a characteristic sequence of furrowed brow, intense stare, and bodily stillness, followed by a sudden smile, a delighted glance at the experimenter, and an expression of self-satisfaction verging on smugness as the infant works out the solution. We don't know precisely what sort of internal phenomenology accompanies these expressions, but it seems at least plausible to us that some of what it is like to be an infant with an object-permanence problem is not, after all, so different from what it is like to be a scientist. Certainly, we suspect that the Fodorian stream of consciousness ("What the hell? Damn, this is hard! Hold on a sec. Jeez, I've got it. Boy, am I smart!") is pretty similar in the two cases. In short, there is little indication that particular types of phenomenology, types not shared by scientists and children, are necessary for theory formation or theory change.

Objections: Sociology

The sociological objections prompt similar replies. The socially oriented view of philosophy of science that developed in reaction to the normative view has always had a difficult time explaining how science gets it right at all. Some of its advocates deal with this problem by simply denying that science does get it right or that there is anything to get right. But if we refuse to take this route and instead espouse some form of scientific realism, then the problem remains and is a very serious one indeed.

Moreover, just as the phenomenological differences between scientists and children may be exaggerated, so may the sociological ones. We suggested that scientists may be less phenomenologically reflective than the usual view would hold. We also suggest that children are less isolated than the term "little scientist" is likely to imply. One of the points of our empirical work will be that children, no less than scientists, develop their understanding of the world in the context of a society that already has much knowledge of the world. They live in a rich social structure with much opportunity for contradiction, instruction, and the linguistic transmission of information. We are dealing with a contrast not between a nonsocial process and a social one but between two different types of social organization. Do these different types of social organization invalidate the analogy?

The most striking sociological difference between children and scientists, the division of labor and the resulting complex system of hierarchical social structure, has more to do with the kinds of problems children and scientists approach than with the processes they use to solve them. We mentioned that scientists typically approach problems where evidence is quite limited. The paucity of evidence leads to the division of labor and to many of the technological and sociological institutions characteristic of science. All you need is a mother and some mixing bowls to find evidence of the spatial properties of objects. To find evidence of Higg's boson you need, quite literally, an act of Congress. When evidence gathering becomes this fragmented, complex social relations become more important, and the whole process of finding the truth becomes drastically slower. (Philip Kitcher has described some interesting examples of exactly how particular social institutions and particular conventions of deference and trust might meet these particular cognitive problems [Kitcher, 1993]).

It is worth noting that the sociological institutions of science have shifted in the direction of increasing specialization and institutional-ization as the problems of science have become more evidentially in-tractable. The institutional arrangements of Kepler or Newton or even Darwin were very different from those of contemporary scientists, and these earlier scientists were typically much broader in their range of em-pirical interests. However, it seems difficult to argue that the basic theo-rizing capacities of current scientists are strikingly superior to those of Kepler or Newton, in spite of the large differences in social organization.

It's easy to see how the division of labor could result from the need for various kinds of evidence and how that structure could lead to par-ticular distinctive problems and patterns of timing in scientific change. What is extremely hard to see is how the hierarchy could lead to the truth or how the division of labor could itself lead to theory formation and confirmation. The division of labor is one consequence of the dif-ferent problems children and scientists tackle, and maybe it gives scien-tists an advantage in solving those particular problems. However, this does not imply that the cognitive resources they use to tackle those problems are different.

Moreover, in other respects the child's sociological organization may actually be superior to the scientist's for cognitive purposes. Infants and children have infinite leisure, there are no other demands on their time and energy, they are free to explore the cognitive problems relevant to them almost all the time. They also have a community of adults who, one way or another, are designed to act in ways that further the children's cognitive progress (if only to keep them quiet and occupied). Finally, this community already holds many of the tenets of the theory that the child will converge on and has an interest in passing on infor-mation relevant to the theory to the child.

In fact, we might argue that much of the social structure of science is an attempt to replicate the privileged sociological conditions of in-fancy. Aside from the division of labor, the social hierarchy largely determines who will get the leisure and equipment to do cognitive work and who other scientists should listen to. The infant solves these prob-lems without needing elaborate social arrangements. These are all differ-ences between children and scientists, but again, they do not necessarily

imply differences in the fundamental cognitive processes that the two
groups employ.

Objections: Timing and Convergence

Another difference we might point to between children and scientists
is that children converge on roughly similar theories at roughly similar
times. It might be objected that scientists do not always show this sort of
uniform development, and that this weighs against the theory-formation
view. The theory theory proposes that there are powerful cognitive
processes that revise existing theories in response to evidence. If cognitive agents begin with the same initial theory, try to solve the same
problems, and are presented with similar patterns of evidence over the
same period of time, they should converge on the same theories at about
the same time. These assumptions are very likely to be true for very
young children developing the kind of ordinary, everyday knowledge
we will discuss in this book. The children will certainly start with the
same initial theory and the same theorizing capacities. Moreover, the
evidence is ubiquitous and is likely to be very similar for all children.
Children the world over may develop similar representations at similar
times because the representations are innate and they mature at the same
rate, or they may converge on the same representations because the
crucial evidence is universally the same and so are children's theorizing
capacities.

Notice, however, that for scientists, these basic assumptions are not
usually going to be true. The assumption of common initial theories and
common patterns of evidence does not usually hold. In science, the relevant evidence, far from being ubiquitous, is rare and difficult to come
by and often must be taken on trust from others. The social mechanisms
of deference, authority, and trust are, like all social mechanisms, highly
variable. Moreover, different scientists also often begin with different
theories and quite typically approach different problems.

In fact, when the assumption of common initial theories and common patterns of evidence, presented in the same sequence, does hold,
scientists, like children, do converge on a common account of the world.
Indeed, even the timing of scientific discoveries is often strikingly similar
when there are independent labs working on the same problem with
a similar initial theory and similar access to evidence (hence all those

shared Nobel prizes). This convergence to the truth itself is the best reason for thinking that some general cognitive structures are at work in scientific-theory change. Scientists working independently converge on similar accounts at similar times, not because evolutionary theory or the calculus or the structure of DNA (to take some famous examples) are innate, but because similar minds approaching similar problems are presented with similar patterns of evidence. The theory theory proposes that the cognitive processes that lead to this convergence in science are also operating in children.

Objections: Magic

So far we have been focusing on apparent differences between children and scientists and trying to show that they do not invalidate the thesis that common cognitive processes are involved in the two enterprises. We might make a different kind of objection. Consider the following three examples of "explanation."

Francis Bacon is trying to refute Galileo's claim that Jupiter has moons. "There are seven windows given to animals in the domicile of the head, through which the air is admitted to the tabernacle of the body, to enlighten, to warm and to nourish it. What are these parts of the microcosmos: two nostrils, two eyes, two ears and a mouth. So in the heavens, as in a macrocosmos, there are two favourable stars, two unpropitious, two luminaries and Mercury undecided and indifferent. From this and from many other similarities in nature, such as the seven metals, etc., which it were tedious to enumerate, we gather that the number of the planets is necessarily seven" (Warhaft, 1965).

Hapiya, a Zuni Indian is explaining his family history. "One day we were eating when two snakes came towards us right together.... They stand up, start fighting. They was all tangled up, fall down, stand up, tangled up, fall down. We was watching them there; we was interested in watching them. Our grandpa came along on the west side and saw snake tracks. Grandpa got mad, he scold us. 'You should have killed them instead of watching' is what he told us.... 'That's danger, too, someday your family will disappear,' that's what he told us. And it really did, too. About four years later, all my folks disappeared. I was the only one that got left. You know, I got no sister, no brother, nothing. I'm the only one I've got left" (Tedlock, 1992).

Alexei, aged four, is talking to himself, trying to understand where babies come from (the Mommy part is easy). "But what does the Daddy do? He uses his penis. [Takes down his trousers and contemplatively wiggles his own back and forth, observing it attentively.] A penis, . . . a pencil, . . . a pencil, . . . a penis, . . . a pencil. [Looks up brightly.] The Daddy uses his penis to draw the baby!"

Faced with these examples of human reasoning, the theory theorist might well be expected to despair. In all three cases we see rather similar kinds of thinking. All three clearly involve deference: central claims in each argument come from authorities rather than experience. In all three there are loose perceptual associations between the premises and conclusion rather than any kind of inference (stars are like parts of the body; the intimate conflict of the snakes is like family conflict; a penis looks [and sounds] like a pencil).

But there is another thing that these examples all have in common, and the last case of Alexei's reasoning brings it out particularly vividly. In all three cases the speakers have no sources of evidence that are relevant to the claims they make. The kind of reasoning Alexei produced is ubiquitous in young children when they answer questions about phenomena of which they are utterly ignorant: Where do babies come from? Why does it get dark at night? Why does the winter come? In fact, these kinds of examples led Piaget to think that young children are intrinsically incapable of logical or causal inference. In similar ways, anthropologists and historians sometimes suggest that people in other places or at other times are fundamentally irrational and certainly very far from possesing the inferential capacities of scientists.

The empirical facts about 4-year-olds, however, show that Piaget was wrong. Suppose instead of asking Alexei about how babies are made, we asked him to explain how his tricycle works or why his friend dragged the stool over to the high cupboard. In these cases he and other 4-year-olds will give a perfectly well-formed causal explanation ("I put my foot on the pedal, and it goes down, and it makes the wheel go around, and the wheel makes it move." "He wanted the cookies, and he thought they were in the cupboard, and so he got on the stool so he could reach the cupboard to get the cookies") (Bullock and Gelman, 1979; Wellman, 1990). (One might also note that Alexei, now 18 years old, did eventually converge on the correct solution.)

These examples reflect an interesting fact about human beings. What happens when the theorizing mechanisms are faced with a causal problem (Why are there 7 moons? Why did one's family all disappear? Where do babies come from?) but have no relevant evidence to operate on? What happens, we suggest, is magic, a combination of narrative, deference, and association. The important thing about these cases is precisely that they involve problems for which the speaker has no evidence: the number of the planets, the death of loved ones, the mystery of conception. In cases where there is evidence, like those of the bicycle and the cupboard, then the genuine theorizing mechanisms can kick in, and we get at least a primitive form of science instead.

There is another interesting fact about these examples. We suggested that science typically applies theorizing processes to cases where relevant evidence is not readily available. It may well be that in just these cases the contrast between prescientific and scientific explanation will be most vivid, and this may misleadingly suggest that scientific methods are fundamentally different from those of ordinary cognition. The explanation a child (or a Zuni or a medieval astrologer) gives of the planet's motions may be wildly different from a scientific explanation. A child's explanation of how a tricycle works, how bread is baked, or why his friend looks in the cupboard for the cookies might be much more similar to a scientific explanation. But in these latter cases scientific explanation would be redundant.

Empirical Advances

The arguments we have advanced so far are really just plausible reasons why cognitive development in childhood might be much like scientific theory change, in spite of the differences between children and scientists. The proof of the theoretical pudding is in the empirical eating. Fortunately, we do not have to provide gastronomic testimonials all by ourselves. Recently, a broader and broader body of empirical evidence in support of this view has accumulated. Cognitive and developmental psychologists have begun to pay more and more attention to the idea that theory change is a model of cognitive development. These empirical projects have been influenced by philosophical ideas, though many of these ideas have come more from other branches of philosophy than from the philosophy of science itself. Philosophers have increasingly drawn parallels between scientific knowledge and language and our everyday knowledge and language, and psychologists have increasingly found evidence in support of these parallels.

Two lines of development have been particularly important. First, in the philosophical literature Putnam extended arguments from scientific change to our ordinary use of "natural kind" terms, such as "lemon" or "cat." Putnam (1975, 215–271) argued that such terms, rather than picking out specific features or properties of objects, pick out underlying causal "essences" that we conceive as responsible for these features. The notion of "essence" may keep the reference of a term fixed, even when radical conceptual changes, such as those that take place across scientific theory change, may entirely alter the term's intension.

Putnam's argument was based on facts of scientific change, but it was also based on our commonsense intuitions about such facts. In psychological studies of categorization it has become increasingly apparent that Putnam was quite right. Our ordinary categorizations of common objects are best understood in terms of our underlying theories of the objects involved. Adults typically give common names to objects that they think have an underlying common causal nature, rather than those that share superficial perceptual features (Murphy and Medin, 1985). In practice, these decisions are based on adults' commonsense theories of the objects.

If we look at young children's classificatory language and behavior, we see a similar pattern. Even extremely young children appear to organize their categorization in terms of "natural kinds," underlying essences with causal efficacy. Moreover, their decisions about which objects belong to these natural kinds appear to be rooted in naive theories of physics and biology (Carey, 1985; Keil, 1987, 1989; Gelman & Markman, 1986; Gelman & Wellman, 1991).

Most significantly, it is possible to chart qualitative conceptual changes in children's categorizations as their theories are constructed, modified, and revised. This point was first made, and has been made most clearly, extensively, and persuasively, in Carey's seminal work. For example, the child's categorization of an object as an "animal" or as "alive" changes profoundly as the child's "folk biology" changes (Carey, 1985). Perhaps the reason that Putnam's arguments have sometimes failed to impress psychologists is that they depend on intuitions about how reference takes place across theory changes in science. Except, in fact, for the case of science, such conceptual changes are quite rare in ordinary adult life. But when we turn to childhood, such changes are the rule rather than the exception, and here Putnam's insights turn out to have quite a lot of explanatory power.

Second, the renewed interest in "folk psychology" has raised the possibility, first formulated in the philosophical literature (Churchland, 1984; Stich, 1983), that our ordinary everyday understanding of the mind should be thought of as analogous to a scientific theory. It is perhaps a little odd that philosophers should have focused on folk psychology as a theory, rather than folk physics or folk biology, since there is so little in the way of scientific psychological theories and so much in the way of physical and biological ones. Nonetheless, this is the context in which the theory theory has been most clearly argued in philosophy.

Again, empirical investigations of the child's developing understanding of the mind have tended to confirm this view. In fact, "the child's theory of mind" has become a catch phrase for this branch of empirical research. Most investigators in the field have argued that the child's early understanding of the mind can be usefully construed as a theory and that changes in this understanding can be thought of as theory changes (Gopnik, 1993a; Gopnik & Wellman, 1994; Wellman, 1990; Perner, 1991; Flavell et al., 1995; though see Harris, 1991; Baron-Cohen, 1995; Leslie & Roth, 1993, for opposing views). In the course of developing an account of the mind, children postulate such mental entities as perceptions, beliefs, and desires as a way of explaining ordinary human behavior. Moreover, there are significant conceptual changes in the child's understanding of the mind. The most well-studied and well-confirmed change is a shift from a nonrepresentational to a representational view of the mind between 3 and 5. There has been extensive and exciting work in the last few years charting the details of this particular conceptual revolution.

Finally, within the philosophy of science itself there have recently been several attempts to integrate ideas from cognitive psychology into accounts of theory formation and change in science. These accounts explicitly aim at developing a cognitive science of science (see Giere, 1992). We are sympathetic with the general tenor of this work. However, it is worth pointing out that in a curious way it has been at cross-purposes with the work in developmental psychology. The philosophers of science associated with this research have suggested that theories are really just instances of quite general cognitive structures, such as meta-phor schemata, production systems, or connectionist nets. In contrast, the developmentalists have been dissatisfied with such general accounts of cognition and turn to the example of science to argue for much stronger and specific theorylike cognitive structures.

Empirically, then, philosophy of science and cognitive psychology, particularly developmental psychology, have come together by way of rather roundabout routes through philosophy of language and philoso-phy of mind. However delayed the union, the consummation of a rela-tionship between philosophy of science and cognitive psychology would be a happy event not only from the perspective of cognitive psychology but also from that of philosophy of science itself. From the point of view of cognitive psychology, the example of science gives us a way of dealing with learning, belief formation, and conceptual change. These are per-haps the most thorny unresolved problems in cognitive science. The rest of this book will really be an elaborated defense of the usefulness of the theory theory for cognitive development. From the point of view of philosophy of science, the idea of largely unconscious theorizing devices, designed by evolution for rapid, powerful, and flexible learning, and exploiting logical regularities to that end, might resolve some of the tensions between the more abstract logical characterizations of scientific change and the actual historical evidence.

So the project, as we see it, is not to show that children do science. Instead, we want to argue that the cognitive processes that underlie science are similar to, or indeed identical with, the cognitive processes that underlie much of cognitive development. It is not that children are little scientists but that scientists are big children. Scientific progress is possible because scientists employ cognitive processes that are first seen in very young children.

What Is a Theory?

So far we have been talking about theories in the vaguest of terms, just waving our hands in the direction of the philosophy of science. In fact, the accounts of theories in the cognitive literature have often been rather vague and underspecified. We would like to remedy this by offering a more detailed and precise account. Within the philosophy of science, of course, there is much controversy about what theories are and how to characterize them. We have taken the modest and emollient route of focusing on those features of theories that are most generally accepted across many different conceptions of science. Our reference list will include strange bedfellows to a philosopher of science, including such classic accounts as those of Hempel and Popper and the more revisionist ones of Kuhn or Laudan. We want for the moment to be as mainstream and middle-of-the-road as possible. Whatever the broader theoretical conceptions and arguments may be, both normative and sociological investigations of science provide us with rich and suggestive data about the nature of characteristic scientific representations and rules.

In particular, we will use much of the vocabulary of the classical normative/logical view of theories. However, we intend that vocabulary to be interpreted as an account of psychological, rather than logical, entities. We crave indulgence from the philosophers when we put their terminology to a use for which it was not originally intended. For example, there are extensive debates between a classical view of theories as a set of sentences in some logical language and a more recent semantic or model-theoretic view (see, e.g., van Fraassen, 1980). However, neither of these detailed logical proposals seem plausible as direct candidates for psychologically real representations and rules, nor, of course, are they intended to be, and so we will not consider such debates here.

Similarly, we will deliberately blur the classic distinction betweeen the "logic of discovery" and "the logic of confirmation" in what follows. The distinction has been seen to be increasingly untenable even in work in the normative tradition (see Kitcher, 1993; Glymour et al., 1987). But it is clearly not a distinction that makes any sense when applied to our psychological project. In fact, we might suggest that in its original form the distinction was really designed to slough off certain particularly hard philosophical problems by referring them to a psychology that was never developed. Perhaps because they felt unconsciously guilty about this abnegation of responsibility, philosophers have customarily supposed that nothing systematic can be said about discovery; the psychologists would end up talking about "genius" or "flashes of insight." There is, as far as we can see, no empirical justification for this claim, though it is certainly true that if you never try to say anything systematic about something, nothing systematic will be said.

We will also focus on those features of theories in science that are most relevant to developmental issues. We will focus on several kinds of distinctive features of theories. First, we'll consider the static, structural features of theories, what theories are. Next we'll consider what theories do. Finally, we'll talk about how theories change. (The account we will offer here was developed in collaboration with Henry Wellman, and a version of it may be found in Gopnik & Wellman, 1994.)

Structural Features of Theories

Theories are always constructed with reference to evidence (Nagel, 1961; Lakatos, 1970; Laudan, 1977; Popper, 1965). One of the morals of modern philosophy of science is that there are no strict separations between all theory and all evidence; evidence, it is said, is "theory-laden." Nor is there some foundational level of experience out of which all other kinds of knowledge are built. Still, in any particular example, we can differentiate between a theory and the evidence on which the theory is based. Moreover, the relation between theory and evidence is a distinctive one.

Abstractness
When we say that theories are abstract, we mean that theoretical constructs are typically phrased in a vocabulary that is different from the vocabulary of the evidence that supports the theory. Theories include entities and laws that are postulated or recruited from elsewhere to explain evidence. Gravity is not itself bodies moving in relation to one another; it is a force postulated to explain the behavior of bodies moving in relation to one another. When we postulate a Darwinian species as a theoretical construct (rather than birds, mammals, etc., as empirical types), we define it in terms quite removed from its apparent features. A green stemmed plant and a woody stemmed one may both be ferns because of their reproductive lineage. Kepler's theory of the planets includes elliptical orbits that are notoriously not visible when we look at the stars' motions in the sky. Theories in biology postulated unseen entities with distinctive properties, like viruses and bacteria, to explain visible symptoms of diseases.

Theoretical constructs need not be unobservable. We can, in fact, see bacteria and viruses through a microscope, and the helical structure of DNA can be observed through X-ray crystallography. But they must be appeals to a set of entities removed from, and underlying, the evidential phenomena themselves. They are entities and laws that explain the data but are not simply restatements of the data.

Coherence

Theoretical constructs do not work independently; they work together in systems with a particular structure. A second characteristic of theories is their coherence. The entities postulated by a theory are closely, "lawfully," interrelated with one another. The classical view of theories captured the coherence of theories by describing two kinds of relations: intratheoretic deductive relations among theoretical entities and "bridge" or "correspondence" relations that connected theories and evidence (Hempel, 1965). More recent conceptions suggest that this is not true; the nature of the theory itself will influence how the theory maps onto the evidence and vice-versa. To say this need not, however, lead us to conclude that theories offer only tautological explanations or redefinitions. There are noncircular ways of specifying both the relations within the theory and the relations between the theory and evidence that allow for an interaction between the two types of laws (Glymour, 1980). This more recent view, in fact, makes the coherent interrelations between parts of the theory even more important.

Causality

A third distinctive feature of theories, related to these two, is their appeal to causality. That is, in theories, we appeal to some underlying causal structure that we think is responsible for the superficial regularities in the data (Cartwright, 1989). Causal relationships are central to theories in two ways. The intratheoretic relations, the laws, are typically interpreted in causal ways. The mass of an object causes other objects to move toward it; selection causes certain mutations to be preserved. But an equally important aspect of theories is that the theoretical entities are seen to be causally responsible for the evidence. The elliptical movements of the planets cause the planets to appear to march across the sky in distinctive ways.

Ontological commitment

Finally, theories make ontological commitments and support counterfactuals (Levi, 1980). An accepted theory is supposed to carve nature at its joints; the theoretical entities and laws are supposed to tell you what there is and what it must do. As a consequence, theories not only make predictions; they also make counterfactual claims. If the sun and earth were a different distance apart, the earth's orbit would be different; if the moth had evolved in a climate without industrial pollution; it would have a different kind of coloration; and so on. A test of theoreticity, which we will return to later, is the nature of our surprise at violations of the theory. If we are committed to the theory, such violations should strike us not only as surprising but as being impossible and unbelievable in an important and strong way. This differentiates theories from other types of knowledge.

Functional Features of Theories

Prediction

The structural features of theories give them a characteristic sort of predictiveness. A theory, in contrast to a mere empirical generalization, makes predictions about a wide variety of evidence, including evidence that played no role in the theory's initial construction. Kepler's account allows one to predict the behavior of new celestial objects, moons, for example, which were quite unknown at the time the theory was formulated. Theories in biology allow us to predict that antibiotics will inhibit many bacterial infections, including some, like scarlet fever, that present none of the symptoms of an infected wound, or some, like Legionnaires' disease, that were unknown when the theory was formulated. They also allow us to predict that such drugs will be useless against viral infections, even when the symptoms of the viral infection are identical to those of a bacterial one (Nagel, 1961; Hempel, 1965).

Some of these predictions will be correct: they will accurately predict future events described at the evidential level. Others will be incorrect. Since theories go beyond the evidence and are never completely right, some of their predictions will be falsified (Popper, 1965). In still other cases, the theory will make no prediction at all.

In fact, the theory may in some circumstances have less predictive power than would a large set of empirical generalizations. This is because explanatory depth and force do not simply equate with predictive accuracy. We can make predictions about things without explaining them. Celestial navigators and astrologers, for example, noticed certain consistent patterns in the movements of the stars, and made predictions on this basis, without having an explanation for those patterns.

There are two differences between these predictions and those generated by theories. First, a few theoretical entities and laws can lead to a wide variety of unexpected predictions. Second, in the case of a theory, prediction is intimately tied to explanation and causal attribution. The ability to produce wide-ranging predictions is perhaps the most obvious pragmatic benefit of science, and it may also be the most important evolutionary benefit of developing theorizing abilities. The evolutionary value of a system that leads to accurate and wide-ranging predictions should be obvious. In fact, making accurate predictions about the behavior of the world and your fellow organisms is the sine qua non of cognition.

Interpretation

An additional characteristic of theories is that they produce interpretations of evidence, not simply descriptions and typologies of it. Indeed, theories strongly influence which pieces of evidence we consider salient or important (Kuhn, 1977; Lakatos, 1970; Scheffler, 1967). It is notoriously true that theoretical preconceptions may lead a scientist to dismiss some kinds of counterevidence to theoretical claims as simply noise or as the result of methodological failures. This is not necessarily a bad thing. On the contrary, deciding which evidence to ignore is crucial to the effective conduct of a scientific research program. Theory-driven interpretations help to solve what computer scientists call "the frame problem." Theories provide a way of deciding which evidence is relevant to a particular problem. This too might be an evolutionary benefit of theorizing.

Explanation

A third function of theories often mentioned is that they provide explanations (Hempel, 1965; Kitcher & Salmon, 1989). The coherence and abstractness of theories and their causal attributions and ontological commitments together give them an explanatory force lacking in mere typologies of, or generalizations about, the data. Explaining the position of the evening star in terms of Kepler's theory or the properties of plants in terms of their evolutionary history is (at least) cognitively satisfying. Explaining the position of the evening star by saying that it always appears there or explaining the properties of plants by saying that one is stemless and the other is stemmed is, by comparison, shallow and superficial.

In fact, it may be that what we mean by saying that we've explained something is simply that we can give an abstract, coherent, causal account of it. Indeed, it is difficult to find a characterization of explanation other than this. From a philosophical point of view this may be fine. Indeed, often philosophical enterprises consist of giving necessary and sufficient conditions for the application of some term. But from a cognitive point of view, there is a puzzling circularity about most philosophical attempts to explain explanation. The cognitive functions of prediction and interpretation seem obvious enough: representations and rules that allow for predictions and interpretations plainly enable an organism to function better in the world. The functional significance of explanation is less clear. On the face of it, it would seem that one of the functions of a theory is to explain, and yet when we define explanation, we often seem to end up by simply saying that to explain something is to have a good theory of it, or to have some aspects of a good theory of it.

A naturalistic evolutionary perspective may help to supply a resolution to this puzzle. What makes having an explanation different from just having a theory? Why does it seem to us that explaining is a function of theorizing, but not that theorizing is a function of explaining? The commonsense notion of explanation, at least, seems to include a kind of affect, a sense of how satisfying a good theory can be. From an evolutionary point of view we might suggest that explanation is to cognition as orgasm (or at least male orgasm) is to reproduction. It identifies the motivational and affective state that serves as a marker for the fulfillment of the underlying evolutionary function. The search for better theories has a kind of internally driven motivation, quite separate from the more superficial motivations provided by the sociology. From our point of view, we make theories in search of explanation, and make love in search of orgasm. It seems sensible to us to say that the function of such activities is to satisfy a certain need. From an evolutionary point of view, however, the relation may be quite the reverse: we search for explanations and orgasms because such searchs lead us to make theories and love. We might speculate that we were designed with a theorizing drive and that explanation is a symptom of that drive in action.

Dynamic Features of Theories

So far we have been talking mostly about the static features of theories, the features that might distinguish theories from other cognitive structures, such as typologies or schemas. We have only begun to mention theory changes. But in fact the most important thing about theories is what philosophers call their defeasibility. Theories may turn out to be inconsistent with the evidence, and because of this theories change. In fact, a tenet of modern epistemology is that any aspect of a theory, even the most central ones, may change (Quine, 1961; Laudan, 1977). The dynamic features of theories, the processes involved in theory formation and change, are equally characteristic and perhaps even more important from a developmental point of view.

Theories change as a result of a number of different epistemological processes. One particularly critical factor is the accumulation of counterevidence to the theory. Again, Popper's classical views in philosophy of science suggested that this was the defining feature of theory change (Popper, 1965). The theory made a prediction, the prediction was falsified, and the theory was rejected. In fact, the real story is much more complicated. As with the relation between theory and evidence, these complexities have sometimes led to a kind of epistemological nihilism, as if theory change was just a matter of caprice (Feyerabend, 1975). But while a precise specification of theory change may elude us, there are certainly substantive things to be said about how it typically takes place. There are characteristic intermediate processes involved in the transition from one theory to another (Kuhn, 1977; Lakatos, 1970; Laudan, 1977).

The initial reaction of a theory to counterevidence may be a kind of denial. The interpretive mechanisms of the theory may treat the counterevidence as noise, mess, not worth attending to (Lakatos, 1970). At a slightly later stage the theory may develop ad hoc auxiliary hypotheses designed to account specifically for such counterevidence. Auxiliary hypotheses may also be helpful because they phrase the counterevidence in the accepted vocabulary of the earlier theory. But such auxiliary hypotheses often appear, over time, to undermine the theory's coherence, which is one of its strengths. The theory gets ugly and messy instead of being beautiful and simple. The preference for beautiful theories over ugly ones (usually phrased, less poetically, in terms of simplicity criteria) plays an additional major role in theory change.

A next step requires an alternative model to the original theory. A theory may limp along for some time under the weight of its auxiliary hypotheses if no alternative way of making progress is available. The ability to fix on this alternative is the mysterious logic of discovery. But as we suggested, it is not clear that this mystery is utterly insoluble. Often the original idea for the new theory is an extension or application of an idea already implicit in some peripheral part of the earlier theory. For example, Darwin took the idea of selection, which was already widely understood and used in the context of animal breeding and horticulture, and applied it to a new problem (Kitcher, 1993). This process may seem like analogy or metaphor, but it involves more serious conceptual changes. The new idea is not simply the old idea applied to a new domain, but rather, the earlier idea is itself modified to fit its role in the new theory. Moreover, the fertility of the alternative idea may not be immediately recognized. Initially it may be applied only to the problematic cases. We may see only later on that the new idea also provides an explanation for the evidence explained by the earlier theory (Giere, 1992).

A final important dynamic feature of theory formation is a period of intense experimentation and/or observation. This period might span both the crisis of the earlier theory (when anomalous results are being produced right and left) and the first stages of the new theory (when a whole range of new predictions become available). The role that experimentation and observation play in theory change is still mysterious, but that it plays some role seems plain. Obviously, experimentation allows the scientist to test the predictions of the theory. But it is worth pointing out that even in science, much experimentation is much less focused and more like what we disparagingly call a fishing expedition. In addition to testing predictions, some experimentation enables scientists to develop a stock of atheoretical empirical generalizations, which in turn will be subsumed and explained by the later theory.

The development of the heliocentric theory of the planets provides some good examples of these processes. Auxiliary hypotheses involving more and more complex arrangements of epicycles were initially invoked to deal with counterevidence. Later heliocentrism was introduced by Copernicus. Copernicus's account, however, still fails to explain many of the empirical regularities and continues to rely on epicycles as an auxiliary hypothesis. Tycho Brahe's account acknowledges many of the flaws of the Ptolemaic accounts and uses the idea of heliocentrism to deal with them (other planets revolve around the sun, which revolves around the earth). But Brahe failed to accept the central idea that the earth itself goes round the sun. Only with Kepler is there a really coherent heliocentric account that deals both with the anomalies and with the earlier data itself. And while, strictly speaking, experimentation on the heavenly bodies was impossible, periods of intense and detailed observation in this transitional period provided a far richer empirical base than had been available before.

Theories in Childhood

We want to claim that infants and young children have cognitive structures like those we have just been describing. All these characteristics of theories ought also to apply to children's early cognitive structures if these structures are really theoretical. That is, children's theories should involve appeal to abstract theoretical entities, with coherent causal relations among them. Their theories should lead to characteristic patterns of predictions, including extensions to new types of evidence and false predictions, not just to more empirically accurate predictions. Their theories should also lead to distinctive interpretations of evidence: a child with one theory should interpret even fundamental facts and experiences differently than a child with a different theory. Finally, their theories should invoke characteristic explanations phrased in terms of these abstract entities and laws. This distinctive pattern of prediction, interpretation, and explanation is among the best indicators of a theoretical structure and the best ways of distinguishing the theory theory from its developmental competitors.

Different aspects of theories will be apparent at different stages of cognitive development. At the very early stage that we are concerned with here, we will emphasize several structural and functional aspects of theories that have correlates in the behavior of infants and young children. These kinds of behavior provide evidence for the theory theory.

Perhaps the most significant piece of evidence is the distinctive pattern of infant predictions. If 18-month-olds develop a theory, we expect them to produce a wide array of new predictions at the same time. In particular, we should see them make predictions even in cases in which simple empirical generalizations would fail. We should see something like inductive and deductive inferences.

The second type of evidence is the pattern of interpretation. If 18-month-olds are using a theory, we expect them to misinterpret and misuse evidence that contradicts the theory. Even if available evidence might solve some pragmatic problem, children in the grip of a theory might ignore the evidence.

A third type of evidence comes from the extensions of early words. If these words encode theoretical concepts, they should give a unifying characterization to events and objects with quite different superficial perceptual features. In particular, they should pick out groups of objects or events with similar causal structures, and these groupings should depend on, and be linked to, the child's particular theories.

Finally, with these very young preverbal children, direct evidence of explanation is obviously hard to come by. We will see, however, that infants show affective and motivational patterns strikingly like those involved in explanation for adults. In making correct theoretical predictions, infants show a kind of motivation and satisfaction that goes well beyond any immediate functional or social reward. Infants seem to have cognitive orgasms.

We also propose that the dynamic features we have described should be apparent in children's transitions from one theory to a later one. Children should initially ignore certain kinds of counterevidence, then account for such evidence with auxiliary hypotheses, then use the new theoretical idea in limited contexts, and only finally reorganize their knowledge so that the new theoretical entities play a central role. When the new theory is, as it were, under construction, they should engage in extensive experiments relevant to the theory and collect empirical generalizations. Over a given developmental period we should be able to chart the emergence of the new theory from the earlier one, and we should be able to predict a period of some disorganization in between.

Theories as Representations

So far we have been using the same kind of language as philosophers of science to describe theories and theory change, and we will continue to use this language in describing children. We could, however, translate this language into the theoretical parlance of representations and rules more familiar in cognitive science. A person's theory is a system that assigns representations to inputs just as one's perceptual system assigns representations to visual input or one's syntactic system assigns representations to phonological input. The representations that it assigns are, however, distinctive in many ways, just as perceptual and syntactic representations are distinctive. We can capture these distinctive structural features by talking about the specific abstract, coherent, causal, ontologically committed, counterfactual supporting entities and laws of the theory, just as we talk about phrase structures when we describe syntactic representations (Chomsky, 1980) or $2\frac{1}{2}$-dimensional sketches when we talk about perceptual representations (Marr, 1982). The representations are operated on by rules that lead to new representations; for example, the theory generates predictions. There are also distinctive functional relations between the theoretical representations and the input to them; theories predict, interpret, and explain data.

We know that the input to our perceptual or syntactic systems is provided by our sensory systems. Exactly what is the input to our theory systems? On one view, we might want to propose that other representational systems translate sensory information into some higher level of ordinary, primary, atheoretical knowledge. On this view, not all our representations are assigned by theories. Rather, an earlier level of processing provides the evidential input to theorizing processes. We could describe a level of "evidence" that is not itself theoretical or affected by the theory but serves as the input to the theory. Some of these systems might correspond to Fodor's (1983) "modules." Alternatively, and more in keeping with the philosophical positions that emphasize the "theory-ladenness" of evidence, the system might simply assign theoretical representations to sensory input without a separate level of evidential representation.

By way of illustration, consider a particular observation, say a particular pattern of tracks in a cloud chamber. On any view there will be some very low level atheoretical perceptual processes that will transform the raw sensory input into some more abstract representational form, say a $2\frac{1}{2}$-dimensional sketch. We might believe that there is also a representational system, distinct from the theory system, that further assigns these inputs an atheoretical "ordinary knowledge" representation. For example, it might represent them as "blue tracks in a white jar on a table." This might then be input to the theorizing system.

Alternatively and, we think, more plausibly, the theory system might itself simply assign the input a particular theoretical representation. It might just represent the input as electrons decaying in a particular way. On this view, there is no atheoretical, evidential, "ordinary knowledge" level of representation, at least not once we get past very low level perceptual processing. All representations will be theory-laden. Even apparently "ordinary" kinds of knowledge, like our knowledge that this is a jar and that is a table, or perhaps even that these are two objects and one is on top of the other, will be the result of the application of everyday theories. For various reasons, this strikes us as a more attractive option than the first one. However, which picture is true is an empirical question, and the truth might differ in different cases.

On both views, the theoretical representation assigned to a particular input would then interact in particular rule-governed ways with the other representations of the theory. Does this input match the predictions of the theory? Do some particular theoretical representations co-occur in a way that suggests some causal link between them, a link not specified in the current theory? The fact that certain representations occurred and not others might lead to changes within the theory itself. This could happen even if there were no separate evidential level of representation outside the theory itself.

The most important and distinctive thing about theories is the fact that the very patterns of representation that occur can alter the nature of the representational system itself. They can alter the nature of the relations between inputs and representations. As we get new inputs, and so new representations, the very rules that connect inputs and representations change. Eventually we may end up with a system that has a completely new set of representations and a completely different set of relations between inputs and representations than the system we started out with. As we will see, this differentiates theories from other kinds of representational systems.

Moreover, this system may be dynamic at yet another level. We have been saying that new inputs to the system change the relation between inputs and representations. It is also possible that the very rules that restructure the relations between inputs and representations may change as a result of new input. That is, as we learn more, we also learn new ways to learn. Certainly this seems to be true in science, and it may also be true in development.

To borrow Neurath's philosophical metaphor, the theorizing view sees knowledge as a boat that we perpetually rebuild as we sail in it. At each point in our journey there may be only a limited and constrained set of alterations we can make to the boat to keep it seaworthy. In the end, however, we may end up with not a single plank or rivet from the original structure, and the process may go on indefinitely.

This kind of system may sound so open-ended as to be uninteresting. But, in fact, the theory theory proposes that the representational system will change in relatively orderly, predictable, and constrained ways. We can try to capture this by talking about the dynamic properties of theory change. For example, the representational system may lead to a particular prediction about a new representation. The prediction turns out to be wrong; the new input, and so the new representation, is not what we predicted. Or the system may accumulate regularities; some representations consistently co-occur in ways that are not predicted by the representational system itself. Events like these cause the representational system to change, and to do so in particular and predictable ways.

Should we think of this relation betwen inputs and outputs as a kind of effective computational procedure? If we know that the system is in state A and receives input B, will we be able to tell what the next set of representations will be like? The answer at this point is simply that we don't know whether there is a procedure like this or not, nor much about how it would operate if there were. What we do know, however, is that there are consistent causal relations between input and representations, both in science and childhood, and the empirical claim of this book is that these relations are similar. We also believe that these causal relations involve, for lack of a better term, the "content" of the input and the representations; they aren't, in any case, like the causal relation between being hit with a hammer and losing consciousness. The best current bet for how a material object like the brain could causally relate inputs and representations in this way is that it is a kind of computer. We subscribe to this faith, though we admit that at this point it is no more than a faith.

There is another, even more profound question to ask, one that we will also not answer. How does such a system get at the truth about the world? We said before, glibly, that it gets at the truth about the world because it is designed by evolution to get at the truth about the world. That is at least a step up from saying that it gets at the truth about the world because of the unique genius of scientists or because some scientists are more powerful than others. But the kind of system we are talking about will certainly suffer from the the the same problems of under-determination that plague the various proposals put forward by philosophers of science in the normative tradition. Given data, the system will arrive at an answer, and given the same data, different instantiations of the system will (eventually) arrive at the same answer. But other answers will still be logically possible, given the same data.

We might say that the space of relations between the input and output will be very much larger than it will be in a modular system, like the visual perception system, but still smaller than the space of logical possibilities. There will be constraints, though very general constraints, on the kinds of relations between inputs and representations that the system will generate. The constraints correspond to the general assumptions that underlie theory formation: that the world has an underlying causal structure, that the structure is most likely to be the simplest one that corresponds to the data, and so on.

The constraints, on our view, come largely from evolution, and at some level this fact is responsible for their veridicality. Presumably, creatures who constructed representations in different ways in childhood, who did not assume underlying causal structure, did not search for the simplest explanation, did not falsify hypotheses when there was counter-evidence, and so on, were at an evolutionary disadvantage. In adulthood, such creatures were less good at predicting which berries were members of a poisonous natural kind, which kinds of minerals would make the most seductive body paint, or when their babies were old enough to be left alone without danger (more germane evolutionary tasks than the proverbial dodging of the sabre-toothed tiger). In this sense nature itself guarantees that the system gets to an understanding of nature.

But, of course, evolution is highly contingent, and for all we know, other systems with different sets of constraints might hit on quite different ways of constructing veridical representations. If quantum-mechanical effects translated into selection pressures, perhaps we would have a cognitive system that derived representations from inputs in quite different ways and would be less frustrated in our attempts to understand the quantum universe.

So the system is veridical because of its evolutionary history. However, *how* the process of evolution, or evolution and culture together, actually manages to hit upon a system that generates representations that match up to the outside world is still profoundly mysterious. Here we don't even have a faith to proclaim, at least not beyond the general faith of realism.

Anyway, it seems to us that if we are ever to answer these questions, we need first simply to empirically specify what the relations between inputs and representations are like. There is nothing mystical or incoherent about the idea of a representational system that revises itself thus. Indeed, we have excellent evidence that just such a system already exists in human minds. Precisely this sort of system generates the representations of science. And we know at least something about how that system characteristically proceeds.

In perception we are beginning to understand the causal relations between inputs and representations. We have an enormous body of psychophysical data. This data underpins the development of algorithms in vision science. We will need a similarly rich store of data about the relations between inputs and representations in conceptual change to even begin to discover the algorithms for theory change, or to discover that there are none.

If we discovered that children's representational system had the features we have been describing, we would, we think, be licensed in saying that children had theories and that the process of theory construction was similar in scientists and children. Suppose that children proposed abstract entities, coherently organized with causal relations among them. Suppose that they made ontological commitments and held counterfactuals. Suppose that these entities served to provide characteristic explanations, predictions, and interpretations and that they changed in response to counterevidence in distinctive ways. Even if we still wanted to deny that children are scientists, we would have to agree that their cognitive processes look remarkably similar to those of science.

3

Theories, Modules, and Empirical Generalizations

So far we have been making a case for the similarities between scientific knowledge and cognition and also between scientific change and cognitive development. However, it is important to say that not all knowledge is like science and not all development is like scientific change. The analogy to science would be of little interest if it were. Our claim is that quite distinctive and special cognitive processes are responsible both for scientific progress and for particular kinds of development in children. Other kinds of cognition and cognitive development may be quite different. We further claim that theories and theory changes in particular are related to and reflected in early semantic development. In this chapter we will consider other types of knowledge and other processes that could be responsible for developmental change. These provide a contrast case to the theory theory. Moreover, these types of cognition and cognitive development may interact with theory formation in interesting and important ways.

We also intend this chapter to serve a somewhat more ambitious goal. In the wake of the collapse of Piagetian theory, cognitive development has been a bit of a mess, with almost theories, half theories, pseudo-theories, and theory fragments floating about in the sociological ether. In this chapter we will also try to present a sort of vade mecum, a road map to the developmental possibilities. We don't want to contend that the theory theory is a better account, in general, than the other accounts we will describe, or that they are somehow incoherent or implausible. Indeed, we want to argue for a kind of developmental pluralism: there are many quite different mechanisms underlying cognitive developments. Our aim is to argue that theory formation is one among them, an important one.

Moreover, we will eventually want to argue that theory formation, rather than these other mechanisms, accounts for the particular cognitive and semantic phenomena we will discuss later. To do this, we need to consider what sorts of evidence could discriminate between the theory theory and alternative accounts. Many different mechanisms could be responsible for different phenomena, but some particular mechanism will be responsible for each particular phenomenon, and we want to know which one it is. (As in politics, being a pluralist doesn't mean being a wimp.)

One particularly significant contrast, given the zeitgeist in developmental psycholinguistics, will be the contrast with innate modules, constraints, or other related structures. We will suggest that the representations that result from such innate structures may have some of the static features of theories—they may be abstract, be coherent, make causal attributions of a sort, and even allow predictions and interpretations—but they will not have the dynamic features of theories. In particular, they will be indefeasible; they will not be changed or revised in response to evidence. The other important contrast will be with what we will call empirical generalizations: scripts, narratives, connectionist nets, and other cognitive structures quite closely related to immediate experience. Here the contrast runs in the opposite direction. Empirical generalizations, like theories, are defeasible; they may and indeed frequently will be revised. However, they will not have the abstract and coherent quality of theories, nor will they support explanation, prediction, and interpretation in the same way.

Modules

One serious alternative to the theory theory is the idea that cognitive structures are the consequence of innate modules. According to modularity theories, representations of the world are not constructed from evidence in the course of development. Instead, representations are produced by innate structures, modules, or constraints that have been constructed in the course of evolution. These structures may need to be triggered, but once they are triggered, they create mandatory representations of input (Fodor, 1983).[1]

Often the contrast between modularity accounts and the theory theory is phrased in terms of a more general contrast between nativism and empiricism. But this general contrast does not capture the distinction accurately. While modules are innate, not all innate structures are modular. We have proposed a distinction between two types of nativism: modularity nativism and "starting-state" nativism (Astington & Gopnik, 1991; Meltzoff & Gopnik, 1993; Gopnik & Wellman, 1994). On the starting-state view, the child is innately endowed with a particular set of representations of input and rules operating on those representations. According to this view, such initial structures, while innate, would be defeasible; any part of them could be, and indeed will be, altered by new evidence. We propose that there are innate theories that are later modified and revised. The process of theory change and replacement begins at birth. To continue Neurath's metaphor, innate theories are the boats that push off from the pier. The boat you start out in may have a considerable effect on the boat you end up with, even if no trace of the original remains.

Innate theories might be important in several ways. If children did not have these initial representations, we might expect them to develop later theories in radically different ways, if they developed them at all. Moreover, the fact that the child begins with an initial theorylike structure, which is then revised and restructured in response to evidence, might help solve some underdetermination problems. Such problems have plagued accounts of conceptual change, both in cognitive psychology and in the philosophy of science. Certainly this type of account seems more tractable than one in which theorylike conceptual structures are constructed from scratch from a disorganized flow of experience.

Modularity nativism, on the other hand, implies a much stronger set of claims. In Fodor's analysis, for example, modules are not only innate; they are also encapsulated. On Fodor's view, the representations that are the outcome of modules cannot be overturned by new patterns of evidence. In Chomsky's (1980) theory of syntax acquisition, the innate universal grammar means that only a very limited set of possible grammars will be developed. It constrains the final form of the grammar in the strong sense that grammars that violate it will never be learned by human beings. The idea that certain syntactic structures are indefeasible is at the very core of the idea of constraints in syntax. Similar claims are often advanced in accounts of perceptual systems (Marr, 1982).

The classic examples of modules are the specialized representations and rules of the visual and syntactic systems. Such modules are supposed to automatically map given perceptual inputs (retinal stimulation or strings of words) onto more abstract set of representations ($2\frac{1}{2}$-dimensional sketches or phrase structures). They automatically mandate certain "inferences" but not others. Outputs from the system may be taken up by other, more central systems, but the relation is asymmetrical. Information from higher systems cannot reshape the representational structure of the module. Once the module has matured, certain representations of the input will result. Other representations simply cannot be formulated, no matter how much evidence supports them.

What kinds of evidence could differentiate between a modularity theory and a theory theory that includes innate theories? Many kinds of evidence that are commonly adduced to support modularity views can't discriminate between these views and the theory theory. In particular, it may be difficult, if not impossible, to distinguish these views by looking at a single static representational system. At least some of the structural and functional features of theories—their abstractness, coherence, and predictive and interpretive force—can also be found in modules.

In particular, both theories and modular representations may involve abstract entities and rules related to sensory input in only very indirect ways. Also like theories, modules allow predictions that go beyond the input. Moreover, they require the mind to represent input in a particular way—a process that may look like interpretation.

In fact, one of the most interesting and important discoveries of cognitive science is that quite automatized, unconscious, indefeasible representational systems can have a very complex internal structure that looks like the complex structure of an inferential system (see Rock's [1983] discussions of the logic of perception for a particularly elegant and perspicuous example of this). The fact that there is some logic in the relations between input and representations is itself not enough to distinguish modular and theoretical structures. Evolution could seize on these relations precisely because they were, at least roughly, the correct ones.[2]

The crucial evidence differentiating the two views lies in the dynamic properties of modules and theories, in how they develop. However, not all the dynamic features of modules and theories will be different. Again, much of the developmental evidence cited to support modularity can't discriminate between modules and theories.

In particular, the fact that there is some knowledge at birth or in very early infancy is compatible with either an innate initial theory or an innate module. The fact that similar representations develop in different children at about the same age also can't discriminate between the two views. The theory theory proposes that there are mechanisms that, given evidence, alter representations in particular ways. If two children start out with the same theory and are given the same pattern of evidence, they will converge on the same theory at roughly the same time.

Theories and Development

If all these kinds of evidence can't discriminate between modules and theories, is there evidence that can discriminate between them? The crucial differences between the modularity theory and the theory theory concern the relation between experience and conceptual structure, between inputs and representations. According to the theory theory, input is evidence. It radically alters the nature of theoretical concepts. Evidence about planetary movements can lead to the transformation of a geocentric conception of the heavens into a heliocentric one; evidence about Galapagan tortoises can lead from Owen to Darwin. Though the relation between the evidence and the change in the theory is, of course, far from simple, the theory theory proposes that there is something about the world that causes the mind to change, and that this fact ultimately grounds the truth of theories.

There is, in principle, a simple experiment that could always discriminate modularity theory and theory theory. Place some children in a universe that is radically different from our own, keep them healthy and sane for a reasonably long period of time, and see what they come up with. If they come up with representations that are an accurate account of our universe, modularity is right. If they come up with representations that are an accurate account of their universe, the theory theory is right. Unfortunately, given the constraints of the federal budget, not to mention the constraints of conscience, this experiment is impossible. In developmental psychology, observation must often do the work of experiment. We can discriminate between modules and theories by observing the interactions of experience and knowledge, of inputs and representations, in development.

A theorizing mechanism is a representational system that reorganizes itself in response to input. It is an inherently developmental system. This leads to a distinctive set of developmental predictions. The theory theory predicts a succession of different theories, each replacing the earlier theory. It predicts that earlier theories will quite typically make incorrect predictions, which are corrected in later theories, which in turn will make different incorrect predictions. Moreover, it predicts that there will be typical intermediate stages in the development of theories that reflect the dynamic features of theory change. Finally and most significantly, it predicts that input from the environment will be a crucially important causal factor in determining the character and sequence of successive theories.

Modules and Development

In modules the relation between input and representation is different: experience is simply represented as the module says it should be represented. Relevant experience can trigger our use of a privileged representational system (or not), but the experience does not reshape or reconstruct the privileged representations themselves, nor does it alter future relations between inputs and representations. Modular representations do not lead to predictions through some set of inductive or deductive generalizations or through a process of theory testing, confirmation, and disconfirmation. They lead to predictions because they are specifically designed by evolution to do so.

A consequence of this is that modularity theories are, in an important sense, antidevelopmental (see, for example, Pinker's [1984] discussion of "the continuity assumption"). Apparent changes in representation occurring over time, on these views, can be accounted for only by processes outside the representational system itself. One possibility is that they reflect the maturation of another innate structure, a later module coming on line. For example, Leslie and Roth (1993) propose at least four separate innate modules in children's representations of the mind, coming on line successively but independently in the first 3 years of life. Similarly, in modular linguistic theories it is sometimes proposed that early language, up until about age 3 or 4, when complex syntax appears, is not really language at all (Chomsky, 1980). It instead reflects the operation of a quite different representational system, supplanted by the maturation of a "real" language-acquisition device at about 3.

Alternatively, modularity theories may invoke auxiliary hypotheses about changes in information-processing ability to explain development. On this view as well, however, development is not the result of internal conceptual changes, as it is in the theory theory, but rather is the result of external, nonconceptual changes in information processing. It is really Chomsky's competence versus performance distinction, and the assumption is that performance, rather than competence, is what develops.

Performance deficits are also often invoked to deal with cases in which the child apparently has incorrect representations at one point, which are replaced by other more accurate representations later on. Such sequences are predicted by the theory theory. They are anomalous, however, for modularity theories. It is easy to see why evolution might have designed a representational system that was inaccurate in some respects. It is much more difficult, however, to see why evolution would have designed a sequence of incorrect modules, each maturing only to be replaced by another. The theory theory predicts that there will be incorrect predictions and that these predictions will lead to representational change. Modularity theories can only account for incorrect predictions by some process external to the module. So modularity theorists tend to interpret incorrect predictions as performance errors. (For two good recent examples of this sort of argument, see Fodor, 1992; Marcus et al., 1992).

There is a third way in which modular systems can account for development. In some theories, several alternative branching routes, so to speak, determine the eventual form the module may take. These are generally described as "parameters" set by the input (Chomsky, 1986). Parameters allow for a somewhat richer developmental story than one in which a module is simply turned on or off. The relation between the input and the setting of the parameter is still, however, a relation of triggering. In contrast, in a theory theory, by analogy with scientific theories, there should be indefinite scope for genuinely novel theories, not simply a choice of several options.

There is an interesting conceptual and formal question about whether a modular system with a sufficiently varied set of parameters and triggers would reduce to a theorizing system, or vice versa. The theory theory, after all, still assumes that not all the logically possible theories compatible with the evidence will actually be constructed. There are some possible theories that will be constructed by human beings, given a particular pattern of evidence, and some that will not. Formally, this may not be profoundly different from the case of a module with a great many parameters differently triggered by evidence. Empirically, however, there is a world of difference between the degrees of freedom that seem to be available in syntactic and perceptual systems and those available in scientific theories as we know them. Theory formation will turn out to involve some set of particular causal principles that get us from patterns of input to patterns of representation. These causal principles must, however, be deeply and radically different from the "parameter setting" principles that have been proposed for modular systems.

Modularity in Peripheral and Central Processing

The canonical examples of modularity are relatively peripheral systems, such as low-level visual and auditory perception and syntax. It may make sense to think of these systems as indeed indefeasible. This is particularly true for syntax, where modularity arguments have been made most strongly. The most distinctive thing about syntax is that it has no reality outside of linguistic behavior itself. There is no syntactic universe independent of us that we develop new and different ideas about. There is just the way we speak. There are no linguistic scientists who discover that language really has unexpected properties not included in any speaker's grammar. If a child incorrectly infers the rules of a language, it is inaccurate to say that he has got it wrong. Rather, he has simply created a new language. In fact, such cases as the development of creoles are often used to support the hypothesis that syntactic structures are innate (Bickerton, 1981). In these cases children are presented with input that is unlike natural language. In particular, they hear a pidgin language that has been created to allow speakers of different natural languages to communicate. The claim in the literature is that the children create a creole, a new natural language like other natural languages, rather than learning the pidgin language they are exposed to, and that this supports the innateness hypothesis.

Chomsky (1980) himself has muddied the waters by describing syntactic structures as our knowledge of a language, rather than as our ability to speak the language. According to Chomsky, universal grammar is therefore innate knowledge of language. If knowledge of language is innate, we might think, why not knowledge of other things as well? As Chomsky himself points out, whether we want to call syntactic competence "knowledge" or not is unimportant; there's no copyright on the term. What is important is that this type of knowledge is very different from our knowledge of the external world. Chomsky (1992) sometimes talks as if he thinks his model of the acquisition of syntax may be quite widely applicable to areas of psychology that are more genuinely cognitive (such as our knowledge of the physical or psychological world). It is worth pointing out, however, that Chomsky himself has resisted applying the same sorts of theories to semantics that he has applied to syntax.

Some perceptual phenomena are similarly indefeasible, though in a slightly different way. Unlike grammar, perception does refer to things outside itself. But when at least some perceptions are inaccurate, we tend to think that they are supplemented by beliefs, rather than replaced by better perceptions. We can arrange situations in which the perceptual system makes false inferences about the world. When this happens, we are stuck with the result, at least perceptually. No amount of knowledge will make the Müller-Lyer illusion go away.

Fodor (1983), the modern originator of the modularity idea, appropriately distinguishes between peripheral and central knowledge. Fodor advocates modules but contrasts them with another type of knowledge, "central process" knowledge, which includes scientific knowledge. In a way, our view is quite Fodorian. We also think there is a distinction to be drawn between peripheral modules and central processes, and that central processes include both ordinary everyday concepts and scientific concepts. And we think these everyday concepts are just as much (or, we would say, just as little) innate as scientific ones.[3]

The relative success of modularity accounts in some areas of cognitive science has led, understandably enough, to a tendency to extend those accounts to other, more central types of cognition and language. In particular, some cognitive psychologists, psycholinguists, philosophers, and developmentalists, have tried to extend the model of syntax to semantics, including lexical semantics. On this view, the possible range of semantic structures, the things we can think or in any case express linguistically, are themselves sharply constrained and limited in ways reminiscent of constraints on syntactic structures. Partly as a consequence of this and partly with the help of still further innate constraints on the relations between syntax and semantics, semantic structures are constrained in much the same way as syntactic structures are.

Such accounts date back to the very beginnings of the Chomskyan revolution, of course, with the early rise and later fall of generative semantics. More recently, however, they have been revived, though in very different forms, by writers like Pinker (1989), Jackendoff (1983), Landau and Jackendoff (1993), Talmy (1985), and Lakoff (1987). (Notice that there is an interesting convergence here of East and West Coast cognitive science.)

Moreover, modularity accounts have been proposed in a variety of cases that appear to involve genuinely conceptual and central knowledge of the world. In particular, Spelke et al. (1992) and Atran (1990) have suggested such a model for at least some aspects of our knowledge of physical objects and living things. Leslie (1988) and Fodor (1992) suggest such a model for our knowledge of the mind. There are even recent accounts proposing that our understanding of quite sophisticated aspects of social life, such as obligation and permission, fits this model (Barkow, Cosmides & Tooby, 1992). These accounts mesh with the accounts proposed in semantics. If there are strong constraints on the possible thoughts we can think and beliefs we can hold, there will also be constraints on the possible things we can say. Spelke et al. (1992) describe their account as "neo-Kantian," and this seems like quite an accurate term for this trend in cognitive science in general. Like Kant, these authors propose that certain conceptual structures are innately given and cannot be overturned by evidence.

Both empirically and conceptually, these applications of modularity to semantics and higher-level cognition have considerably less support than modularity accounts of low-level perceptual, motor, and syntactic abilities. There is, moreover, an important respect in which a modular account of semantics, particularly lexical semantics, and high-level cognition will be different from modular accounts of syntax or perception. The representations of syntax and perception are, at least plausibly, the end of the line. We may indeed have relatively fixed syntactic and perceptual representations. We may not be able to overthrow these structures without abandoning perception and syntax (as we do in scientific and formal languages).

In the case of concepts, beliefs, and words, however, such structures cannot be the end of the line. Our concepts and beliefs and the meanings of our words can and do change all the time, and do so in radical ways in science. Historically, it was the very fact of these radical changes in science that led to the abandonment of the Kantian view in philosophy. If we want a modularity view of conceptual structure to work, we must have, at the very least, some mechanism by which it feeds into a revisable, defeasible conceptual system, like the systems of science. Constraints must eventually be overthrown, biases rejected, conceptual organs reshaped.

But if there is such a mechanism, then the underdetermination arguments used in support of modularity in the first place become much weaker. The standard claim used to support modularity is that certain kinds of knowledge must be innate, since it is difficult to see how such knowledge could be learned. In answer to this claim, we might ask whether children could acquire these kinds of knowledge if they had a learning mechanism as powerful as that of science. Is a particular concept more underdetermined by evidence than scientific theories are? If we think that the cognitive devices of science are powerful enough to allow such learning to take place, we would need some very clear and strong reasons for believing that children do not have such cognitive devices. We would need to draw a sharp and clear line between our everyday cognitive mechanisms and the cognitive mechanisms of science. Otherwise, the underdetermination arguments would not go through. In any particular case it would then be an open empirical question whether a concept was the result of a module or a theory.

Empirical Generalizations: Scripts, Narratives, and Nets

Recently, nativist accounts of cognition have been more prevalent than empiricist ones, particularly in semantics and in discussions of cognition in infancy. However, there are also accounts in cognitive science and in cognitive development that are much more in the empiricist tradition. These accounts explain cognition in terms of the accumulation of particular pieces of information about the world.

We know, in fact, that even in science there are many cases where we know about things without having a theory about them. We may simply have a collection of observations with some regularities among them. Almost all of scientific medicine has this character. We notice a constant (or even inconstant) conjunction between treatment and cure.

Such conjunctions can be powerful enough to be the bases for whole professions and industries (physicians make a lot more money than physicists). In our discussion of theories in the last chapter, we used the philosophy-of-science term "empirical generalizations" to describe this kind of knowledge.

Some theories in cognitive science have proposed that knowledge consists of these sorts of empirical generalizations. "Scripts" are a good example. Scripts were originally proposed by Schank to provide an account of our everyday knowledge (Schank & Abelson, 1977). Scripts are cognitive structures that are supposed to have some predictive or generalizing force, but they are very different from theories. Nelson (1986) has argued that much of the child's early knowledge is organized into "event structures" much like scripts. Similarly, Bruner (1990) suggests that much of our ordinary knowledge is organized in terms of narratives. Narratives, at least on Bruner's view, are another example of a relatively atheoretical type of knowledge, of a kind of empirical generalization. Narratives may sometimes involve "theoretical" notions like causality, but the real constraints in narratives are simply the unities of time and place. As someone once said about the philosophy of history, a narrative is one damn thing after another. It is likely that some of our knowledge of the world has this character. It consists of a set of fairly narrow generalizations about which events typically follow which.

In the area of development, these theories propose that children combine primitive representations of events into more complicated ordered structures. They discover, for example, that a telephone conversation consists of more than just "hi" and "bye," or that something as apparently simple as eating dinner in fact consists of a number of actions with a characteristic order (no dessert until you finish your peas). This process of combination is often quite context-specific, and factors like familiarity and repetition play an important role.

A rather different empiricist account comes from psychologists working with connnectionist models (Bates & Elman, 1993; Clark, 1993; Karmiloff-Smith, 1992) or dynamic systems (Thelen & Smith, 1994). There are two aspects to connectionist modeling. One is that connectionist systems involve a (somewhat) more neurologically realistic kind of computation than classical computational systems. From this perspective, connectionist systems are simply an alternative way of implementing particular models of the mind and could be used to implement any such model.

But there is also a more substantive version of connectionism. On this view, connectionist systems imply a different model of the mind than classical implementations. On these connectionist views, knowledge is a distributed collection of quite particular and concrete pieces of information. Connectionist systems suggest a picture of cognition in which particular pieces of evidence or input are compared and weighted to form a single network. There are no broader and more abstract representations that would correspond to the entities and laws of a theory. Moreover, these accounts stress the fact that representations in connectionist systems often "emerge" from the input as a result of repeated training. Dynamic-systems theories propose an even more radical view: there are no representations, only complex dynamic causal relations between input and output.

While these accounts are not so clearly phrased in terms of empirical generalizations, the general type of explanation is similar. In essence, these connectionist and dynamic systems are designed to detect complex statistical patterns of regularity in the relations between inputs. These patterns may be considerably more complex and powerful than, say, the patterns that would be proposed in classical associationist accounts. This is what makes these systems interesting. Nevertheless, the basic kind of model is similar.

How can we tell whether we have an empirical generalization or a theory? Like theories, but unlike modules, empirical generalizations, scripts, narratives, and nets are defeasible. However, empirical generalizations contrast with theories on the structural and functional dimensions we described in the last chapter. In empirical generalizations the vocabulary of claims is just the same as evidential vocabulary; such generalizations don't posit separate abstract entities and laws. By themselves, empirical generalizations make few, if any, causal claims. At the most, they invoke a very general notion that there is some causal link between the antecedent and consequent. They do not make ontological commitments or support counterfactuals. As a result, the predictions they can generate are quite limited, basically of the form that what happened before will do so again. Similarly, they lead only to very limited constraints on the interpretation of new data. Finally, they generate, at best, rather limited and shallow explanations.

For example, consider "the restaurant script," Schank and Abelson's (1977) classic example of a cognitive structure that organizes our knowledge of the sequence of events in a restaurant. (As anyone who has dined out with a toddler is aware, it is a script that children acquire only gradually.) It could almost be taken as the paradigm of atheoretical knowledge. Knowing what happens in a restaurant is entirely a matter of fairly arbitrary generalizations about particular events (ordering, receiving the food, paying) and their order. The parts of the script are described in exactly the same terms one would describe the events themselves, not in terms of some underlying abstract entities. Moreover, the connections between the parts are not lawlike or even causal at all. There is no causal law that ensures that paying must come after eating; this is just how it usually happens. Indeed, the order may easily be overridden or changed. Similarly, the discovery, say, that a particular restaurant requires that you pay in advance has no empirical consequences for your other restaurant experiences. Going to a restaurant like Legal Seafood, where you pay first and eat afterward, isn't counterevidence that makes you doubt your understanding of all your other dinings out.

These features of scripts and other empirical generalizations mean that they can be distinguished from theories. We could contrast our everyday restaurant script and our everyday restaurant theory. Our restaurant script tells us what the restaurants we encounter are typically like. Our restaurant theories provide us with deeper and more abstract predictions, explanations, and interpretations of restaurants.

Suppose that we wanted to predict how not a local restaurant but, say, one on alpha centauri might serve its food. We would have to resort to some causal folk theory, rather than simply relying on a script. An episode of *Star Trek* featured a Klingon restaurant, newly opened on a space station, in which a large and aggressive waiter served up handfuls of wriggling live animals called "rastkh" to customers at a counter. A frail female human customer says "I can't eat that," speaks in Klingon to the waiter, and is instead presented with an even more actively wriggling mass. "Good," she says. "Nothing worse than half-dead rastkh." The joke depends partly on the simple violation of our restaurant script, in which animals (by and large) are killed before they are eaten, and on the mockery of self-consciously exotic sushi eaters on our planet. But at least for the attentive and faithful Trekkie, the joke also calls on complex, underlying theoretical anthropological generalizations about the kinds of creatures Klingons are (for the *Star Trek* uninitiated, they are militarist, macho, humorless, courageous, loyal, and melodramatic [the restaurant also features opera]) and about the kinds of restaurants they would be likely to run. We may never have seen a Klingon restaurant, but our folk theory enables us to predict what one would be like.

Similarly, we typically go beyond scripts precisely when we feel motivated to provide an explanatory account of phenomena. If we were to ask, Why do we eat first and pay later at restaurants? simply repeating the script would be an inadequate reply. We suggest that even the unscientific would grope for some folk-psychological or economic theory rather than being content with the script itself. The same is true of interpretive effects. If we go to a restaurant where we pay first and eat later, the data, though surprising, are acceptable: that's how they do it here. If we went to a restaurant in which the food suddenly appeared on the table out of nowhere, like the magic dining room in Jean Cocteau's *La belle et le bête*, we would reinterpret the data. The restaurant must be run by conjurors good at special effects; the food can't *really* appear out of the blue. The point is that when we want deeper explanatory adequacy or wider predictive power, we turn from scripts to theories, even when we are talking about restaurants.

These differences in the static organization and function of empirical generalizations and theories should allow us to distinguish between the two types of cognitive structures in any particular case. Moreover, while both theories and empirical generalizations are defeasible, the characteristic patterns of developmental change may also be different in the two cases. In the case of a theory, we will typically see a pattern in which the child holds to a particular set of predictions and interpretations for some time; the child has a particular theory. Then we may expect a period of disorganization, in which the theory is in crisis. And finally, we should see a new, equally coherent and stable theory emerge. In contrast, in the case of an empirical generalization, the child manifests a more piecemeal, contextually specific pattern of development. Very familiar and frequent pieces of information are learned first, and other pieces of information are gradually added to this store.

Interactions among Theories, Modules, and Empirical Generalizations

So far we have been considering the epistemological relations between theories, modules, and empirical generalizations. How can we tell when we have one or another? What kinds of evidence can discriminate between them? There is also another question to ask. Assuming that theories, modules, and empirical generalizations all are possible cognitive structures, and assuming, as the developmental pluralists we are, that all. three types of structures exist in us, we can try to understand the developmental relationships among them. How do these kinds of knowledge interact with each other in development?

Modules must help to provide the input to theorizing processes. On any view, there are encapsulated atheoretical processes that take us from patterns of stimulation at the retina to patterns of representation in the visual cortex. There may also be some encapsulated atheoretical phonological and syntactic processes that take us from patterns of stimulation at the cochlea to meaningful linguistic strings. Obviously, both what we see and what we hear from other people are important sources of evidence for theory construction. How far up, as it were, do these modular processes go? Where is the border between modules and theories, between the periphery and the center? If you seriously believed in the modularity of all commonsense conceptual knowledge, if you believed that there is what Spelke et al. (1992) call "core knowledge," the answer would be that the border lies at the dividing line between regular people and scientists. If you believe that our commonsense knowledge is at least partly theoretical, however, then this becomes an interesting and important empirical question.

One way of answering it might be by distinguishing modular perceptual processes and central cognitive ones. We might make a principled distinction between perception and cognition by saying that perceptual processes are those that lead to unrevisable representations, representations that are not, in Pylyshyn's (1984) phrase, "cognitively penetrable." These representations are the input to theories, which assign further representations, in this case highly defeasible representations.

It is important to notice that this way of making the distinction between perception and cognition doesn't map onto our phenomenology in any simple way. As we said earlier, a cognitive view of theories is not committed to any particular phenomenology that accompanies them. In fact, a lesson of the cognitive revolution is that phenomenology does not, in general, recapitulate epistemology. On this view, many representations that are theoretical, in the sense of being revisable and defeasible in theorylike ways, might have much of the direct, vivid phenomenology of perception.

In fact, there is good reason to believe that this is true. We know that in cases of expertise where we have a really extensive, worked-out theory that we regularly employ, claims that call on conceptual and even theoretical knowledge (the black king is in danger of check, the electron decayed, the patient has cancer) may be accompanied by very direct perceptionlike phenomenology. Conversely, it is possible that higher-order cognitive representations might be indefeasible and modular and yet not have the phenomenology of perception at all. For example, this is Spelke et al.'s (1992) suggestion with regard to "folk physics," and this is why she denies that the structures of "core knowledge" are perceptual (see also Gopnik, 1993a, 1993b, and discussion in *Cognitive Development* 8, no. 2 [1993]).

In particular, it seems very likely that such low-level visual representations as those of texture and distance are cognitively impenetrable. On the other hand, it seems very likely that such high-level visual representations as the perception of an object's identity are penetrable and often even theoretical. But there is a large intermediate area, for example, the representations involved in perceptual organization, where the answer is unclear. It might take extensive experimental and developmental work to sort out which representations were the result of modules and which were the result of theories (Rock, 1983).

While modular systems can provide input to theorizing systems, in some respects the two types of structures will simply coexist and develop in parallel and independently. Modules provide input to theories, but they are not replaced by theories. Modular representations may contradict theoretical representations and yet coexist with them. Certain perceptual illusions are, of course, the classic example of this. In something like the Müller-Lyer illusion (figure 3.1) our conceptual system overrides the perceptual system. Nevertheless, the perceptual system seems to continue to generate its modularized representations.

Figure 3.1
The Müller-Lyer illusion. Though the top line looks shorter, because of the outward-pointing arrowheads, the two lines are actually the same length.

Notice, however, that the perceptual illusions generated by modules determine our phenomenology, and perhaps our visual attention or reflexive behaviors, but not our actions or our language. If we want a long stick, we will reach for the stick that we know is longer, not the one that simply looks longer. If someone asks us which stick is longer, we will mention the stick that is really longer. In fact, we need to construct a very special "looks like" vocabulary even to express the perceptual phenomena linguistically at all. In contrast, our conceptual system, our beliefs, our theories are central to both our language and action. When modular and theoretical representations coexist, the theories underwrite a different and much wider range of other mental phenomena than modules.

Sometimes the representations and rules involved in a module may simply remain impenetrable and encapsulated forever. Fourier analysis is a good case in point. We know that at low levels of processing, the visual and auditory system perform fairly complex dynamic analyses of inputs that conform to Fourier analyses (DeValois & DeValois, 1988). We also know that these computational mechanisms are dedicated to these tasks. No process of reflection will give us access to these mechanisms for other purposes. Do we know the principles of Fourier analysis? Whether we want to call the representations of such a module "knowledge" or not is up for grabs; as we said before, there's no copyright on the term. We might say that the eyes, like the heart, have their reasons that reason knows not of. But, however much semantic tolerance we want to extend to modularity theorists, we would at least want to say that the defeasible central representations governing action and language are knowledge if anything is.

There is another possible relation between modules and theories, however. At some stages of development, information from within the originally modular peripheral systems may indeed become available to the central theorizing system. This is not the same as the proposal that the output of the modular systems serves as input to the theorizing systems. Instead, the idea is that at some point the internal structure of the module, its internal representations and rules, become subject to the same kinds of revision and restructuring as more theoretical kinds of representations and rules. In this way a module could be rewritten as an innate theory. We might say that we open up the module, look at what's inside, and turn it into a theory. Karmiloff-Smith (1992) has made extensive and interesting arguments for a role for this kind of "representational redescription" in cognitive and linguistic development. Both Karmiloff-Smith (1992) and Bowerman (1982) have convincing examples of such phenomena in the acquisition of syntax. Later we will point to several areas of cognitive development where a similar representational-redescription account may be useful.[4]

Like modules, empirical generalizations could be an important source of input to theorizing mechanisms. A sufficiently rich set of observations and generalizations could provide a child with an important initial knowledge base from which new theories could later be constructed. In fact, empirical generalizations often seem to play a crucial role in theory change. Almost by definition, empirical generalizations are the kind of knowledge that provides us with counterevidence to the predictions of the theory. The theory itself can't directly generate the counterevidence, though theory-internal considerations of simplicity or coherence may also play a role in theory change. In later chapters we will repeatedly see a pattern in which a theory makes inaccurate or insufficient predictions about some phenomena, the child goes through a period of intense experimentation, including the construction of empirical generalizations, and the resulting generalizations are then integrated into a new and more powerful theory.

Unlike modular representations, however, empirical generalizations, we suggest, are deeply influenced by theories. Indeed, as we said, earlier empirical generalizations may be, and, we think, usually are, phrased in the vocabulary of an existing theory. Once we get past the modular level, we suggest, we may always represent the world in terms of the representational vocabulary of our theories.

In both science and everyday cognition, however, the fact that a statement is phrased in theoretical terms doesn't mean that it is a theoretical statement. For example, astronomers using the Hubble telescope recently discovered that a number of distant stars are much older than they should be according to the big-bang theory. Similarly, there appears to be much less matter in the universe than there is supposed to be. The facts about the age of the stars and the missing matter are phrased in theoretical terms. They are extremely far removed from any perceptual inputs that might be specified by modules, such as the astronomers' reports of their visual perception of the Hubble's printouts. Nevertheless, we suggest that these are not theoretical claims; they are not predicted by the theory; they cannot be explained in terms of the theory. In fact, they contradict the theory. We all hope that a succeeding theory can be found that will predict and explain these empirical generalizations, but we don't have one yet.

Similarly, empirical generalizations, we suggest, will typically be phrased in terms of whatever theory the child currently holds. Nevertheless, the generalizations themselves may not be predicted by the current theory. In fact, when they are not predicted by the current theory, they may help induce the succeeding theory. It is also possible, however, that some empirical generalizations are never incorporated into new theories; they just sit around being scripts and narratives, and one damn thing after another (or, if this sounds too pejorative, they just sit around being the rich empirical texture of everyday life, autobiography, literature, and history).

It might be tempting to suppose that modules, empirical generalizations, and theories are ordered: that modules lead to empirical generalizations, which lead to theories. It also might be tempting to suppose that this ordering is reflected in development: that children begin with modules, proceed to empirical generalizations, and end up with theories. This might be a kind of developmental recapitulation of the philosophical attempts to develop a foundationalist epistemology in the 1920s and 1930s.

We think, however, that this is not the correct picture at all. On our view, modules, theories, and empirical generalizations are all in play literally from birth. Innate theories will assign powerful, abstract, and predictive representations to the outputs of modules. New information coming into the cognitive system will be represented in terms of these theories. Some relations among the inputs will not, however, be predicted by the theories; they will constitute empirical generalizations. Eventually, some of these kinds of inputs will lead to a revision of the theory, the modular outputs will be assigned new representations by the new theory, and so on. To return to Neurath's metaphor once again, children are never in dry dock; they never have a chance to construct their boats from scratch. Instead, like scientists, they employ their theories and revise them simultaneously.

Nonconceptual Development: Information Processing and Social Construction

Information processing

If we are genuinely interested in cognitive development—how we develop representations that provide us with a veridical view of the world—variants of the three views we've described above seem to us to be the only games in town. These are the most plausible current accounts of how we might arrive at substantive, accurate accounts of the world. Two other types of developmental accounts should be mentioned, however, since they are widely viewed as alternatives to those we have described above and since the mechanisms they propose could indeed play a contributing role to these more central cognitive engines.

The first is the idea that changes in broad information-processing abilities—such as motor skill, memory, the ability to construct hierarchies or deploy strategies, and so on—may be responsible for changes in development (Case, 1985; Siegler, 1990; Fischer, 1980). This position is sometimes called neo-Piagetian. Some of the advocates of this position believe, like Piaget, that there are general stage changes in cognitive development (Case, 1985). This is in contrast to the domain-specific predictions of all three of the accounts we have just considered. For Piaget, however, the general stage changes were due to changes in the deep logical structure of the child's cognition. Logical changes are, by definition, far-reaching and general, but unlike information-processing changes, they are themselves genuinely cognitive: they are changes in both the structure and content of our representations of the world. In contrast, the information-processing accounts do not contain mechanisms for making representations. Cognitive development involves changes in the information we have, not just in the way we use the information. Changes in information-processing abilities can, however, enable or disable other conceptual mechanisms such as modules, theories, or empirical generalizations.

As we mentioned in our dicussion of modularity, one of the most common uses of information-processing arguments in development is the idea that innately generated concepts are disabled by information-processing limitations. A typical argument is that children's errors on some allegedly cognitive task are really the result of some information-processing deficit. Conceptual structure is present, but it can't manifest itself because of information-processing limitations.

An alternative, and to our minds more interesting, way in which information processing might play a role is as an enabling device in a theory theory or empirical-generalization account. That is, it is conceivable that changes in information-processing abilities, broadly conceived, could give children more access to evidence than they had before such changes took place. Learning to walk or crawl, for instance, might plausibly give children access to important new kinds of information, which they could use in the creation of new theories of objects and space. Such abilities could also give children considerably more scope for experimentation than they can muster earlier on in development.

More subtle changes in mnemonic or hierarchical capacities might play a similar role. For example, both Karmiloff-Smith (1992) and Perner (1991) explain new conceptual advances in terms of the development of general capacities for metarepresentation. While Karmiloff-Smith and Perner elsewhere advocate the theory theory, it is worth pointing out that there is nothing intrinsically theoretical about this kind of meta-representational development. The mechanisms of change they propose are not theoretical mechanisms. From the point of view of the theory theory, the developmental work is done not by the fact *that* you represent your own representations but by the particular things that you represent about them.[5] Again, however, one might imagine that these sorts of architectural developments could play an enabling role in theory change.

The relation between information-processing changes and theory changes in childhood seems analogous to the relation between technological changes and theory changes in science. Technological innovations, by themselves, are notoriously inadequate for scientific progress. Buying a telescope doesn't make you Galileo. Moreover, such innovations are as often the consequence of theory change as the cause. This also often seems to be true in development. Chi, Glaser, and Rees (1982), for example, have shown that increases in memory span are often consequences of the child's increasingly sophisticated knowledge of a particular domain rather then the reverse.

Nevertheless, it might be argued that without the telescope, Galileo's advances in astronomy could not have been made. Similarly, it was recently argued that the supercolliding superconductor was necessary for advances in very sophisticated areas of theoretical physics. This is not because 47 miles of tunnels in Texas would provide a simple test of theories in particle physics and certainly not because anyone thinks that the tunnels would make up a new theory of particle physics. Rather, it is because the supercollidor would provide unseen and unprecedented kinds of evidence relevant to those theories. In the same way that technological advances enable or facilitate change in science, so information-processing advances might enable or facilitate theory change in children.

Social construction

A similar argument applies to the role of social interaction in cognitive development. As in the philosophy of science, "social constructivist" views of cognition have also been influential in cognitive development (e.g., Rogoff, 1990). Here the analogy to science is even more evident. At least for realists, social interaction by itself can't be a mechanism for cognitive change. Social interaction can as easily lead to the internalization of radically false conceptions of the world as true ones (as in the case of religion and magic). However, social interactions could be important enabling (or disabling) conditions in the development of a scientific theory. (All those conferences must have some function other than assortative mating.)

Social interactions might play a similar role in development. For example, a child might have developed a particular structure through one of the other processes we have mentioned and yet be unable to communicate that theory effectively to others because of limitations in their interactive, linguistic, or communicative competence (see Donaldson, 1978).

Alternatively and more interestingly, we can imagine many ways in which participation in a social community might enable or facilitate other mechanisms of conceptual change. Clearly this happens in science (see Kitcher, 1993), and we can imagine that it would also happen in childhood. As in science, social interaction may be particularly important as a way of gathering evidence. Other people might structure the child's life so that particular kinds of evidence are especially salient. For example, giving 18-month-olds particular objects to play with may often highlight particular phenomena. A child who plays with mixing bowls will be gathering evidence about different sorts of phenomena than a child who plays with clay, or spears and arrows.

Adults may also use linguistic devices to draw the child's attention to particular phenomena. While parents, unlike scientists or professors, don't lecture, they do talk, and their talk embodies their own conceptions of the world. As we will see, changes and differences in that talk, even just changes in emphasis or focus, can have important consequences for the children's cognitive development. As in the case of science, however, social interaction, by itself, can't produce veridical theories or genuine theory change, any more than merely attending our lectures can, alas, instill an understanding of cognitive development in our students. All such interactions can do is to provide information to some other cognitive mechanisms.

Of course, there are areas of development where social interaction plays a more central role than this. In areas where there is no fact of the matter, children may indeed develop by simply internalizing the structures provided to them by those around them. There is a wide variety of distinctively human normative and conventional practices where there is no fact of the matter. There is simply a way that people behave. Learning those practices may be a very complicated and interesting developmental process. We suggest, however, that such cases are really instances of socialization rather than cognition. Moreover, there are some domains, such as "theory of mind" understanding, where the line between cognition and socialization may sometimes be quite difficult to draw. Interestingly, syntax may be another such domain. As we mentioned above, other than practice there is no fact of the matter about syntactic structure. The most significant alternative to modularity accounts in syntactic development is not the theory theory but rather various functionalist theories that emphasize the role of social interaction in language acquisition (e.g., Tomasello, 1992). Assimilating *all* cognitive development to the model of socialization is, however, a dreadful mistake, allied to the dreadful mistake of postmodernism in general. The crucial fact about cognitive development, and cognition in general, is that it is veridical, it gives us a better understanding of the world outside ourselves. Purely social-constructivist views discount this fundamental link between the mind and the world.

Though we won't always systematically compare all these accounts in what follows, they do constitute the world of alternative possibilities in which we will place our discussion of the evidence. We will try to show that certain particular types of cognitive and semantic development are best explained in terms of theory formation, and not in terms of the triggering of modules or the accumulation of empirical generalizations, in terms of simple changes in information-processing skill, nor in terms of social interaction. At the same time we will also try to show how modules, empirical generalizations, information-processing abilities, and social interaction play a role in the formation of these theories.

II

Evidence for the Theory Theory

In chapter 2 we mentioned that several areas of children's cognitive development had proved to be particularly amenable to theory-theory explanations. In particular, investigators have looked at children's theory of the mind and their understanding of object kinds. Most of this work has involved children in the school-age and, more recently, pre-school-age group. The youngest children in these studies have been about 3. Interestingly, theories of mind and object kinds also turn out to be two of the most important domains in the 18-month-old child's cognition and language. Part of our strategy in this chapter and the following ones will be to work backward from what we know of 3-year-olds' theories to help infer the theories that children have at 18 months and to describe the differences between these theories and the later ones.

But we will also be working upward from infancy. Some of the words in the child's early vocabularies fit well, perhaps better, with what we know of infants' conceptions of the world than with what we know of those of older children. In fact, one aim of these chapters will be to give an account of children's theories that bridges the nonverbal infancy data, the data about very young children's spontaneous language, and the experimental studies that start at around age 3.

We suggest that there is a continuous line of development from the understandings of object appearance and disappearance involved in infant "object permanence" tasks, to the early understanding of visual perception, to the later understanding of belief and representation reflected in theory-of-mind tasks. A less well researched domain that is nevertheless equally important from the point of view of young children is the understanding of desires, plans, and intentions. Here we will suggest a line of development from an early understanding of the relations between actions and goals, to an early nonrepresentational understanding of desire and intention, to a later fully fledged understanding of desire as a representational state. Similarly, we will argue that there is a continuous line of development that bridges early object manipulation, early naming, and later "natural kind" understanding.[1]

We will suggest that these sets of problems—the nature of appearances, actions, and kinds—are at the core of the child's cognitive and semantic development in the period between late infancy and early childhood. This is reflected in children's nonlinguistic problem solving, in their spontaneous language, and later in their performance on verbal experimental tasks.

At the same time that we make this argument for continuity, we will also argue for deep conceptual changes in how children understand each of these domains. In particular, we will suggest that their early conceptions are quite different from their later conceptions and that their ideas about these domains change in a way that is like theory change. Moreover, we will suggest that even very early infant conceptions have some of the character of a theory: they involve abstract, coherent systems of entities and rules, which give rise to predictions, causal attributions, and interpretations and are revised in response to evidence.

In addition, we will argue that these domains may be relatively independent of each other in development. That is, though there are changes in all of these areas at around 18 months on average, the changes are not highly correlated and do not constitute a cognitive stage in Piaget's sense. Independent factors, including the acquisition of language itself, may emerge at 18 months to accelerate the changes. Nevertheless, conceptually, they are relatively independent of one another. In this sense our argument will be in line with many recent suggestions that development is domain-specific. Indeed, we have called this idea "the specificity hypothesis" (Gopnik & Meltzoff, 1986a). There is a fairly close relation between the theory theory and the idea of domain-specificity. In particular, the version of the view we suggest does not predict across-the-board logical changes of a Piagetian sort. Instead, we will chart a specific sequence of changes in each domain.

On Piaget's view, basic cognitive abilities involved in scientific theorizing—such as the ability to make inductions and deductions, the ability to consider evidence, the ability to entertain hypotheses, and other general logical capacities—are gradually developed over the course of childhood. As each of these developments occur, there is a very general restructuring of children's knowledge. On our view, these capacities are available from the very start of development. Developing a particular set of inductions and deductions, however, depends on having a particular body of knowledge organized in a theorylike way.

Thus on our view we would expect to see inferences about the behavior of objects and people from birth. Some inferences might be specified by innate theories. Others, however, will become possible only as the infant restructures and extends those theories. Moreover, developing theories of different domains may enable the child to make quite different kinds of inferences. Similarly, in developments in science, while the processes of theorizing may be generally similar, different domains may proceed quite independently. Advances in biology need not reflect advances in physics and vice versa.

In another sense, however, we will be arguing against domain-specificity. Some traditions in linguistics have argued that linguistic development is quite separate from nonlinguistic conceptual development. We, however, will argue that conceptual and semantic developments within each domain are closely related to one another, though neither conceptual nor semantic developments are closely related to conceptual and semantic developments in other domains.

A general caveat here. We want to present a quite detailed account of the particular theories that infants and young children hold at particular times, as well as we can on the basis of the present evidence. We have every expectation that the details of these accounts will change as we accumulate more empirical data. However, our overarching aim in these chapters is to show, in general, how describing development in terms of the theory theory can offer good explanations and substantive predictions. The best way to do this, on our view, is to make quite specific claims about the sequence of particular theories, claims that can and will be tested and revised. This enterprise should, we hope, support the general framework of the theory theory, even if more research eventually leads to changes in the details of the particular theories that we will advance here.

4

The Child's Theory of Appearances

The Adult Theory

The development of infants' understanding of object appearances and disappearances is one of the most thoroughly researched areas of cognitive development. At the same time, however, the very pace and intensity of the research has left this area in some ways less clearly understood than other areas of development. Piaget's original account (1954) is the jumping off place for later accounts, and work in the Piagetian tradition is an important part of the data base. But more recent research requires that we abandon both Piaget's empirical claims and his theoretical conclusions. Moreover, more recent research at least begins to let us see how the work on infants is related to later developments in early childhood, such as the development of visual-perspective taking.

Many discussions of object permanence treat it as a single concept that develops at some single point in infancy. The question then becomes when the child develops the concept. An alternative view would be to see adult object permanence as part of a complex and tightly interwoven theory of objects, space, and perception, rather than as a single concept to be discovered. On this view, our ordinary concept of a continuing, permanent object is an abstract theoretical entity that, among other things, explains sequences of object appearances and disappearances at the evidential level. The underlying properties of the object and other objects cause the object appearances and disappearances to have certain regularities. These properties are related to one another in coherent ways.

There are four factors in our adult theory explaining how permanent objects moving in space lead to sequences of object appearances

and disappearances. First, there are the laws governing the movement
of objects. Second, there are the properties of the objects themselves.
Third, there are the spatial relations between stationary objects. Finally,
there are the laws that govern the perceptual relations between observers
and objects. The theory of object appearances is an interesting bridge
between "folk physics" and "folk psychology." It involves ideas about
objects and the relations among them, but just as crucially, it involves
ideas about the way that we and others perceive objects.

With full knowledge of all these factors, we can make quite accurate
and wide-ranging predictions about when an object will disappear and
reappear and when it will be visible or invisible to a particular observer.
Moreover, we can construct intelligent alternative hypotheses about
apparently mysterious disappearances, since the theory leads us to interpret evidence about disappearances in particular ways. Finally, the theory
allows us to explain disappearances and reappearances.

Conjuring tricks are an interesting illustration of our use of this sort
of adult theory of object appearances. The general principle of conjuring
tricks is that they violate our deep ontological commitments about the
nature of the world. Conjuring tricks are designed, first of all, to cause
certain perceptual illusions. Our perceptual system tells us, for example,
that the silk handkerchief has disappeared into thin air or that the rabbit
has leaped from the box to the hat without moving through the intervening space. These odd events capture our attention.

But merely creating perceptual illusions isn't enough for magic.
When we are faced with these illusions, we use our higher-level theories
to devise alternative explanations for the perceptual appearances. As we
say, we can't believe our eyes. Much of the conjuror's art is devoted not
just to producing the appearances but also to frustrating the explanations.
For example, we might propose that the rabbit was really in the hat
all along, though out of sight, and so the conjuror collapses and re-
constitutes the hat in front of our eyes first. Or we might think that
our perceptual capacities were being undermined, say by distracting our
attention, and so the conjuror finds an audience member and instructs
him under no circumstances to take his eye off the box. The postmodern
magicians Penn and Teller are famous for "explaining" the tricks to the
audiences. But in fact what they do is to take this process of frustrating
explanations one step further: they give possible "trick" explanations that
someone with little knowledge of conjuring might not immediately

think of; they add, as it were, to our theoretical stock. Then they frustrate these explanations too. One point about a theory is that it doesn't necessarily give just one answer to a specific question like "Where's the rabbit?" It gives a range of possible hypotheses, which are then subject to further confirmation. These alternative explanations lead to detailed and constrained predictions about where the object might really be (up the magician's sleeve, rather than in his hotel room) and to interpretations, in fact rejections, of the apparently deviant evidence.

It is interesting to contrast the case of a conjuror and the case of a clown. The clown violates all our familiar scripts of behavior or events: he throws custard pies at people at random, eats his necktie, and wears a banana round his neck, generally acting silly. But while he may evoke a kind of moral or social unease, he doesn't evoke the ontological unease that a conjuror does. Commonsense adult theories make ontological commitments and counterfactual supporting causal claims in a way in which empirical generalizations or scripts do not. One test of whether a particular belief was the result of a module, an empirical generalization, or a theory might be to think about how we would react to an event that violated that belief. If our knowledge was really modular in a strict sense, we should not be able to represent the event at all, as our perceptual system can't represent the reality in a perceptual illusion and children can't represent the syntax of a pidgin language. If the event violates a script or an empirical generalization, we might find it weird or surprising. However, only if it violates a theory, with all its ontological commitments, will we think it's magic.

So our adult understanding of permanent objects seems to have some of the structural and functional characteristics of a theory. It involves a system of abstract causal entities and rules related to one another in coherent ways. It allows a wide variety of coherent predictions, and it leads to interpretations and explanations.

Does object permanence, however, have the dynamic character of a theory? Is it defeasible? Recall our earlier discussion of modularity. Some object disappearances seem to be handled at this perceptual–modular level. For example, when I blink, an object may technically disappear but I continue to represent it. It seems very likely that my continued representation of the object and my predictions about its location in these cases are simply specified by the perceptual system itself and do not involve any sort of central belief system or commonsense theory.

Can this be true more generally? Is what we have been calling our commonsense theory of object disappearance specified not by a system of defeasible beliefs but by a sort of "object module"? Spelke et al. have made vigorous and interesting arguments for this view (Spelke, 1994; Spelke, Breinlinger, Macomber & Jacobsen, 1992; Spelke & Van de Walle, 1993). They argue that we innately represent certain perceptual events in particular ways. These representations constitute a "core knowledge" that does not substantially change later in development, and this core knowledge operates as a kind of constraint on our conceptual system.

Clearly, our perceptual system is an extremely important source of information about objects, and clearly that information is already represented in an abstract form. At the very least, the perceptual system already "smooths over" our blinks, for example. There may well be modular systems that also lead to more complex, abstract representations of objects. But while the perceptual representations themselves may be largely constrained and indefeasible, it's also clear that we can override these perceptual representations in theorylike ways in our ordinary life and that we could override them still further with further evidence.

Think again about the conjuring cases. The point in those cases is not only that we can make predictions about where the object will appear, of a sort that might be specified by an object module. It is also that even when these predictions are disconfirmed, when the perceptual system, as it were, is assuring us that the rabbit really did vanish from the box and appear in the hat, we can formulate alternative possibilities and make other predictions. We attribute the apparent disappearance to a deeper underlying cause, usually some sort of movement. The conjuring cases involve a conflict between the representations generated by our perceptual system and the representations generated by our theories. The fact that we can override the illusions already suggests that our representations of the objects are defeasible.

In the conjuring cases, we seem to use a theory to override our perceptual representations. But could we also override the theory? Could our whole theory of object appearances and disappearances be disconfirmed? In some sense, of course, this already happens when we learn about physics. Even Newtonian physics disconfirms some of the basic postulates of our "folk physics," let alone Einsteinian physics. And the division of labor means that we are ontologically committed to the theories proposed by science.

Well, we might reply, as Spelke (1994) does, even when we believe that theories in physics tell us the real truth about objects, such theories may not have direct consequences for our everyday experience; it is possible to treat the two sets of beliefs as complementary rather than contradictory (see also Atran, 1990).

But notice that even in ordinary life there are many cases where our predictions about objects and disappearances would plainly have to override any innate core principles. In particular, our knowledge of properties and processes informs our predictions. To use a simple and ubiquitous example, when we eat things, we do not assume that they will reappear at the location where they disappeared. Instead, we assume that they will be transformed or destroyed. Spelke (1994) also discusses the analogous case of shadows. Shadows violate our ordinary account of objects. Interestingly, infants initially seem to pay special attention to these violations. Eventually, of course, we learn that these violations are not really surprising. We modify our theory to account for them.

Moreover, we can also perform a sort of thought-experiment version of the forbidden crucial experiment we proposed in the last chapter.[1] Suppose, for example, that the "transporter beams" on *Star Trek* became a ubiquitous reality. We might have difficulty saying whether we thought the object really ceased to exist during transport or was simply hidden from view in a very peculiar way. Transporter beams would disconfirm our current adult commonsense theoretical view that objects must trace a continuous spatiotemporal path as they move from one location to another. Moreover, since our understanding of permanence is part of a wide-ranging and coherent theory, the disconfirmation of the theory would have consequences for other parts of our understanding of objects (and people) as well. Indeed, one episode of *Star Trek* was devoted to the romantic complexities that followed when a single person was accidentally transported to two different planets simultaneously. Notice, however, that the very fact that we can make coherent sense of the *Star Trek* world implies the capacity to override fairly fundamental parts of our commonsense object theory. If the core knowledge thesis is correct, then this intuition about the results of our thought experiment should be wrong. On the core knowledge view, if we really were on the

Enterprise, we would be permanently stymied in our attempts to represent the effects of transporter beams, and indeed, we should be permanently stymied in our attempts to explain eating in this world.

So our normal representations of object appearances and disappearances not only have the synchronic character of theories. In addition,
and unlike the representations given directly by the perceptual system,
they are also defeasible and disconfirmable, at least in principle. But we
can also ask the dynamic question of theory change the other way
around. If the theories are defeasible at one end, are they defeasible at the
other end too? Is there a history of theory formation and revision that
leads to their eventual appearance? And if so, when and how does this
theory develop?

The Initial Theory

As we argued in the last chapter, the theory theory is more than compatible with the idea that there is a rich, abstract, innate structure to the
child's understanding of the mind and the world. Indeed, we think these
structures are rich enough and abstract enough to merit the name of
theories themselves. Unlike modularity theorists, however, we also think
these structures are themselves defeasible; they are revised and restructured in important ways as the child accumulates more evidence about
the world.

There is considerable evidence that infants have a much more
highly structured initial view of objects than we previously supposed. For
example, one classic question that had long been debated in the literature
was whether our understanding of distance is innately specified or is
the result of some inferential process. There is now fairly solid evidence
that at least some distance cues are specified innately (Bower, 1982;
Caron, Caron & Carlson, 1979; Slater, Mattock & Brown, 1990; Slater
& Morison, 1985; Yonas & Granrud, 1985). Similarly, there is strong
evidence for innate links between information picked up from different
sensory modalities (Bahrick, 1983; Bower, 1982; Kuhl & Meltzoff, 1982;
Meltzoff & Borton, 1979; Spelke, 1976, 1979, 1987). In these studies an
understanding of distance and cross-modal mapping was demonstrated
by more passive measures of whether infants look more at some displays
than others (as in habituation and preferential-looking paradigms). But
these abilities can also be demonstrated in experiments that use more

active measures of the infants' behavior, such as reaching and imitation. In these experiments newborns use perception to govern their actions. The results are consonant with the looking-time studies: they show both an understanding of distance and cross-modal mapping within the first month of life (Bower, 1982; Butterworth & Hopkins, 1988; Hofsten, 1982; Meltzoff, 1993; Meltzoff & Moore, 1977, 1983).

The research we have just described suggests that infants are born assuming a world of three-dimensional, amodal objects. Their representations of the world are abstract and interrelated, and they license certain kinds of inferences and predictions. For example, infants make appropriate inferences about whether their reaches will make contact with an object and about the relation between size and distance (Bower, 1982; Hofsten, 1982). They correctly and productively infer that if an object has certain visual features, it will have certain corresponding tactile or auditory features (Kuhl & Meltzoff, 1984; Meltzoff, 1990; Spelke, 1976, 1979, 1987). These extremely early representations are plainly much richer than Piaget supposed, and than we often suggest when we talk about purely "perceptual" capacities.

More directly relevant to object appearances, within the first six months of life, infants are capable of responding to an object that has disappeared from sight. Piaget himself noticed this. For example, if infants lose sight of an object because they turn their head away from it, they will move their heads back again to recover sight of the object (Piaget, 1954). Similarly, young infants will move an object they hold into their visual field (Piaget, 1954). There is also some evidence suggesting that young infants who are looking at an object when the room lights are extinguished may continue to reach for the object that they saw before (Bower & Wishart, 1972; Clifton et al., 1991; Hood & Willatts, 1986). In these cases it is clear that even these very young infants predict something about where the object will reappear after it has disappeared. Indeed, in the reaching-in-the-dark cases, the infant must continue to represent the object even when it is out of their immediate sight. If we use this minimal notion of object permanence, then even very young infants seem to have object permanence.

By the time they are 6 months old, young infants also demonstrate a great deal of systematic, coherent knowledge about the movements of objects. Infants seem to be able to project the visible trajectory of an object. That is, if they see an object moving on a trajectory, they predict that it will be at the appropriate place at the appropriate time later in that trajectory. If an object disappears at one edge of a screen infants will look in anticipation at the far edge of the screen, and if the object does not appear at its expected place at the right time, the infant's tracking will be disrupted, and they may even look back to the original edge of the screen (Bower, Broughton & Moore, 1971; Moore, Borton & Darby, 1978). Infants also show anticipatory reaching to the place an object will be on a visible trajectory (Hofsten, 1980; Hofsten & Lindhagen, 1979). Infants show similar kinds of knowledge in some habituation studies. Under certain circumstances, they also seem to know that solid three-dimensional objects will not be able to move through each other if they are on the same path (Baillargeon, 1986, 1987a, 1987b, 1993; Bower, 1982; Bower, Broughton & Moore, 1970; Spelke et al., 1992; Spelke et al., 1994; Spelke & Van de Walle, 1993; but see Cohen, 1995).

This knowledge, like the earlier knowledge of distance and cross-modal regularity, also has the abstract and predictive quality of a theory. Thus infants can make predictions about the novel trajectories of novel objects. Moreover, the knowledge is manifest in a variety of tasks with a variety of measures, including active measures like reaching and visual tracking, as well as more passive measures of looking times.

Interestingly, however, very young infants do not seem to show disrupted tracking if an object disappears behind a screen and a completely different object emerges at the far edge of the screen on the same trajectory, nor are they surprised by these events (Bower, 1982; Bower et al., 1971). Similarly, young infants do not show surprise if an object under a cloth is surreptitiously replaced by another object (LeCompte & Gratch, 1972). In fact, according to Bower, very young infants do not show disrupted tracking even if an object visibly changes its features, so long as it continues on the same trajectory. In contrast, they do show disrupted tracking when an object suddenly stops or changes its trajectory, and their specific pattern of tracking suggests that they are continuing to search for the object along its original trajectory in these cases. Meltzoff and Moore found similar phenomena in very young infants' individuation of people. Infants' seemed to have some difficulty identifying individuals strictly on the basis of their static perceptual features, without relevant evidence about their continuous movements (Meltzoff & Moore, 1992, 1995b). The phenomena seem to appear for both people and things.

Similarly, both Bower (1965; 1982) and Spelke (1990) suggest in general terms that very young infants use primarily movement information (such as common fate) to individuate objects rather than such static Gestalt properties as proximity or similarity. Moreover, Kellman and Spelke (1983) found, in particular, that young infants did not treat a stationary continuous object that was partly occluded by another object as a single object, although adults in similar settings would treat it as a single object. When the two parts of the object moved together, however, the infants did treat it as a single object (see also Johnson & Aslin, 1995; Kellman, Spelke & Short, 1986; Spelke, 1990; Slater et al., 1990).

These young infants apparently use the place or trajectory of an object to individuate it, rather than its static perceptual features or properties. Their predictions about the behavior of objects center on an object's movements, rather than its properties (Bower, 1982; Moore, Borton & Darby, 1978; Meltzoff & Moore, 1995b). By 5 or 6 months of age infants may begin to take static features into account in their individuation of objects. For example, they appear to show disrupted tracking of objects if a new object appears on the far side of a screen (Bower, 1982; Moore, Borton & Darby, 1978). By 9 months, though not earlier, infants show some mild surprise when an object is surreptitiously replaced by another object, though they show more extreme surprise at 16 months (LeCompte & Gratch, 1972; Gratch, 1982). However, until around 12 months these infants do not seem to infer that when one object with one set of features disappears and a different object emerges, there must have been two different objects behind the screen (Xu & Carey, in press). They make similar inferences based on object movements much earlier. The process of integrating features and movements and using features to individuate objects seems to develop gradually in the first year.

In one sense, this research indicates a very early and surprisingly sophisticated understanding of objects. This includes the ability to extrapolate trajectories of objects and the assumption that solid objects cannot pass through each other. A priori, we might not have thought it likely that these conceptions of the world would appear at such an early stage of development, just as we might not think, a priori, that cross-modal links or an understanding of distance would be innate.

On the other hand, other aspects of the theory that would appear a priori to be as central to the adult theory as these principles do not appear to be innate. In particular, as adults we individuate and reidentify objects by using both place and trajectory information and static-property information. We also use property information to predict and explain appearances and disappearances. If the same large, distinctive white rabbit appears in the box and later in the hat, I assume its the same rabbit, even if I don't immediately see a path of movement for it. In fact, I infer an often quite complex, invisible path for the object. If I see the green scarf turn into a bunch of flowers as it passes through the conjuror's hand while maintaining its trajectory, I assume it is a different object. On the other hand, if an object changes its trajectory, even in a very complex way, while maintaining its properties, I will assume it is still the same object. For the very youngest infants, the opposite assumption seems to be true: they reidentify objects by their movements rather than their properties, and they predict that paths of movement will remain constant but not that properties will do so.

Notice, moreover, that the difference between the place and trajectory theory and our adult theory of objects is not just that the first theory is a more limited subset of the second. It is not just that the addition of property information enriches the object theory. Instead, the two theories postulate substantively different entities and make substantively different predictions. The place and trajectory theory predicts that objects can change their features but not their trajectories. The feature theory predicts that objects can change their trajectories but not their features.

It seems strange to say that an understanding of objects in which it is odder to see an object change its trajectory than to change its features is core adult knowledge. In fact, ironically, some of Spelke's own findings should be problematic for her "core knowledge" hypothesis. To use an example from Spelke's own research, it is odd to say that infant "core knowledge"—in which the principle of common fate individuates objects but proximity, similarity, and the principle of good form do not—is fundamentally identical to adult understanding. For adults, the continuity of a partially occluded stationary object is as compelling an inference as any we make.

The Paradox of Invisible Objects

An important and interesting question is whether these young infants sometimes apply their theory of object movement to objects not immediately visible. There is some evidence that they do this. Infants show distinctive looking patterns if they are first shown objects moving in a normal way and are then shown similar but anomalous events. These include events such as a screen slowly descending backwards without interfering with the object (Baillargeon, 1987a, 1991; Baillargeon, Spelke & Wasserman, 1985), an object appearing to move through another object behind a screen (Baillargeon, 1986; Baillargeon & DeVos, 1991; Spelke et al., 1992; Spelke et al., 1994) and an object moving behind a screen in a way that implies a discontinuous trajectory (Baillargeon & Graber, 1987; Moore, Borton & Darby, 1978; Spelke et al., 1995).

These infants may indeed be applying their theory of visible movement to these cases. They may be making the assumption that even when they lose perceptual contact with objects, the objects will continue to be at the places or along the trajectories where they were when last seen. The infants may represent a world of objects moving in particular visible ways and believe that the objects continue to exist even when some portions of the events are occluded.

A number of other results suggest a different picture, however. These same young infants do not show disrupted tracking when an object smoothly moves from right to left, disappears at one edge of a screen, then fails to appear at a gap in the middle of the screens, but reappears at the opposite edge of a second screen. This suggests that young infants do not represent the object as necessarily continuing through the gap. This behavior only emerges at around 9 months (Moore, Borton & Darby, 1978). Moreover, these same young infants are at a loss when an object, even a highly desirable object like a bottle or toy, disappears under or behind a screen (Piaget, 1954; Uzgiris & Hunt, 1975). In spite of their apparent perceptual expectations, 6-month-olds do not search for the object.

Piaget's result that 6-month-olds fail to search for hidden objects is, of course, a classic and highly replicated finding. Some more recent studies using slightly different techniques may also support this finding. The same 6-month-old infants who seem to anticipate an object's invisible trajectory in looking studies do not anticipatorily reach toward the object, though they will reach for objects on visible trajectories (Hofsten et al., 1994). Finally, infants will not even perform a simple action, well within their competence, to obtain a hidden object, though they will perform such an action to obtain a visible object (Munakata et al., 1994). All of these behaviors do emerge later, at around 9 months.

So we seem to be faced by a contradiction in the young infant's abilities. Some kinds of knowledge that seem to appear in one paradigm, the looking-time paradigm, do not appear when we use other measures, such as surprise, visual tracking, or search. Notice that it is not simply that these measures always yield different results. It is not simply that habituation measures are more sensitive than measures of action. Contra Piaget, there is now general agreement that by 9 months infants predict that an object will be at the location where it disappeared. These predictions are manifest in habituation measures, and in a wide variety of search behaviors, but also in infants' surprise reactions and in their tracking behavior. Similarly, there is concordant information from a variety of measures for the young infant's early understanding of distance and cross-modal matching, and for the infant's theory of visible-object movements. In the particular case of the child's application of this theory to invisible objects and the particular period of between about 3 and 9 months, however, there seems to be a discrepancy between measures. When we look at the child's visual attention, as measured in habituation studies, we seem to see one kind of knowledge, and when we look at the child's search or tracking behavior or reaching or surprise reactions, we seem to see quite another kind.

This is a real and important empirical problem, but the debate it has generated is in some ways unfortunate. The sound bite is that we used to think that object permanence develops at 18 months, but now, with more sensitive tests, we think it develops much earlier. This is very misleading, however. There is not a single object-permanence achievement. Many changes occur in children's understanding of appearances and disappearances, and they are well documented throughout infancy. In particular, as we saw, there are other early changes, and as we will see, there are still other later changes, in the child's understanding of appearance and disappearance. However, we will pause for a moment to consider the problem of the young infant's understanding of invisible objects, since it raises interesting issues about the relations between theory formation and other types of knowledge. There are a number of different approaches we might take to resolving this paradox.

Information-processing limitations?

One common way to resolve the discrepancy is to invoke information-processing limitations: to claim that the child has the relevant knowledge of object permanence but fails to express it in search behavior because of other limitations. However, no one has ever been able to propose a coherent account of just exactly what these information-processing limitations are or to provide much independent evidence for them. Simple memory or motor deficits are clearly not the problem. For example, 6-month-olds can and will successfully search for an object under a transparent cover (Bower & Wishart, 1972). Slightly older children search for a partially occluded object, which indicates that their motor skills and motivation are intact (Moore & Meltzoff, 1978; Piaget, 1954). In the experiment by Munakata et al. (1994), infants failed to perform an extremely simple bar press, which they would produce when the object was visible. Note also that there is converging evidence from studies of several different behaviors—not just search but also surprise, reaching, and visual tracking—for the idea that there is a significant change at 9 months.

Habituation limitations?

The information-processing view suggests that we overinterpret the later difficulties in action. We might also want to take the alternative view and suggest instead that we are overinterpreting the early habituation studies in arguing that they demonstrate an understanding of genuine permanence. The studies are congruent with other studies in suggesting a much richer initial conception of objects than Piaget supposed, but it is still unclear precisely what they allow us to infer about infants' early understanding of invisible objects. In particular, the studies depend on a single paradigm in which infants are first habituated to particular events and then often quite small shifts in visual attention are recorded. It is not clear how much these findings are limited to particular types of stimuli, and more generally, the theoretical work has yet to be done that completely specifies the relation between these visual-attention measures and underlying cognitive competence.

Modularity

Another path toward the resolution of these difficulties might be to invoke the distinction between central theories, perceptual modules, and empirical generalizations. As we saw in the last chapter, there may be cases in which these different kinds of cognitive systems assign contradictory representations to the same input. Something like this might be the explanation for the contradictions in the child's behavior at this point in development.

Some fairly abstract perceptual representations may well be the result of indefeasible systems. Some of these very early predictions about disappearances may similarly be the result of modular systems. As we argued above, innate perceptually based representational systems may be theorylike in many ways: they may involve quite abstract representations, related to the actual input in abstract ways, which then may allow predictions.

There may be reasons to suppose that some of the very early phenomena reported by Spelke et al. (1992), Baillargeon (1993), and Bower (1982) have this kind of character. Again as Spelke et al. (1992) themselves point out, these findings give us little evidence that the child is making predictions or registering surprise, nor do they indicate the strength of the child's conviction about the violations or show whether the child is capable of entertaining alternative hypotheses. Such predictions, deductions, and ontological commitments are characteristic of both theoretical knowledge and, we will argue, of the 9-month-old's and the 18-month-old's understanding of invisible objects. They are also, we would argue, characteristic of the very young infant's understanding of distance and movement. It is possible, however, that the shifts in visual attention recorded by these investigators reflect the innate calculations of a modularized perceptual system. Like other modularized systems, these representations may strictly control visual attention and not other more central cognitive processes.

In fact, Spelke suggests this in her recent work (1994). She suggests a discontinuity of the sort we are describing between the infant's knowledge as reflected in action and that reflected in habituation experiments. She draws a rather odd conclusion from this, however. Her conclusion is that the kinds of representations involved in the shifts in visual attention in habituation experiments are "core knowledge" and the kinds of representations that govern purposive, goal-directed actions are not. As we have repeatedly said the term "knowledge" is up for grabs. Still, surely if we were choosing which kinds of knowledge were likely to be modular and peripheral and which central and core, we would not say that knowledge that governed small shifts in visual attention was core and knowledge that governed goal-directed action was not.

There is a kind of ambiguity about the term "knowledge" in many discussions of modularity. The problem is that the more truly modular the systems are, the more inflexible and fixed, and the more narrowly they are limited to a few outputs and inputs, the less they look like what we would usually call knowledge. But the interest and excitement about modularity comes because it promises an explanation of knowledge in the usual sense. If Chomsky talked about innate syntactic abilities instead of innate knowledge of language, his claims would be both less controversial and less interesting. The same would be true if Spelke talked about innate constraints on the visual-attention system instead of core knowledge.

Representational redescription

Yet another alternative is that the representations of the perceptual system, rather than remaining utterly encapsulated, might later feed into the more conceptual central theorizing systems by a process like "representational redescription." Indeed, Karmiloff-Smith (1992) has suggested this. The idea is that the earlier representations and rules of the modularized perceptual system might become available to the more centralized theorizing mechanism at a later point. They could then be susceptible to experimental test, reorganization, confirmation, and disconfirmation in a way that they are not when they are simply encapsulated in the module. At the same time, though, this very process might take some time developmentally, and this might contribute to the lag between the earlier perceptual capacities and their later expression in intentional behavior.

Empirical generalization

Finally, the habituation results might represent a particular empirical generalization about the behavior of objects. It is striking, in this regard, that the tasks depend on giving the infant a set of consistent experiences in the initial phase of the experiment, experiences that the infant must relate to the experiences in the dishabituation phase. The habituation paradigm asks the baby not "Could this happen?" but "Is this like what you just saw?" The ingenuity of the experimental design is in showing that the infant doesn't make this empirical discrimination just on the basis of superficial perceptual features of the situation. Infants do not dishabituate to events that are equally perceptually different from the habituating event but are not anomalous. The difference between these two cases underpins the claims about the infant's knowledge.

The infants may, in fact, be noticing that objects behave in particular ways and not others, in particular, that there is regularity in the appearances and disappearances of objects. These regularities are reinforced by the technique in the habituation experiments. The regularities may even be phrased in terms of the earlier movement theory. The infant may be saying to herself, in effect, "I have seen things like this before, and in some ways they are like what my object-movement theory says," or alternatively, "This is completely new to me and is very much unlike what I just saw or anything my object-movement theory says." But this recognition need not imply that the infant makes any active inferences about the objects, nor that she uses her knowledge to control actions.

Compare the scientific case. A celestial navigator can recognize that an event is similar to an event he has seen before, the stars were in a similar configuration last fall. Alternatively, he can recognize that another event is completely novel; nothing like this has appeared in the skies before. But neither of these reactions of familiarity or unfamiliarity necessitates prediction or inference. Similarly, the knowledge that some object configurations are familiar or not may not be part of the infant's theory of objects at this point, and so may not be used to control actions. Infants may notice when these regularities are violated without postulating that an object exists in the fully powerful and causal way that allows them to make predictions about trajectories or to postulate a permanent object later on. We might imagine that just these sorts of empirical generalizations play a role in the formation of the more powerful theoretical understanding of invisible objects at 9 months.

An Alternative: A Theory-Change Account

The modularity, representational-redescription, and empirical-generalization views would say that the habituation experiments really do reveal something about the young infant's representations of objects. Moreover, these kinds of representations might play an important role in the formulation of the fuller theory of object appearances and reappearances later on. This knowledge, however, would not be theoretical, as early knowledge of trajectories is theoretical or as later knowledge of object permanence is. It would not allow predictions and inferences in the same way, nor would it govern action and language.

Yet another possibility is that both habituation studies and action studies are tapping genuinely theoretical representations in this case as well as in others. We might interpret the longer looking times in the habituation studies as an indicator of a response to theoretical violations: they might be the closest a 5-month-old can get to exploring counter-evidence. The apparent discrepancies between earlier and later competence and between looking-time and action studies might indicate a genuine conceptual shift rather than multiple simultaneous representations, one for observation and another for action. The younger and older infants really might represent the objects differently, though this difference might not be immediately apparent, given the presuppositions of the adult theory.

The conceptual shift would rest on a distinction between representing an object when it is hidden and representing an object as being hidden. Consider the case of an infant reaching for an object when the lights are turned off. It seems at least plausible that these infants may continue to represent the object at the same location, even though they have no immediate perceptual access to the object. However, these infants presumably have no representations of why or how they have lost sight of the object. If they wanted to regain visual contact with the object, they would have no way of doing so. The thought of reaching for the light switch would never occur to them. They would represent the object that was out of sight but not represent how, or why, or in the strongest case, perhaps even that, it was out of sight.

Young infants faced with occluded objects may be in a similar situation. They may continue to represent the object at the place or along the trajectory at which they last saw it, even though they no longer have direct perceptual evidence that it is at that location or along that trajectory. This is an important ability and certainly implies a much richer representation of objects than Piaget supposed. They may, however, have no theoretical account of why the object is no longer visible. In particular, they may not represent it as being behind the occluder. More tellingly, they may not know that the relation between their own body, the occluder, and the object is responsible for the disappearance. Without such a representation they have no way of knowing what to do to change the relationship between the occluder and object so as to regain sight of the object. Hence, they fail to search for the object behind the occluder. The failure is a theoretical failure, but it involves the infant's theory of spatial relations and appearances rather than her theory of objects per se. It might also be consistent with this account that, as we will see, the first signs of a primitive understanding of the relation between spatial position and perception emerge at about 9 months, at the same time that infants begin to search for hidden objects. For example, at about this age infants begin to point objects out to other people and to follow the points of others.

This account is also consistent with tracking studies. In the Moore, Borton and Darby (1978) tracking study, 5-month-old infants are presented with two occluders with a gap between them. The "impossible" event involves an object that disappears behind one screen, does not appear in the gap, and then magically appears "on time" at the far edge of the other screen. The young infants appear to continue to represent the object's trajectory both across the occluders and across the gap between them; the infants visually track the object even though they have no direct perceptual contact with it. However, they do not appear to distinguish between the disappearance caused by the occluder and the "magical" disappearance of the object in the gap. They accept the objects' reappearances at the far edge of the screen in both cases. From the baby's point of view, the disappearance of an object for a brief interval seems no more and no less surprising than its occlusion, and the baby seems to continue to represent the object in terms of its previous trajectory in both cases.

The interesting change at 9 months is that the infant now does discriminate between the occluder and the gap. They will continue to track happily across the occluder but not across the gap. In fact, when the object fails to appear in the gap, they look back to the first occluder. This suggests that the infants now have a richer understanding of appearances and disappearances, one congruent with their manual search behavior. They understand that the object is invisible *because* it is occluded.

Does the younger baby have object permanence on this view? Well, yes and no. The baby represents objects as continuing to exist even when they are out of sight. On the other hand, the baby does not continue to represent the object as continuing to exist behind the screen. The baby has an important part of our adult theory of permanent objects but is missing an equally important part.

This theory-theory account has the advantage of presenting a unified conceptual story, a single set of developing representations, throughout infancy, rather than having different representations for attention, search, and inference. If it is correct, it suggests that we should be able to find evidence for this conceptual shift in both habituation and action experiments. It also suggests an appealing continuity between earlier and later developments: as we will see, many of the later object-permanence developments can be understood as further developments in the child's theory of space and perception. However, differentiating between these alternatives clearly awaits further research.

The Nine-Month-Old's Theory

Whatever the explanation for the earlier results turns out to be, by around 9 months infants seem to have a genuinely theoretical understanding of hidden objects. They typically can find an object under a single cloth, even a novel object hidden in a novel way at a novel location. They do react with disrupted tracking if the object fails to appear in the gap between two screens. They are surprised if the object under the cloth disappears or is replaced by another object. They even shake the cloth as if they expect the object to appear there. All this suggests that these infants genuinely postulate that the object will be behind the occluder where it disappeared. More significantly, it also suggests that the infants know that the disappearance of the object is due to the spatial relations between the object, the occluder, and perhaps the child herself. To regain sight of the object, the infant has to manipulate these relations. The 9-month-old seems to believe that the object is at the place or trajectory at which it disappeared *and* that it is behind the occluder *and* that the fact that it is behind the occluder is what makes the object invisible.

However, these children still make incorrect predictions. The most celebrated error has come to be called the *A*-not-*B* error. If the object is hidden and recovered several times under cloth *A* and then hidden under cloth *B*, the 9-month-old infant will often continue persistently to search at *A* (Piaget, 1954; Uzgiris & Hunt, 1975; Wellman, Cross & Bartsch, 1987; Butterworth & Jarrett, 1982).

Piaget thought that the *A*-not-*B* error was an indication that the infant did not, in fact, represent the hidden object at *A* (Piaget, 1954). Instead, the infant had a sensory-motor scheme that she repeated because it had been effective in retrieving the object on previous occasions. This explanation, however, does not seem to be correct. Indeed, Piaget's claim that during infancy representation takes the form of instructions for action has in general turned out to be false. For one thing, infants make the *A*-not-*B* error even if they have never retrieved the object themselves but have simply seen it hidden at *A* and then *B* (Butterworth, 1977; Wellman, Cross & Bartsch, 1987). For another, the explanation leaves a puzzle about why children correctly search at *A* on the very first trial when they have never retrieved the object there before. If Piaget's explanation is wrong, why do children make this error?

Again, there have been suggestions in the literature that the *A*-not-*B* error is simply a result of information-processing or memory limitations (Diamond, 1985, 1990). However, no one has been able to make a coherent and convincing story about such limitations. Young infants may indeed have difficulty with certain complex memory or inhibition tasks, but these difficulties do not fully account for their behavior toward hidden objects. Other studies show that 9-month-olds can remember and act on events that took place as much as 24 hours earlier, to say nothing of the few seconds involved in object-hiding tasks like *A* not *B* (Meltzoff, 1988b). Moreover, under some circumstances, 9-month-olds make the *A*-not-*B* error even when the object at *B* is still clearly visible, which indicates that it is not simply a memory problem (Harris, 1987), and as noted above, they make the error when they simply see the object hidden first at *A*, without having searched for it at all, which indicates that it is not simply a matter of inhibiting an earlier action (Butterworth, 1977; Wellman, Cross & Bartsch, 1987). The most committed advocates of information-processing limitations (e.g., Diamond, 1990) have had to posit some complex and ad hoc mix of motor-planning incapacities, memory deficits, inhibition difficulties, and other problems to explain the phenomena. Such accounts also do not speak at all to the earlier developmental changes between birth and 9 months and the later changes we will see between 12 and 18 months.

More significant, the *A*-not-*B* error is not the only error children make in this period. In fact, even after the *A*-not-*B* error disappears, at about 12 months, infants are still not capable of predicting where a hidden object will reappear in many circumstances. In particular, infants seem unable to deduce the location of objects by considering complex possible invisible paths of motion, rather than simple extrapolations of visible trajectories. Thus if an object is hidden under a hand and then the hand is placed under a cloth and brought out empty, 12-month-olds will typically not look under the cloth; they will only look for the object in the hand, that is, under the occluder where they saw it disappear (Piaget, 1954; Uzgiris & Hunt, 1975). This is a highly replicated finding. More-over, 9-to-18-month-old infants make similar incorrect predictions in a wide variety of tasks. If an object is placed under one of two cloths and the cloths are rotated, the infants are as likely to search under the wrong cloth as the right one (Bremner, 1978). Similarly, if an object is placed in a closed hand and placed under one cloth and then the same hand is opened and disappears under a second cloth, 18-month-olds will predict that the object must be under the first cloth, whereas 12-month-olds will not make such predictions (Haake & Somerville, 1985).

Notice that these are not problems that can be solved by extrap-olating from the object's visible trajectory or location, in the way that infants seem to do in the straightforward hidings from nine months old and in the earlier habituation experiments. Even if infants could extend their knowledge of the object's earlier visible location or trajectory, it would do them no good in these instances. In these cases, the objects are, as Piaget puts it, "invisibly displaced." The idea of invisible displacement is in a way ambiguous. In the earlier studies, the object may be said to be invisibly displaced in the sense that it moves invisibly. However, it is not invisibly displaced in the sense that it changes its trajectory and traces an invisible path of movement that cannot be extrapolated from its visible path. In the difficult invisible displacements, it is not just that an object moves along a constant trajectory, part of which is hidden. Rather, the very trajectory of the object changes invisibly. It is interesting to note, for example, that the "impossible" sequence in some of Spelke's and Baillargeon's tasks actually is produced by making an object trace a complex invisible trajectory. In the invisible displacement tasks, we are presenting infants with just this "impossible" situation, except that in this case it is not only possible but actual.

Notice also that from the point of view of the adult theory, these inferences about invisible displacements are as obvious, compelling, and central as inferences about the extrapolation of trajectories. If anything, they are more central. As adults, we are not committed to the fact that objects will continue to move along the same trajectory. We are com-mitted to the fact that an invisible object inside a container (like the hand in these experiments) will share the movements of the container. Once again, the younger infants' theory seems qualitatively different from our commonsense adult theory.

The *A*-Not-*B* Error as an Auxilliary Hypothesis

It is clear that even when, at 9 months, the infant unambiguously begins to make predictions about hidden objects, these predictions are still limited in important ways. A number of authors (though not Piaget) have suggested that by around 9 months the infant develops a rule for predicting where the object will be (Bower, 1982; Harris, 1987; Moore, 1975; Moore & Meltzoff, 1978; Wellman, Cross & Bartsch, 1987). It says, "The object will be behind the occluder where it disappeared." We would suggest that this rule is itself part of a rich and abstract conception of objects developed in the previous 9 months of infancy. It is, we would argue, a kind of theoretical law: it applies across a wide range of empirical instances, and it allows the child to make new predictions.

There are, however, a number of disappearances and reappearances that this rule, and indeed this theory, cannot deal with. Take the following example. Alice sees her teddy bear fall toward the floor after she throws it out of her crib. Even though she doesn't see it, she can represent its location and even project its invisible trajectory. It is somewhere on the path on which it was moving when it disappeared, but the path is temporarily occluded by the crib. Some time later she is lifted out of her crib, and the teddy bear is not on the floor. She crawls over to the toy box, and there it is. Her earlier theory may ensure that she notices that the bear is no longer on the floor and perhaps even ensure that she is surprised that it is no longer there. But it gives her no way of dealing with the bear's reappearance in the toy box.

As we noted above, any case like this where the object's trajectory changes out of Alice's sight will not be handled by the theoretical principle about looking behind the occluder where the object disappeared. To solve these problems, Alice not only has to represent the object that is out of sight; she also has to represent the invisible movements of the object, and not only a single set of movements but a number of possible trajectories. (An adult in similar circumstances, for example, may try to reconstruct the movements, not to mention the psychology, of the cleaning lady.) Moreover, Alice has to have some idea of the spatial relations or other factors that led her to fail to perceive the invisible trajectories in the first place. As we have seen, the 9-month-old's theory doesn't allow her to do this. One might draw the analogy here to many cases in science where a theory works well in a limited domain but fails to work in a more complex one. The 9-month-old's theory can handle invisible objects and even project invisible trajectories. Nevertheless, it cannot handle this sort of invisible displacement.

What can the baby do in these circumstances? There is a rule that can handle the teddy bear case and many others where invisibly displaced objects reappear at places that were not part of their original trajectory. Moreover, the rule doesn't require that you have a theory of invisible displacements. Many objects, especially in the child's world, have habitual locations. The rule is, "The object will be where it appeared before." A number of authors have suggested that children also develop this rule (Bower, 1982; Harris, 1987; Wellman, Cross & Bartsch, 1987). It is very difficult to see how the second rule could be innately specified. For one thing, the rule is, of course, profoundly wrong. From the point of view of the adult theory, it doesn't matter how often an object has appeared at *A* before, it can only be at *A* if it followed a path of motion that led it there. And the rule, at least as used by the infants, seems to be atheoretical. The rule "It will be behind the occluder where it disappeared" calls on a variety of central facts about how objects move in relation to one another and their locations in space. In particular, it draws largely on the idea that there is a location where the hidden object is, namely behind the screen or under the cloth, that the object got there by moving (visibly) along a particular trajectory, and that the object will continue to have its other properties and features. The rule "It will be where it appeared before" works because of regularities (like conventions of parental tidiness) that are completely outside of the scope of the child's knowledge.

On the other hand, the rule "It will be where it appeared before" will receive a great deal of empirical confirmation. We might think of it as an example of a purely empirical generalization, like the knowledge that aspirin reduces fever or that we eat first and pay later at restaurants. But from the point of view of the adult theory, and arguably of any coherent theory, both this generalization and the theoretical prediction cannot simultaneously be true; the object can't be under both cloth *A* and cloth *B*. An infant who believes both these rules has a view of the world that is qualitatively different from the adult view.

Notice also that this contradictory empirical generalization may be made possible by the very theoretical advances that lead to the initial integration of features and movements. Sometime during the first year, infants seem to start to notice that objects maintain the same features across movements. By 12 months they even begin to use this featural information to override common movement information in individuating objects (Xu & Carey, in press). But infants do not seem to use this information initially. The 3-month-old infant does not find invisible displacements troubling or develop the rule "It will be where it appeared before," because he does not use features to reidentify objects at all. It would not occur to him to identify the teddy in the toy box with the teddy in the crib, and so the relation between the two appearances is not problematic. As in science, the very advances a theory makes set up the empirical generalizations that will eventually lead to its downfall.

In fact, the evidence suggests that infants may also develop other often contradictory empirical generalizations in the 9-to-15-month period. Moreover, children may shift from using one rule to using another rather easily, depending on the particular details of the context of the hiding. This situation is analogous to similar situations in science where, without a theory to resolve them, contradictory generalizations may proliferate. The 9-month-old is like a scientist who attempts to save the theory by adding ad hoc auxilliary hypotheses. The central theory of object movements leads to apparent anomalies when objects are invisibly displaced. The ad hoc rule "It will be where it appeared before" is invoked to deal with these anomalies.

In fact, infants abandon this rule by around 12 months; they stop making the *A*-not-*B* error. Why do they abandon it? The fact that the rule is sometimes directly disconfirmed, as in the *A*-not-*B* situation, probably plays a part. We suspect, however, that the lack of consistency between this rule and the centrally developed theory of objects that leads to the rule "It will be where it disappeared" plays an even more important role. To return to our earlier account, the child is analogous to a scientist who is disturbed to discover that her ad hoc auxilliary hypotheses lead to contradictory predictions.

The *A*-not-*B* situation not only provides disconfirmation. More significantly, it is a situation in which the ad hoc rule is placed in direct conflict with the more central theoretical prediction. In almost all cases where the object reappears at its habitual location, it will be because it was invisibly displaced (as in the teddy bear example). Such cases do not directly conflict with the theoretical prediction, since the 9-month-old's theory makes no predictions in these cases. Empirical generalizations that contradict the theory can be "bracketed" by ad hoc auxilliary hypotheses. In the *A*-not-*B* situation, however, the theory and the auxilliary hypothesis are brought into direct conflict. The object both appears in a location habitually (because of the experimenter's intention) and is visibly displaced. It is no wonder that children's behavior in this situation is labile, changeable, and both confused and confusing.

The Eighteen-Month-Old's Theory

Infants 18 months old consistently and productively solve the kinds of invisible-displacement tasks we described earlier. Presented with these kinds of problems, they will infer the correct solution, as an adult would. Notice that it is very unlikely that the infant will have had much specific experience with these particular kinds of disappearances. The infant is unlikely to have seen an object hidden in a hand, placed under a cloth, and then removed, for example. Instead, the infant seems to use the new theory of objects productively to make inferences and predictions in quite new situations.

This becomes even clearer when we make the object disappear in a complicated way that the infants are almost certain never to have seen before. For example, the experimenter may put the object in her hand and then under three cloths in succession and then take out her still closed hand (the serial-invisible-displacement task). Then she opens her hand and there is no object there. From a purely perceptual point of view, the child has no clue about what happened to the object: it was in the experimenter's hand and now is there no longer. The 9-month-old's theory is also no help: it leads the infant to search in the hand (and 9-month-olds do search there), but it provides no other solutions. Moreover, the child has had no specific knowledge of this kind of disappearance of a sort that would lead to empirical generalizations. In fact, in this case there is no single prediction that will necessarily be correct. However, the 18-month-old infant, like the adult at the magic show, can and does make a variety of intelligent predictions about where the object might be by systematically searching under the cloths on the table.

In fact, we can present the infant with a real conjuring trick by surreptitiously replacing an object placed in a box with another object or by leading her to expect the object will be at one location and actually placing it at another location. As we mentioned earlier, 9-month-olds show some surprise in these situations. The 9-month-old's theory tells her that the original object should be in one location, and then she sees that it is not there. However, 9-month-olds have no alternative hypotheses about where the object might be; they do not search for it (Gratch, 1982; Uzgiris & Hunt, 1975). Moreover, in a sense this sort of thing is happening to the 9-month-old all the time. Since she has no theory of invisible displacements, all the common events that involve such displacements should be as mysterious as the magic trick.

In contrast, 18-month-olds react to such a trick much as an adult would. First, they are very surprised, giving both the toy and the experimenter suspicious glances (that is, they reject the perceptual evidence). But also, and more significant, they systematically search at many reasonable locations for the missing toy. They do not search at unreasonable locations. They interpret the counterevidence as an adult would, in terms of a theory of invisible paths of motion, paths of motion that have been occluded. In particular, the 18-month-olds, but not the 9-month-olds, assume that the object will be along a particular invisible path of motion (Piaget, 1954; Gopnik & Meltzoff, 1986a; Uzgiris & Hunt, 1975).

The point is not just that 18-month-olds can make one particular kind of prediction while 9-month-olds can't. It's that they suddenly produce a wide variety of predictions in a fundamentally new way. They also interpret countervailing evidence in terms of the theory: they treat the mysterious disappearance of the object as an invisible displacement. Notice, moreover, that an explanation of this shift in terms of motor or memory ability becomes very implausible. Infants 9 or 12 or 15 months old can search in exactly the same way under exactly the same covers for objects. They simply search in the wrong place.

Where does the new theory come from? One obvious source of the theory is the empirical generalizations and incomplete or incorrect predictions of the earlier theory. We suggested earlier, however, that mere disconfirmation of a theory is not sufficient for theory change. The infant must also have some positive source for the alternative theory. Positive information from other aspects of the child's understanding of objects plays an important role in the development of the full theory at 18 months or so. We mentioned that the adult theory includes information about movement, properties, and spatial and perceptual relations between objects and observers. All these kinds of information seem to be accumulating in the period from 9 to 18 months.

In particular, the theory of visible-object movement, which is already present much earlier, gives the child a fairly easy way of conceiving of invisible movement. If the child can extrapolate a visible trajectory and can represent an invisible object with particular features at a location, then he has come some way toward conceiving an invisible object, with those features, moving invisibly along many different trajectories, which have the same basic properties as visible trajectories. Thus an important part of the explanatory structure of the theory, the idea that objects move in space in particular ways and not others, is already in place.

We suggested earlier that the infant also has to represent the mechanism by which the path has been occluded. The infant must figure out what movements would lead simultaneously to the change in the object's location and to that change's being invisible. There is evidence that the child's conception of spatial relations and of perception also changes in this period. Understanding invisible displacements involves understanding a wide variety of spatial relations, not just the distance relations (*A* is behind *B*) that underwrite the 6-month-old's and 9-month-old's theories. In particular, it is important to understand that objects can be completely contained by other objects and that this relation has certain properties. For example, an object must move inside another object before it can be located there. Containment is also transitive: if *A* is in *B* and *B* is in *C*, then *A* must be in *C*. And perhaps most significant, contained objects share all the movements of the objects that contain them. Notice that this represents an interesting exception to the common-fate principle for individuating objects. Spelke (1990) suggests that common fate represents a core principle of object knowledge, while contiguity does not. Notice, however, that when one object is contained in another, the two objects share common movements but are not the same object. Understanding this fact, and so overriding the common-fate principle, is necessary for the 18-month-old to solve the invisible displacement problems. Even these very young children already seem to be able to override "core principles." There is some evidence that children come to appreciate spatial relations of this sort in the period from 12 to 18 months (Bower, 1982; Caron, Caron & Antell, 1988; Piaget, 1954).

An additional piece of the theory comes from the child's increasingly sophisticated conception of visual perception. There is a substantial body of evidence that suggests that a first understanding of visual perception may have its roots even in infancy. Even very young infants pay special attention to eyes. Moreover, a number of writers have pointed out the significance of joint attention and social-referencing behaviors, which emerge between about 9 months and 12 months and become more sophisticated up to 18 months. At about this age infants develop the ability to follow the point or gaze of another person toward an object (Butterworth, 1991; Baldwin & Moses, 1994). They begin to use points to get someone else to look at an object (Bates et al., 1979). They also draw attention to objects in order to discover another person's attitude toward them. Faced with an ambiguous situation, infants look to their mother's face for information and may draw her gaze to the objects in question (Campos & Stenberg, 1981).

These behaviors imply a primitive but genuine understanding of visual perception. These infants seem to know that the direction of the eyes, or perhaps just the direction of the head and body, indicates something about the person's visual contact with an object. There seems to be some connection in these children's minds between the visual display of another person's head and eyes and the phenomenal experience of vision.

Moreover, at least by 18 months, infants seem to be able to disciminate between cases where the other person is, and cases where he is not, in visual contact with an object. In "social referencing" studies, Repacholi (1996) showed infants two closed boxes. The experimenter looked in one of the boxes and made a disgusted face and looked in the other with a happy face. Infants were more willing to put their hands in the "happy" box than in the "disgusted" box. The only difference in these cases was the direction of the experimenter's gaze. Similarly, Baldwin and Markman (1989) found that 18-month-olds would assume that a spoken word named the object an adult looked at, even if the child was not looking at that object.

These advances in understanding the relation between the line of sight of another person and their access to objects may also provide an important part of the full object theory.

Other Evidence for the Theory Theory

So far we have largely focused on the infants' changing predictions about the location of the object, as manifested in their search and tracking behavior, and on their interpretation of deviant evidence, as manifested in their reactions to anomalies. But infants between 12 and 18 months old engage in other activities relevant to theory formation. Many of these activities have not been systematically studied, though they would repay such study. They have been apparent to us, however, in the course of ten years of observations of hundreds of infants in this period and in the naturalistic observations involved in our linguistic studies.

Experimentation

Infants actively experiment with disappearances. Indeed, hiding and finding games become almost an obsession with infants between 12 and 18 months old. Lifter and Bloom (1989) systematically studied this aspect of babies' behavior and found significant changes in infants' spontaneous hiding games in this period that seem to reflect the developing theory (see also Bloom, 1993). Moreover, by 12 months the infant obsession with active hiding and finding extends to a wide variety of appearances and disappearances caused by a wide variety of events. In our spontaneous naturalistic language data from 15-to-21-month-olds, we often find sequences of many hidings and uncoverings of the same object in a sequence, each accompanied by "gone." In one typical sequence, for example, an 18-month-old hides a ring under a cushion and then uncovers it thirteen times in a row, saying "gone" each time (the fourteenth time he hides it in his mouth) (Gopnik, 1980).

Similarly, we commonly find that in our search tasks children will spontaneously replicate particularly difficult types of hidings, such as invisible displacements. Or the children will retrieve an object and return it to us with verbal or gestural instructions to repeat the game. Most charming, perhaps, infants who solve a task will often themselves hide the object in the complex way and indicate to the experimenter that she should search for it. It is clear in these cases that the child is not primarily concerned with retrieving the object but with understanding the problem. We suggest that these activities are similar to experimentation in adult science. To return to our previous analogy, we might think of the infants' affection for elaborate hiding games at this period as analogous to physicists' affection for cyclotrons. If the really interesting problems concern object disappearances and reappearances or subatomic particles moving at high speeds, it makes sense to expose yourself to these phenomena as much as possible.

The affect of explanation

Second, children's expressive behavior undergoes interesting shifts in our longitudinal studies. These shifts are very striking to anyone watching the same child over a period of time. Typically, 15-month-old children are relatively unperturbed by mysterious invisible displacements. They fail to solve the tasks, but their failure is not particularly disturbing to them. Over the succeeding months, as the child becomes more successful at the tasks, their affective behavior, paradoxically, often becomes more distressed. We have become familiar with testing sessions in which the child performs insightfully on several trials and then apparently falls apart. (In a number of studies, we recruited infants from La Leche League clubs, which promote the breast feeding of toddlers, and some children at this stage would take a few trials on a difficult hiding task, turn desperately to the mother for a brief nursing break, and then, comforted and refreshed, turn back to the problems. The analogy to scientific cigarettes and snacks is striking.) When the infants do solve the tasks, however, the solution itself is often accompanied by expressions of utter joy. Most interesting, this expressive behavior typically comes *before* the baby actually picks up the cloth, often before the baby makes any movement at all. The typical pattern is that the baby looks at the correct cloth, smiles to himself and sometimes radiantly at the experimenter, and then searches. By the time the children are 20 or 21 months old, their former insouciance returns. They solve the problems quickly and even routinely, and we see much less ecstasy as well as agony.

Notice that this pattern of affective change is not explicable by any simple functional story. The infants are better at finding the objects at 18 months than at 15 months and worse than at 21 months. Both maximum agony and maximum interest and satisfaction, however, take place in this intermediate stage. We don't know that the infants have the internal phenomenology of explanation, but they certainly have its outward affect.

Interpretation

Similarly, there is an interesting and quite typical pattern of changes in interpretative behavior that we and others see in our longitudinal studies. The very youngest infants are often susceptible to rough empirical generalizations of the sort "It will be where it appeared before." They may, for example, continually look under a cloth of a particular color. In contrast, as we have seen, as the children grow older, they seem increasingly resistant to such atheoretical interpretations. Their abandonment of the *A*-not-*B* strategy is a good example of this. This is true even when such interpretations could be quite useful pragmatically.

These interpretative effects emerge fortuitously in situations in which we give children multiple trials of object-hiding tasks. In all our studies we begin with a simple hiding task, to ensure that the child is motivated to find the object. 15-month-olds easily solve such tasks. Moreover, in the standard invisible-displacement procedure, the object is hidden under the experimenter's hand and placed under one of three cloths. The hand then emerges empty. And this task is repeated several times. There is, in fact, a simple procedure for succeeding at this task. The procedure is to pull all the cloths on the table, preferably at the same time. And some of the younger children will occasionally do this.

In fact, however, most children do not engage in this kind of behavior at all. Instead, they may search persistently in the experimenter's hand without approaching the cloths at all. Similarly, in the serial, invisibly displaced, hiding task, the object is placed in the experimenter's hand, is then placed under several cloths in succession, and is left under the last cloth. Again, one might think that children who succeeded in earlier tasks involving objects hidden under these same cloths would simply search the cloths in this more difficult task. While some children do engage in this sort of random search behavior, most simply search in the experimenter's hand, or search under the first cloth in the series and then refuse to search under the others. Just as infants eventually abandon the *A*-not-*B* rule, these infants resist a purely empirical generalization that is inconsistent with their developing theory, even when it is very useful pragmatically.

We argue that somewhere between 15 and 18 months the infant develops a new theory of objects. This theory posits that all object disappearances are a consequence of movements, including invisible movements, either of objects or of the observer. The development of this theory allows infants to do two things. First, it allows them to consolidate all the information about disappearances that has been accumulated over the preceding year and a half into a single model. This includes the earlier theory of visible movements and trajectories, the theory of invisible objects, new information about spatial relations and visual perception, and information captured by the various empirical generalizations that infants construct between 9 and 18 months.

Second, the theory allows them to make new predictions and deductions that were not possible before. These predictions include predictions about simple disappearances, like visible displacements. But more significant, the new theory also allows the infant to deal with disappearances, like trick disappearances or complex invisible displacements, in an intelligent way.

The younger infant seems to conclude that if an object disappears and that disappearance cannot be accounted for by the theory of visible movements and trajectories or by particular empirical generalizations, the object is gone for good. Like the adult, the 18-month-old, on the contrary, seems to believe that in general, objects continue to exist and their temporary disappearances can be explained in spatial terms. Recall that 18-month-olds, though not younger children, continued to search for the original object when it was mysteriously replaced by a different object. We might capture this difference by saying that before 18 months infants would be unimpressed by such conjuring tricks, even if they recognized their empirical oddity, because for them, mysterious disappearances are just part of life. After 18 months, on the other hand, infants, like adults, will be impressed by mysterious disappearances but will also be pretty sure that the conjuror has something up his sleeve. Their knowledge of movements, spatial relations, and perception lets them make at least a pretty good stab at just what it is. They immediately interpret disappearances in terms of invisible displacements. Of course, the 18-month-old will still be ignorant of other aspects of disappearances—like the effects of attention or distraction, or the possibility of disintegration or destruction—which an adult would apply to solving the conjuror's problem.

The 18-month-old's theory of objects does all the things a good theory should. It revises a previous theory so that it includes a new body of empirical evidence, evidence that considered by itself might seem confusing and contradictory, it restructures the previous theory so that it becomes a special case of the new theory, and it allows inferences and predictions about new situations that were beyond the scope of either the previous theory or the empirical generalizations.

Moreover, from a dynamic point of view, in the period between 9 months and 18 months we can see many of the processes involved in theory formation and change. Children start out with a theory (the theory that objects are behind the occluders where they disappear) that explains a limited set of phenomena. However, the theory makes inadequate or just plain wrong predictions about other phenomena, particularly invisible displacements. Children then make a number of empirical generalizations to deal with the new data, some of which are contradictory. They use both these empirical generalizations and their already developed theories as a basis for the new theory. They engage in a period of intense experimentation and evidence gathering. They suffer.

Moreover, as with theory change in science, there is a certain incommensurability between the concepts of the old and new theories. The 18-month-old's theory depends on the idea that there are permanent objects in locations and that all disappearances, including complex invisible displacements under many cloths, are due to changes in location. This abstract concept of objects is not simply a combination of the earlier theory and additional information about invisible displacements, nor is it simply a matter of adding additional empirical rules or motor routines to the theory. Rather, developing the 18-month-old's theory involves developing qualitatively new abstract conceptual structures, structures that appear to be irreducible to earlier conceptual structures. Of course, as in science, we may feel that there is some principled relationship between these structures and the earlier concepts.

Semantic Development: "Gone" as a Theoretical Term

So far we have been discussing infants' nonlinguistic problem-solving behaviors. But 18-month-olds' adoption of the new theory is also accompanied by important semantic developments. We can also see evidence for the new theory in changes in children's spontaneous language that are empirically closely correlated with the changes in predictions we described above. Infants very consistently begin to use a word for disappearance, in English usually "gone," just about when they first demonstrate the 18-month-old's object theory in their behavior.

"Gone" is part of the category of "relational" words, first described by Bloom in 1973. These words have been rather neglected in the semantic literature. Very likely, this is because such words appear to be conceptually rather different from those that have been taken to be central by theories of the semantics of the adult language. Nevertheless, such terms are extremely common, in fact, nearly ubiquitous, in early lexicons. In a study of over 500 English-speaking 18-month-olds, for example, over 75 percent of the children were reported to use "allgone," one of the highest reports of any lexical item (Fenson et al., 1994). Children learning other languages also use some word or other for disappearance in their very early speech, for example, "parti" in French or "epta" in Korean (Gopnik & Choi, 1990).

Moreover, this word captures precisely the generalization that is crucial to the 18-month-old theory. In an early study one of us recorded the contexts of all the 378 uses of "gone" of 9 children, who were recorded longitudinally for over a year (Gopnik, 1980, 1984a). Table 4.1 shows some typical contexts in which "gone" is produced. "Gone" was applied to disappearances of all types, including those caused by the babies' head turns, those that involve visible displacements, and those that involve invisible displacements. It is particularly interesting to note that nearly half the occurrences of "gone" came in contexts in which babies searched consistently for a missing object. That is, they occurred in classic invisible-displacement situations. Moreover, babies also applied "gone" to hypothetical disappearances. They said "gone," for example, searching for objects they had never seen but whose existence they had deduced. For example, a baby who was given a set of nesting blocks would decide that there must be a still smaller block to nest in the smallest block in the set. (In fact, there was no such block). They would say "gone" as they systematically searched for this block. This is significant, since in these contexts the children never had the perceptual experience of seeing the object disappear, or indeed of seeing the object at all. Interestingly, there were even a few very early uses of "gone" when objects were suddenly "destroyed" in a mysterious way, when, for

Table 4.1
Typical uses of "gone" by nine 12-to-24-month-old children

General situation	Examples
Child turns away from an object.	Child turns away from video camera.
	Experimenter unfolds a large shawl in front of child. He turns his back to it.
An object moves away.	Child throws a block over her shoulder.
	Child places a car behind his back.
	Child gives experimenter her watch, walks away.
	Ball rolls away into the kitchen.
Object moves behind, under, or inside another object.	Child closes the flap of a tape recorder, hiding the wheels.
	Experimenter holds a mask in front of her face.
	Child turns over a piece of paper with brown sugar sticking to it.
	Child places a doll inside a shoe.
	Child closes a drawer full of blocks.
	Child pushes a block through the hole of a toy mailbox.
	Child turns the page of a book.
Child searches for a real object.	Child searches for a block to put in the mailbox.
	"Teddy gone." Child searches for his teddy bear.
	Child searches for the correct hole of the mailbox.
	Child searches for a missing piece of a jigsaw puzzle.
	"Baby gone." Child searches for her doll.
	Child searches for a battery that he has been playing with (and which was surreptitiously removed by his mother).
Child searches for a hypothetical object.	Child searches for a pocket in his mother's apron. There is no pocket.
	Child places some small Fisher-Price dolls in the holes in a truck. There are some empty holes left, but no more dolls. He searches for one.
	Child searches for a glove to put on the glove rack. There is an empty peg on the rack, but there are no more gloves.
Empty containers	Child pours all the pegs out of a tin.
	Child takes a doll out of its crib, looks in the empty crib.
	Child looks in the empty cab of a toy tractor.
Destructions	A Lego construction falls apart.
	Child's mother folds up the ironing board.
	The cars of a toy train come apart.

example, an ironing board was rapidly folded up. Even more interestingly, these uses quickly disappeared.

In fact, in our later studies children frequently used "gone" during the object-permanence-testing sessions themselves. When they did so, they applied the word, just as in their spontaneous speech, both to visible and invisible displacements and to "trick" disappearances.

What does "gone" mean? These uses of "gone" are quite unlike the adult uses of "gone." "Gone" does not simply encode perceptual or functional features of an object, nor does it reflect a particular "script." There is no simple perceptual way of characterizing the contexts in which the children choose to use the term. They involve any object and almost any mode of disappearance, and sometimes involve contexts in which no perceptual "disappearance" event took place at all. They do not involve a single script or a simple, common pragmatic or functional feature. Sometimes the child wants to retrieve the missing object, but more often he doesn't, as when, for example, the child himself has hidden the object.

How would we characterize moving your head to turn away from an object, turning a piece of paper over repeatedly, searching for a hypothetical block, etc.? The only way to describe these events is by saying that the child points out that an existing underlying object is not currently visible. The best characterization of "gone" seems to be that it is a theoretical term in the 18-month-old's theory of object appearances. "Gone" does not unite contexts that are functionally or perceptually similar. In a sense, "gone" refers to the fact that perceptions do not occur. It does, however, unite events with a similar underlying causal structure. The underlying causal structure is the one central to the object-appearance theory: all these events involve an object that is temporarily not visible. "Gone" catches a particular contrast between ontology and phenomenology; between the fact that the world is one way and that it looks another way (see Gopnik, 1984a, and Gopnik & Meltzoff, 1986b, for further discussion).

Other words can emerge well before the infant has developed the full 18-month-old's object theory (Gopnik, 1988b). In our studies a few children initially used "allgone" exclusively in the particular context of finishing meals. These uses could appear well before the development of the object theory. Such very early uses seem to encode something like a script. Interestingly, however, these uses actually disappear and are replaced by the more sophisticated and general use of "gone" of the sort we describe above. Such general uses seems more closely connected to the development of the concept of objects. Following Bloom, 1973, we predicted that these more general uses of "gone," with their distinctive conceptual content, would be specifically related to the nonlinguistic behaviors that emerge at about 18 months, and involve the same content.

We have found precisely such a relation. Moreover, similar findings have been reported by a number of different investigators, using different methods. Children first begin to use "gone" to encode disappearance, that is, as a theoretical term, when they first demonstrate nonlinguistically that they have acquired the object theory, that is, when they solve complex invisible-displacement tasks (Corrigan, 1978; Gopnik 1980, 1984a; Gopnik & Meltzoff, 1984, 1986a; Lifter & Bloom, 1989; McCune-Nicolich, 1981; Tomasello & Farrar, 1984, 1986). We compared children's performance on object-permanence tasks in the lab and their mother's reports of their spontaneous language. In our longitudinal data, the word "gone" generally emerged within two weeks of the time when the child first solved the serial-invisible-displacement task, though the two developments could take place in either order. Moreover, the two developments are highly correlated: children who deduced the location of invisibly displaced objects early also acquired "gone" early. We found similar patterns in cross-sectional studies.

Significantly, these relationships between cognitive and semantic development are very specific, the development of "gone" is not closely related to other cognitive developments in this period, and other semantic developments are not closely related to the development of the concept of objects (Gopnik & Meltzoff 1984, 1986a). This pattern of results is important because it rules out what might otherwise seem to be a "third cause" responsible for the correlation, such as a causal relation between general linguistic skill and cognitive ability. As we will see in chapter 7, there is in fact, little evidence for such general correlations of any sort, but in any case, they could not be responsible for these results. There is something distinctive about acquiring a word for disappearance and the specific development of the object theory at 18 months.

This relationship between lexical and cognitive development provides independent evidence for the idea that there is some significant conceptual change underlying the changes in problem-solving behavior at this point. Otherwise, it would be extremely difficult to see why these changes would be specifically correlated with the spontaneous production of a particular lexical item. In particular, this relationship undermines any more superficial information-processing explanations for the problem-solving changes. Motor or memory or means-ends skills might be responsible for developments in search. It is, however, extremely difficult to see how they could be responsible for the emergence of a single lexical item in the child's spontaneous speech but not for other lexical items that emerge at about the same time. Similarly, while we might think of many possible explanations for the emergence of the word "gone" at this particular point, it has only its semantic content in common with the problem-solving changes. Whatever development takes place at this point is something that is linked particularly to solving invisible-displacement problems and to saying "gone," and not to other cognitive or lexical developments. Only a conceptual change fits this pattern.

A final significant point about these relations is that "gone" typically emerged in our studies right in the midst of the behavioral developments that indicate the emergence of the object theory. Like others, we have found a sort of minisequence in the child's understanding of invisible displacements. Children typically solve simple-invisible-displacement tasks slightly before they solve more complex serial-invisible-displacement tasks, and they solve such tasks slightly before they solve "trick" tasks. In our longitudinal studies (and in those of others, such as McCune-Nicolich, 1981; Tomasello & Farrar, 1984; Corrigan, 1978) "gone" emerged just after the simple invisible displacements were solved, before the "trick" disappearances were solved, and either just before or just after the serial invisible displacements were solved. Moreover, children typically still made errors on the task when they began to use "gone." "Gone" emerged not when the child fluently and routinely applied the theory but at the rather tortured intermediate stage we described above.

We have used a particular serial-invisible-displacement task in our more complicated studies as a convenient nonlinguistic index of the emergence of the 18-month-old's theory. We would emphasize, however, that we do not identify the acquisition of the theory with the solution of that particular task or any particular task. Indeed, part of the point of the theory theory is that the acquisition of the theory underlies abilities in a variety of different tasks, and that developing a complete theory is a developmental process that takes some time and involves intermediate stages. The word "gone" is not just related to a single object-permanence task. Instead, it appears at a particular, and particularly crucial, point in the child's development of the full theory of object permanence. The emergence of this linguistic form is itself part of the linked pattern of new predictions, interpretations, and explanations that constitutes the theory change.

Later Developments: From Object Permanence to Perspective Taking

If understanding object-permanence is part of a continual process of theory revision, then the developments at 18 months should not be the end of the story. In fact, we argued that the developments in infancy involve only part of the adult theory; futher important parts of the adult theory have yet to be developed. For example, an important facet of the adult theory of appearances and disappearances is the fact that it applies equally, but differentially, to ourselves and others. The same theory that allows you to predict where to search for an object allows you to predict how to hide it from someone else, it allows you to predict when and whether the object will be visible to someone else, and it allows you to predict differences between your own view and the view of others. In contrast, the 18-month-old still needs to work out the complexities of how visual perception works in herself and others. One way of thinking of the highest-level of the 18-month-old's object-permanence abilities is to say that the child discovers that all (or almost all) disappearances are due to changes in the spatial relation between the child's eyes and the hidden object. Appropriately generalizing this discovery, however, is more complex.

The acheivements of social referencing and joint attention suggest that by 18 months infants begin to understand some of the simpler relations between their own perceptions and those of others. They seem to understand, for example, that they and others may share the perception of an object and that they can make objects invisible to others visible by pointing or showing. There is some interesting evidence that suggests, however, that children only begin to understand the more complex relations and differences between their own perceptions and those of others later in their development. Lempers, Flavell, and Flavell (1977)

report that very young two-year-olds failed to effectively reproduce situations in which their visual perceptions were discrepant with those of
others. For example, a child who was asked to hide an object from her
parent behind a screen sometimes produced the egocentric response of
hiding the object on the far side of the screen.

In our studies we have observed similar, quite consistent, errors in
24-month-olds. We developed a more controlled version of Lempers,
Flavell, and Flavell's task using an imitation paradigm (Gopnik, Meltzoff,
Esterly & Rubenstein, 1995). Children were trained to reciprocally
imitate the actions of another person, such as giving objects to the experimenter after the experimenter gave them to the child. We included
linguistic control tasks to ensure that children understood the meaning of
"to," "from," and "hide." In the crucial experimental task the children
saw the experimenter manipulate an object so that it was visible to the
experimenter but not the child or vice versa. We used a range of different objects and different types of showings and hidings. The experimenter then handed the toy to the child and asked her to reciprocally
imitate her action by showing it to the experimenter or hiding it from
the experimenter. The children were able to show the objects in a nonegocentric way; that is, they showed them to the experimenter even
when this required losing sight of them themselves. As for hiding from
the experimenter, however, 24-month-olds consistently hid the object
egocentrically, either placing it on the experimenter's side of the screen
or holding it to themselves so that neither they nor the experimenter
could see it. In contrast, 36-month-olds were at ceiling on this task, and
30-month-olds were intermediate. The infants made the wrong predictions about when and how the object would be hidden from the
experimenter.

While we have used the word "egocentric" to describe these behaviors, we want again to emphasize that this is not egocentricity in
Piaget's sense. Piaget thought of egocentricity as a very-wide-ranging
logical feature of the child's cognition, one that was in place, moreover,
until quite late in childhood. In contrast, we say that children have a
quite specific and specifically mistaken theory of how visual perception
and spatial location are related to one another. The infants are not generally egocentric: they quickly grasp the idea of reciprocal imitation, and
they show objects to others in a nonegocentric way. Their theory builds
on the achievements of the earlier theory of object permanence to make

more extended predictions about the vision of others, but it also makes some particular incorrect predictions. By about 3 years of age this theory is revised to become something more like the adult theory.

In support of this idea, the 24- and 30-month-olds in our study showed a variety of experimental behaviors, reminiscent of the 1-year-old's hiding games. For example, children would sometimes move the toy from one side of the screen to the other several times, finally settling on the correct perspective. Several children got the task right and then walked over to the other side of the table to check that the toy was indeed invisible from that perspective. To us as adults, this inference would seem immediate and compelling. To the 2-year-olds, in contrast, it seemed in need of testing and confirmation.

By $2\frac{1}{2}$ to 3, however, children do seem to firmly understand these aspects of visual perception. That is, they explicitly understand that an object may be visible to them but invisible to another or vice versa. Flavell has referred to this phenomenon as "level 1" visual-perspective taking (Flavell, Everett, Croft & Flavell, 1981). Children show a similarly advanced understanding of other perceptual modalities, such as hearing and touch (Yaniv & Shatz, 1988). Also, 3-year-old children are near ceiling in understanding that they may now see an object that they did not see before and vice versa. They understand level 1 changes in their own visual perspectives (Gopnik & Slaughter, 1991).

However, children of this age notoriously have difficulty in understanding other more complex kinds of mental states, notably belief (Wellman, 1990; Perner, 1991; Astington, Harris & Olson, 1988). The classic indicator of this difficulty is the "false belief" task (Wimmer & Perner, 1983). In one such task we showed children a candy box and then revealed that the box was actually full of pencils. The 3-year-old children report that they always believed there were pencils in the box and that another person who sees the box will also think there are pencils inside it (Gopnik & Astington, 1988). As we mentioned earlier, there is extensive evidence for a theoretical change in the child's understanding of belief between $2\frac{1}{2}$ and 4 (Gopnik & Wellman, 1994).

This change builds on the theory of perception, which is itself constructed between 2 and 3. We have argued that this understanding of visual perception is itself further transformed to provide a basis for the child's later understanding of belief (Gopnik, Slaughter & Meltzoff, 1994; Gopnik & Wellman, 1994). Just as 18-month-olds use their theory of visible movements as a model for their theory of invisible movements, 36-month-olds use their theory of perception as a model for their theory of belief. Perception and belief have many features in common: Both have a mind-to-world direction of fit—they involve changing representations to fit the world. Both are only indirectly reflected in action and behavior. Most significant, both perception and belief may be subject to misrepresentation—with perceptual illusions we see what is not the case, just as with false beliefs we think what is not the case.

At the same time, perception may be easier to understand than belief. In particular, many perceptual misrepresentations involve changes in the spatial relations between observer and object. We see something differently from one angle than from another or from one "point of view" than another (notice how pervasive perceptual metaphors are in belief talk). As we have seen, this causal framework is familiar even to 2-year-olds, and builds on ideas that are first apparent even in 9-month-olds. The causal framework involved in generating and explaining false beliefs is much more complex.

In fact, we have shown that children understand perceptual misrepresentations well before they understand false beliefs. In one set of studies we showed children a cat that looked black when viewed through a red filter but turned out really to be green. Even young 3-year-olds said that the cat looked black through the filter and green without the filter. Moreover, children were more able to understand false-belief tasks when they involved perceptual misrepresentation: they said that they at first thought that the cat was black and that another person would think that the cat was black. Pointing out the analogies between the two domains made the false-belief task substantially easier for 3-year-olds.

More powerfully, Slaughter has shown that giving children relevant evidence about perception over a period of time improves their performance on false-belief tasks and on other tasks indexing the development of a representational theory of mind (Slaughter, 1995; Slaughter & Gopnik, in press). In her experiments she selected 3-year-olds who initially failed false-belief tasks. Over the course of the following two weeks the children were exposed to several perceptual tasks of the black-cat versus green-cat sort. In each case children received feedback about their responses: "Yes, you did see a black cat," or "No, you saw a black cat." Children who received this perceptual training did better on false-belief tasks *and* on other theory-of-mind tasks than a control group who received training on other tasks. They did not do better on tasks that did not involve their theory of mind. This study also suggests that an understanding of perception may be the basic model on which a later understanding of belief is constructed.

Later Semantic Developments: "Gone" and "See"

Are these changes in cognition during this period also reflected in semantic changes? Both the conceptual developments that underlie deduction at 18 months and the semantic content of "gone" are particular to this stage of the child's conceptual development. As we have seen, the child's theory of object appearances at 18 months is still incomplete and limited in many respects. In particular, the child has yet to master the complexities of the many relations between the perceptions of different people, the fact that an object behind a screen, say, is visible to one person but not another. These conceptual limitations are reflected in incorrect predictions, like the children's behavior in our perspective-taking task. These theoretical limitations are also reflected in the extension of "gone," just as the theoretical advances of 18 months are. The child does use "gone" to link visible and invisible displacements, just as the 18-month-old theory does. But she does not apply "gone" to the perceptions of other people, nor does the 18-month-old theory. These children often used "gone" when an object was invisible to them but not to other people, after placing an object behind their backs, for instance. They never used "gone" in the opposite case.

As the infant develops cognitively and linguistically and moves away from the 18-month-old's theory, we can see parallel changes in semantics as "gone" is used differently and is to some extent replaced by such mental-state terms as "see." In an analysis of the child's early use of "see" based on the CHILDES archives, for example, we found consistent semantic changes that appear to parallel the cognitive developments between 18 months and $2\frac{1}{2}$ years (see table 4.2). "See" typically emerged shortly after "gone," and its first uses applied to the child's own attempts to see objects. References to the sight of other people and to failures to see emerged only later. However, by $2\frac{1}{2}$ to 3 such references were common. Semantically, children seem to move from using "see" and "gone" initially to refer to their own perceptions or failures to perceive objects

Table 4.2
Seven children's uses of "see" for their own and others' vision

Child	Age in yrs., mos., days	Use
Naomi	1, 6, 16	See, Mommy.
	1, 11, 6	Come see water, Daddy. Daddy, look at the water.
	2, 3, 19	I can't see, I can't see.
	3, 4, 10	I gonta put this right here so you can see. Oh, look at this.
	3, 4, 10	Would you tear this off so I won't see it?
	3, 5, 7	You come around the side and you can see.
	4, 9, 3	The moon is shining, but its too bright to see the stars, and its too bright to see the clouds too.
Sarah	2, 3, 5	See dolly.
	2, 7, 28	You yawn. I yawn too. See?
	2, 8, 25	See hand, see hand, Mummy? See hand? (Mother: Yes, I see the hand.)
	3, 2, 2	He see talking.
	3, 2, 23	I can't see it.
	3, 4, 16	Did you see that?
Ross	1, 8	I want to see.
	2, 6	I know where it is. Daddy can't see it. You get your glasses?
	2, 6	Tiger going to see me again.
	2, 6	Giraffe wanted to see snake.
	2, 8	I haven't seen Star Wars.
	2, 8	I never see a movie.
	2, 9	That's blood. If you get blood in your eyes, you won't see.
Eve	1, 6	I see it.
	1, 10	Papa come see Eve.
	1, 11	I can't see you.
	2, 0	Fraser not see him. He outside.
Nathaniel	2, 5, 18	See apple. Enne see a fire truck.
	2, 6, 25	Nanna see the trolley. (Unclear referent)
	3, 0, 22	Adrianna's gonna see me?
	3, 4, 8	I never see bears and crows.
	3, 4, 21	So why can't he see you?
	3, 7, 14	I can ... the eyes are makin' cause the sun is makin' me see.
Nina	1, 11, 16	Let's see.
	2, 1, 29	You see him.
	2, 1, 29	Him can't see.

Table 4.2 (cont.)

Child	Age in yrs., mos., days	Use
	2, 2, 28	That turn around. There see train.
	2, 4, 12	Can't see it. (Nina places egg cartons on her eyes and adult's eyes and then systematically takes them off.)
Shem	2, 2, 16	Want see.
	2, 2, 23	Wanna see my puzzle? (To his sister)
	2, 3, 2	I can't see it.
	2, 5, 9	You can't see it.

to using these terms more generally to refer to the perceptions of anyone. This parallels their cognitive acquisition of level 1 visual-perspective taking. Of course, we have not yet done the detailed longitudinal studies required to demonstrate specific links between the linguistic and cognitive changes, but the general age parallel is nevertheless striking.

Finally, Bartsch and Wellman (1995) have documented the emergence of belief words like "know" and "think" during the fourth year of life, after "see" is well established. In this case as well, changes in the children's spontaneous extensions of these terms parallel changes in their predictions and explanations. The developing theory of mind is apparent both in semantic change and in conceptual change.

Conclusion

We have claimed that the 18-month-old's conception of objects is a theory and that this theory is different from earlier and later theories. We have argued both that the child's knowledge at various stages has the structural and functional characteristics of a theory and, perhaps more significant, that the changes in this knowledge have some of the dynamic character of theory change. Children develop a sequence of related theories, each of which makes some incorrect predictions. In chapter 3 we suggested that this pattern of development would tend to support the theory theory.

The reader will doubtless have noted that the quality of our evidence for various aspects of the theory theory varies considerably. We have good evidence for the distinctive pattern of predictions about object appearances and reappearances at each point in infancy and early childhood and the changes in those patterns. We have good evidence that at 18 months children use "gone" to make an abstract theorylike generalization, which is consistent with our interpretation of their predictions, and that these semantic developments are empirically closely related to those predictions. We have good evidence that children make and abandon at least one empirical generalization, the *A*-not-*B* rule, that functions much like an ad hoc auxilliary hypothesis.

Our evidence for other aspects of the claim is weaker. We hope, however, that it suggests several new and promising areas of research. We ourselves find the changes in infants' expressive behavior subjectively convincing, but we must confess that others are likely to find them merely anecdotal. Much the same is true of the interpretive effects and the infant's early experiments. There is, however, no reason why these phenomena cannot be investigated more systematically. It would also be helpful to have stronger converging evidence from surprise, tracking, and looking-time studies of 18-month-olds for the claims we have made on the basis of search data.

What about the ultimate forbidden *Star Trek* experiment? Ideally, we would want to show that infants in a world where objects disappeared and reappeared in some extremely odd way would learn the principles that explained such disappearances. We do not have evidence that is that strong. But it would also tend to confirm the theory if we showed at least that exposure to the relevant evidence accelerated the development of the theory. Not every kind of exposure will be effective, of course. The interpretive effects of the theory may make small amounts of counterevidence simply be ignored. However, if we presented the child with extensive and varied counterevidence at just the right point in the theory crisis, we could expect to accelerate the development of the new theory. Slaughter's studies show this kind of acceleration of the representational theory of belief at age 3 (Gopnik, Slaughter & Meltzoff, 1994; Slaughter, 1995; Slaughter & Gopnik, in press).

Would a similar study work earlier in infancy? There are several suggestive findings in the literature that are relevant. One is Bower's (1982) claim that extensively exposing children to particular relevant types of experiences of objects leads them to make the shift from a place and trajectory theory to a feature theory more quickly. Infants who repeatedly saw objects starting and stopping advanced through the early stages of the object theory more swiftly. The second is that the onset of crawling has been found to be related to developments in object permanence. While this finding might simply indicate some sort of maturational synchrony, other studies suggest that this is not the case. In particular, children who have more opportunities for early mobility, for example, by using walkers, solve object-permanence problems earlier than other children (Bai & Bertenthal, 1992; Bertenthal, Campos & Kermoian, 1994; Kermoian & Campos, 1988). From our point of view, the relevant effect of self-produced locomotion might be that it enormously increases opportunities for the observation of counterevidence. A baby who crawls will observe many more systematic appearances and disappearances than a baby who doesn't. Third, there are suggestions in longitudinal studies that children who have more exposure to the relevant evidence develop these conceptual abilities slightly before children who do not have this longitudinal experience. More systematic and specific experiments investigating the effects of evidence can also be done, and we are currently investigating this possibility.

5

The Child's Theory of Action

While the study of object permanence has become a minor industry, the child's understanding of action has been investigated much less. Nevertheless, there is reason to think that this kind of understanding is very important to infants and young children. In fact, in Piaget's original investigations he was at least as deeply concerned with children's understanding of actions as with their understanding of objects.

Moreover, understanding action underlies the child's later development of a theory of mind. First, an understanding of action provides the basic evidence on which any theory of the mind must be based, since we infer mental states from actions. Second, many of the fundamental concepts of our theory of mind share important features with concepts of action. John Searle (1983) makes a helpful distinction between mental states with what he calls "world-to-mind" direction of fit and those with "mind-to-world" direction of fit. In world-to-mind states, states like desire, the mind alters the world to fit its representations. In contrast, in mind-to-world states, states like belief, the mind alters its representations to fit the world. There is considerable evidence that world-to-mind states, particularly desire, are among the earliest and most central concepts in the child's theory of mind. Wellman, in particular, has demonstrated that 2-year-olds show a surprisingly sophisticated understanding of desire, an understanding that substantially predates their understanding of belief (Bartsch & Wellman, 1995; Wellman, 1990; Wellman & Woolley, 1990). The early understanding of perception revealed in object permanence, social referencing, and visual-perspective taking is the child's first conception of mind-to-world states. The early understanding of actions, plans, and goals might be the child's first conception of world-to-mind states.

The Adult Theory

Our adult theory of action has many complexities but also a few basic causal tenets. We believe that the world contains both psychological agents and inanimate physical objects. Psychological agents centrally include ourselves and other human beings, and we assume that we and others act in the same way. Psychological agents have internal mental states (desires, plans, intentions, and so on) that cause bodily movements. In turn, bodily movements cause things to occur in the world in particular and predictable ways. We also believe that, partly because of the difference between agents and objects, the causal consequences of bodily movements will be different when we are interacting with other people and when we are acting on objects. We influence people by communication and objects by contact. Finally, we believe that the events in the world that result from our movements will "satisfy" our mental states. That is, the events in the world that are the consequences of our actions will be the events we wanted to happen in the first place.

Just as with the concept of objects, we use this theory both to generate wide-ranging predictions about human action and to generate causal explanations. These tenets are perhaps best summarized by the "practical syllogism": "If a psychological agent wants event y and believes that action x will cause event y, he will do x." Many philosophers have argued that the practical syllogism is the basic explanatory schema of folk psychology.

Just as conjurors play on our ordinary theory of object appearances in a way that reveals its depth and extent, so they play on our ordinary theory of action. In addition to disappearances, "mentalist" feats are a standard part of the conjuror's stock in trade. The magician appears to make objects move simply by talking to them, looking at them, or waving his wand at them, without making any physical contact. Or he makes inanimate objects behave like animate ones. Or he has a member of an audience express an intention ("Pick a card, any card"), of which the conjuror is ignorant, and then proceeds to show the intention is fulfilled by his own action rather than the audience member's. Or, as in one Penn and Teller routine, a dozen members of the audience make a series of apparently arbitrary decisions, which seems to lead to the fulfillment of the conjuror's original intention. Among the conjuror's most persuasive tricks are to appear to act on people without communication and to act on objects without contact.

As with object appearances, however, the conjuror doesn't stop there. He also frustrates the causal explanations of these events that we construct using our folk psychology. Perhaps the audience member is a confederate, so he has one member of the audience pick out another. Perhaps the audience members have inadvertently communicated their intentions to him, so he is elaborately blindfolded. And so on. The events in a conjuror's show violate both our familiar scripts and any innately given predictions we might make. But, given our ordinary theory of action, these facts don't make the events utterly incomprehensible. On the contrary, they provide us with a stimulus to generate new predictions and explanations. The conjuror's technique is to provide counterevidence to those predictions and to frustrate those explanations.

Also, as with object appearances, we can imagine patterns of evidence that would force us to revise our ordinary theory. Scientific psychology, like physics, itself forces us to revise our views of the relations between inner states, actions, and events. For example, consider the notion of ambivalent or self-defeating actions, actions that apparently fulfill one desire but actually fulfill another. Or consider materialism, the doctrine that all psychological events can be explained in physical terms. These notions pose some challenge to our ordinary theory and yet have become widely and even popularly accepted.

Again, however, these scientific cases may be too abstract to influence our everyday life. So take the *Star Trek* examples once more. Two of the long-running plots on *Star Trek* involve creatures who deeply violate our ordinary theory of action. Q is an omnipotent creature who can cause his desires to be satisfied simply by willing them, without intervening actions. The Borg is (or are) a collective species who all share the same intentions (generally malign). Both Q and the Borg are long-running "guest stars" because the données (as Henry James would say) of their special attributes cascade through the rest of our coherent theory of human action. Q's powers call into question fundamental ideas about will, desire, morality, and time. The Borg calls into question ideas of personal identity, responsibility, and agency.

Like the conjuror, *Star Trek* invokes our sense of wonder by violating the deep tenets of our ordinary theory of actions. But while, in the conjuror's case, these violations force us to call on the theory for alternative explanations (since we know that the conjuror is part of our real world), the *Star Trek* cases present us with worlds containing genuine counterevidence to our ordinary theory. The theory theory predicts that if we were born into a universe actually inhabited by Qs or Borgs, we would develop alternative accounts of human action.

The Initial Theory

Interactions with persons

We suggested before that certain kinds of information about objects are represented at birth in an abstract and coherent way. The child possesses initial theorylike structures for organizing the world, which he then modifies and reshapes in later theorizing. In the case of objects, the initial theory includes the information that three-dimensional objects move through space in particular ways. We suggest that the same is true for certain kinds of information about actions. In particular, one aspect of our ordinary theory of mind that has often seemed inferential or learned is, we will argue, innately given.

We mentioned that part of our adult theory is that both we ourselves and others are psychological agents and that internal states cause actions in both ourselves and others. In classical terms, the connection between our own internal mental states and the perceived actions of others has seemed particularly problematic, just as our ability to infer three-dimensional space from two-dimensional images seemed problematic. Phenomenologically, the causal link between our internal states and our actions seems self-evident. But the inference that there are similar links in other people is far from evident. Many philosophers and psychologists have suggested that we need to learn about this similarity between ourselves and others. The problem of "other minds" is a problem about inferring the internal states of others from their behavior.

There is considerable evidence that from an extremely early age infants distinguish between inanimate objects and people and respond in a distinctive way to human faces and voices (de Boysson-Bardies et al., 1993; Meltzoff & Kuhl, 1994; Meltzoff & Moore, 1993; Morton & Johnson, 1991; Trevarthen, 1979). This parallels the distinction between objects and psychological agents in the adult theory. This fact by itself, however, does not tell us how the infant conceives of people or whether she identifies other people with herself. We want to make a stronger claim about the infant's initial theory. We claim that infants already know that they are like other people. We suggest that from birth, information about action that comes, literally, from inside ourselves is coded in the same way as information that comes from observing the behavior of others. There is a fundamental cross-modal representational system that connects self and other (Meltzoff & Gopnik, 1993; Meltzoff & Moore, 1995a). This initial coding then becomes the basis for the child's further acquisition of a theory of action.

As we saw in the last chapter, there is good empirical evidence that very young infants map information from different sensory modalities onto the same representation. In particular, young infants can recognize equivalences between tactile and visual representations of objects (Bryant et al., 1972; Meltzoff & Borton, 1979; Streri, 1987). These abstract cross-modal representations could allow a kind of inference about what the features of the object will be in one modality, given its features in another. If I know that an object feels bumpy, I can represent how it will look.

We suggest that something like this picture also applies to our perception of actions. Information about action may come to us from many different sources. In particular, it may come from observing the behavior of others or, literally, from within ourselves, through our kinesthetic sensations. However, all this information is represented similarly. There is an abstract representation, a kind of body scheme, that allows an innate mapping from certain kinds of behavioral observations of others to certain kinds of perceptions of our own internal states. In particular, we innately map the visually perceived motions of others onto our own kinesthetic sensations (Gopnik & Meltzoff, 1994; Meltzoff & Gopnik, 1993; Meltzoff & Moore, 1995b).

Evidence for this claim comes from studies of the early imitation of facial gestures. Imitation is a particularly interesting and potent behavior because it implies recognition of the similarities between the self and the other, the imitator and the imitated. The imitation of facial gestures, in particular, requires a mapping from visually perceived physical movements to internally felt kinesthetic sensations, the most fundamental of action representations. To genuinely imitate another person sticking out his tongue, for instance, I have to recognize the equivalence between the visual spectacle of his face, an oval with a protruding moving cylinder in

its lower portion, and the set of feelings that make up my own kinesthetic image of my invisible tongue.

Meltzoff and Moore (1977) demonstrated that 12-to-21-day-old
infants differentially imitated tongue protrusion, mouth opening, and lip
protrusion. Later they found similar imitation in newborns, including
babies as young as 42 minutes old (Meltzoff & Moore, 1983; Meltzoff &
Moore, 1989). These findings have since been replicated in more than a
dozen different laboratories and studies. Moreover, several features of the
studies demonstrate that the behaviors are indeed genuine imitations and
not simply reflexive behavior. The infants productively produce particular types of actions in response to particular types of actions they see in
others. Since infants cannot see their own faces, this implies some kind of
cross-modal mapping (Meltzoff & Moore, 1977, 1995b).

Infant imitation also implies some ability to map very simple motor
plans onto perceived actions. When the infant imitates a facial expression, she not only recognizes the link between the state of her own face
and that of the person she is imitating; she also translates her perception
of the face of the other into an intentional action, a kind of simple plan.
She acts to bring her face into accord with the face of the other person.

There is an empirical aspect of infant imitation that is particularly
revealing in this regard. Infants do not immediately produce the imitative
responses in their full-fledged form. Rather, they produce responses that
slowly converge on the gesture to be imitated (Meltzoff & Moore, 1994,
1995b). An infant who sees another person stick out his tongue, for
example, might begin by making small tongue movements, then tenta-
tively stick the tip of her tongue outside her mouth, and only later produce full-blown tongue protrusions. Again, this suggests that infants
recognize the relationship between their plan to produce the action and
the action they perceive in others. It also suggests that these actions are
the product of inferencelike processes and are not merely reflexive.

Finally, in addition to linking the self and others, early imitation
links internal states to perceived actions. We might wonder whether
kinesthetic sensations and simple motor plans ought to count as "mental"
states. Plainly, these states are not the same as sophisticated mental states
like desire or intention. However, kinesthetic sensations do have a great
deal in common with classic mental states like pain. In fact, a kinesthetic
sensation, like that of holding your arm in a particular position, will
actually become a pain if the position is maintained for long enough. We

seem to innately link these internal sensations to the visually perceived expressions and actions of others. Similarly, simple motor plans, like the intention to move your tongue, seem to be a primitive kind of mental state, and we seem to map these plans onto perceived actions.

Imitation, then, suggests an innate link between mental states and actions, though this link is much more primitive than the links among desires, intentions, and actions that underpin the adult theory. Newborn imitation is nature's way of solving both the problem of other minds and the mind-body problem at one fell swoop.

We have direct evidence that newborn babies less than 1 hour old can imitate facial expressions, just as we have direct evidence that newborns can perceive objects in three dimensions. Imitation is surely innate if anything is. As with the concept of objects, we see other more complex but similar abilities emerging in the first few months of life. These abilities may be part of the initial theory of action or they may develop from the earlier capacities.

A number of very early interactive behaviors have been described under the rubric of "primary intersubjectivity" (Trevarthen, 1979; see also Brazelton & Tronick, 1980; Bruner, 1975, 1983; Kaye & Fogel, 1980; Tronick, Als & Brazelton, 1980). There seems to be an affective and temporal coordination between the infant's gestures and expressions and those of other people. Very young infants gaze at the faces of significant (or even not-so-significant) others and vocalize and gesture in a way that seems "tuned" to the vocalizations and gestures of the other person. When they engage in these behaviors, the infants seem to detect the temporal structure and some of the affective quality of the other person's facial expressions and to respond in a harmonious way (Trevarthen, 1979). (If we saw adults behave in this way—smiling, gesturing, and cooing in rhythm with another person—we would say they were flirting.) When the infant's predictions about the other person's response are violated, when, for example, the mother responds to the baby's flirtatious overtures with a perfectly still stone face, babies behave in a distinctively distressed way (Tronick, Als, Adamson, Wise & Brazelton, 1978; Murray & Trevarthen, 1985). These behaviors seem to reflect the same initial mapping between the behavior of others and our own internal states that is first and, to our minds, most convincingly demonstrated in early imitation.

One possibility is that such facial imitation and other behaviors reflect the same initial underlying representation that unites our visual experience of the actions of others and our kinesthetic experience of our own actions. Such a representation might include information about timing and affect as well as gestural structure.

Another possibility is that the gestural mapping is primary and the other representations are derived from it. In particular, the very mechanism of imitation itself might establish links between the perceived affect of others and the infant's own internal affective state, or between the timing of the infant's own actions and those of others. Ekman, Levenson, and Friesen (1983) have demonstrated that the mere physical experience of certain facial expressions is itself enough to induce a parallel internal affective state, which thus substantiates all of Dale Carnegie's advice about smiling when you're depressed and whistling when you're scared (see also Zajonc, Murphy & Inglehart, 1989). Infants may begin by "affectlessly" imitating gestures and then, through Ekman et al.'s mechanisms, find that the internal affective state they produce in this way is distinctive. They might then further map the internal affective state onto the behavior of the other, as well as onto their own kinesthetic experience.

In either case, very young infants represent a variety of aspects of human action—its structure, its timing, and perhaps even its affective tone—in a single code that represents both their own actions and those of others in similar ways. This suggests that information acquired about the self is generalized to others, and vice versa, from early in development. Moreover, these representations involve links between internal "mental" states, like emotions, motor plans, kinesthetic sensations, and perceived behavior.

Furthermore, infants can make inferences on the basis of these representations. They can recognize which movements of their own faces and bodies will correspond to the observed movement of the other's face and body and then produce that movement. They also seem able to infer the appropriate affective and temporal responses to the behavior of others. Later they can also apparently make some inferences about what behaviors another person is likely to produce in response to their own behavior.

This capacity to map her own actions and internal sensations onto the actions of others provides an important, and in some ways unexpected, groundwork for the infant's theory of action. Just as we might not have guessed a priori that infants would be able to project trajectories or locate objects in three-dimensional space, so we might not have guessed that they would be able to map their own internal states onto the perceived behavior of others. In the case of both objects and actions, the initial theory allows an important generative set of predictions, based on rather abstract representations (an object scheme in one case and a body scheme in the other). In both cases infants respond distinctively if they are presented with events that violate these predictions. Their initial states are theorylike in this regard.

As in the case of the concept of objects, the initial theory of action is not identical to the later theory, nor is it even just an incomplete version of the later theory. The infant's initial notion of the link between the self and others is qualitatively different from our adult notion in several ways. First, it seems particularly intimately tied to the similarity between our bodies and the bodies of others. Rather than having a concept of psychological agents, young infants seem to have a concept of persons, which combines mind and body. For us as adults, it isn't necessary to have a face in order to have a mind. Moreover, the kinds of internal states that infants seem able to relate to actions, kinesthetic sensations, motor plans, and emotions seem rather different from, and more primitive than, the desires and beliefs of the adult theory.

Second, infants seem initially to assume similarities and parallelisms, perhaps even identities, between themselves and others, rather than differences. It is conceivable that young infants think that persons are rather like the *Star Trek* Borg; that is, they think of themselves and others as fundamentally sharing the same psychological states (Trevarthen [1979] and Hobson [1993] both suggest this sort of picture; it also features in some psychoanalytic accounts). This rather Rousseauean view turns the problem of other minds on its head: we start out deeply identifying with our fellow human beings and need to develop an understanding of separation and conflict. Certainly, when we adults engage in flirtation with very young infants, the impression of rapport, mutual understanding, and deep commonality is extremely powerful, despite the enormous differences between us (the analogy to adult lovers springs to mind). We still lack the evidence to demonstrate conclusively that it feels that way to babies too, and there is some evidence that infants differentiate between the actions they see and do (Meltzoff & Moore, 1995a, 1995b). Nevertheless, it seems likely that the infant's notion of the relation between herself and others is significantly different from the adult notion.

We will argue, moreover, that, just as in the case of the concept of objects, the infants' innate understanding of action is not the end of the story. Important aspects of the adult theory still have to be constructed.

Actions on objects

So far we have been discussing one facet of our commonsense theory of action, namely our assumption that the actions of ourselves and others are linked to internal states in the same way. If we are right, very young infants in the first few months of life understand the basic commonalities between the feeling of their own intentional bodily movements and the sight of the movements of others. The commonsense notion of action, however, involves more than just bodily movements. It also involves the effects of those movements on objects. An infant's account of persons may enable some predictions about the character, timing, and affective significance of actions, but importantly, actions are also correlated with events in the world. Persons make objects do things.

There is evidence that infants become sensitive to the consequences of their actions on objects within the first 2 or 3 months. Very young infants are highly motivated to attend to and reproduce events that stem from their own actions. These very young infants already seem to appreciate some aspects of the causal connection between their actions and events in the world. They are very sensitive to the temporal links between actions and events and to the patterns of contingency between them. Their appreciation of these relations enables them to make a primitive kind of inference: if a particular type of event followed a particular type of action before, it will do so again (Bower, 1989; Watson, 1967, 1972).

The initial theory enables these contingencies to be constrained and interpreted in particular ways. Not all contingencies in the world capture the infant's attention or interest, nor will the infant learn about any arbitrary contingency. Rather, infants seem particularly interested in events that are closely linked to the temporal structure of their own actions. In fact, it seems that there is a temporal "window" of about three seconds between the young infant's action and the resulting event.

When the action and the event are not this closely linked, infants seem unable to appreciate the contingencies (Watson, 1967).

Moreover, infants seem particularly likely to attend to and learn about contingencies when the structural properties of their actions parallel the structural properties of the events that follow them. For example, infants are particularly likely to learn that shaking their legs leads to the shaking of the object and that a strong kick leads to a larger displacement of the object than a weak one. Thus we can find particularly clear, strong, and swift examples of learning in early infancy with the technique Rovee-Collier (1990) calls "conjugate reinforcement," where every action the child makes is immediately temporally linked to a structurally parallel following event.

Finally, infants seem to learn these contingencies best when the salient events that follow the actions are events that are well represented in the child's early theory of objects, such as continuous movements of objects along trajectories. The bodily movements specified by the infant's theory of action are linked in specific temporal and structural ways to the object movements specified by his theory of objects.

Some of these behaviors might look at first like classical or operant conditioning, and in fact much of the empirical work on early contingency learning comes from researchers working in this tradition. A closer look at the data, however, suggests a rather different and richer view. First, there is evidence that it is the very contingency of the consequences that captures the children's attention, and not some intrinsically reinforcing aspect of the outcome. In one experiment, for example, Papousek (1969) found that very young infants would rapidly detect the contingency between a particular pattern of head turns and a display of flashing lights and would reproduce these actions, even when the display itself had ceased to capture their interest. Second, as we have pointed out, there are substantial constraints on the kinds of actions and events that infants will link. (Of course, this is probably also true of many of the animal behaviors that were originally supposed to be explained by classical learning theories [see Gallistel, 1990].) These contingencies are more like empirical generalizations constrained by theoretical presuppositions than like the unconstrained connections of some versions of classical learning theory.

The evidence also suggests, however, that young infants only have a sketchy sense of the full underlying causal structure of these contingencies. In particular, they do not appear to understand that only some events that are temporally connected to actions or structurally parallel to them are actually caused by those actions and will reliably occur again. Conversely, they do not appreciate that there can be causal links between actions and events that are not temporally or structurally parallel. In particular, they do not initially appreciate the role of spatial contiguity in causality. Contingency-learning experiments themselves support this suggestion. Infants appear to be as willing to accept an utterly arbitrary contingency, such as the connection between head turning and lights in the Papousek (1969) experiments, as they are to accept a more causally motivated one. Similarly, techniques standardly used in testing very young infants presume that infants will search for highly arbitrary contingencies between their actions and events and reproduce the actions that produce events (Lipsitt, 1990; Rovee-Collier & Lipsitt, 1982). Interestingly, these techniques become ineffective with older infants.

Behaviors that Piaget (1954) called "magical procedures" are a further dramatic example of the limitations of this early view. Infants do not initially act in ways that respect the spatial structure of causal events. Simply using temporal contingency and structural parallelism as marks of causal efficacy leads to some strikingly inaccurate predictions. In one observation, for example, Piaget moves a book back and forth as the infant shakes her perambulator. When the infant is presented with the stationary book, she again shakes the perambulator, looking at the book to see if it will move. In a classic later experiment (Uzgiris & Hunt, 1975; Piaget, 1954), 6-month-old infants who had learned to pull a cloth toward them to obtain an object on top of it, pulled the cloth even when the object was placed to one side of it, out of any spatial contact.

We might argue that many of the behaviors involved in infant-learning experiments are magical procedures in this sense. Carolyn Rovee-Collier has provided more detailed and experimentally controlled examples of similar phenomena in very young infants. Infants in her studies rapidly learned rather arbitrary contingencies between actions and consequences and generalized them to new instances. For example, infants who had a foot attached to a crib mobile with a ribbon rapidly learned to kick in such a way as to activate the mobile. When the ribbon was no longer attached, infants still generalized this response to similar new mobiles (Rovee-Collier, 1984, 1990; Rovee-Collier & Gekoski,

1979). Notice that in both these and Piaget's classic cases, the actions and events are temporally and structurally parallel; the problem is that there is no spatial contiguity between them. The infants begin by making overly general predictions about the connections between actions and events.

Of course, infants do eventually learn that only some links between actions and events are reliable. Initially they seem to do so by constructing specific empirical generalizations. Rovee-Collier notes, for example, that infants who learn a contingency between kicking a foot and making a mobile move will not reproduce that contingency if a fairly arbitrary aspect of the context is changed, like the stripes on the crib liner (Amabile & Rovee-Collier, 1991; Borovsky & Rovee-Collier, 1990; Rovee-Collier, Griesler & Earley, 1985). Nor will infants who learn to kick the mobile with one leg readily generalize that action to another leg (Rovee-Collier et al., 1978).

At the same time, there is unsystematic but suggestive evidence that young infants are collecting similar information about the consequences of their actions in the psychological realm. The face-to-face interactions of "primary intersubjectivity" provide rich information of this sort. Aside from the innately given mapping of their own actions onto those of others, infants must also learn the idiosyncratic action patterns of the people around them, particularly their actions in response to the infant's own behavior. One reason that the amount of strict imitation apparently decreases in this period is that infants become involved in these more complicated interactions with others (Meltzoff & Moore, 1992). The baby, like any effective flirt, must learn not only that his mother responds to his smile with her own smile but also that she responds to his frown with a sympathetic "There" or to his particularly charming cross-eyed expression of concentration with her own mock-serious gaze.

We suggest that within the framework of their general appreciation of contingency, these infants are accumulating empirical generalizations about the relations between actions and events. They begin to recognize that only some subclasses of relations between actions and events are actually reliable over the long run. In a natural setting, subpatterns of regularity will gradually become apparent in the course of the infant's experimentation. Watson (1979) has given an interesting account of how different patterns of contingency could give the child fundamental information about the structure of the physical and psychological world.

At this time infants are also learning that some of their initial predictions about the world are false.

The Nine-Month-Old's Theory

Actions on objects

We suggest that as a consequence of accumulating this sort of information, the infants develop a new theory of action. In particular, by around 8 to 10 months infants start to appreciate the role of spatial contact in determining the consequences of their actions on objects and to appreciate the role of communicative interaction in determining the consequences of their actions on people. In both cases, we suggest, children start out with the earlier and more limited theory plus an accumulation of empirical generalizations and replace this information with a new and more powerful theory.

A number of distinctive behaviors that emerge at around 9 months suggest that by this point infants have begun to abstract some of the underlying causal structure of both physical and psychological causality. The theory theory suggests that this causal understanding replaces infants' earlier set of empirical generalizations about which events follow which actions. Just as children give up arbitrary object-permanence rules, like searching for the object where it appeared before, as they develop a more sophisticated object theory, so they give up arbitrary contingencies as they develop a more sophisticated theory of actions and consequences.

In particular, somewhere in the second half of the first year, infants begin to appreciate the fact that their actions can affect objects only if they are spatially in contact with those objects. This new understanding leads them to abandon the more arbitrary, magical procedures of the earlier period. It also allows them to shape quite individual and well-adapted solutions to particular problems.

At this point in their development, infants begin to ignore the contextual effects we see in their earlier behaviors: at 9 months they will generalize their earlier action across crib liners and feet (Aaron et al., 1994; Rovee-Collier, 1990). They also stop producing magical procedures to obtain the object on the pillow (Piaget, 1952; Willatts, 1984). Most significant, children only attempt solutions that obey the rules of spatial contact. This enables their problem solving to be both more constrained, since a wide array of actions are ruled out, and more general at the same time. Infants can now see a new problem, like obtaining an object by pulling at the end of a horizontal string, and immediately hit on one of several appropriate solutions. They can appropriately predict that only actions that make contact with the object will affect it and that a wide range of such actions, including new actions they have never produced before, may have this sort of influence (Piaget, 1952; Willatts, 1984, 1985).

These sorts of behaviors led Piaget (1952, 1954) to propose that only at this point do infants produce genuinely goal-directed actions. But this characterization is not really accurate. In an important sense, earlier behaviors are quite goal-directed. What is true is that at this point the goal-directed behaviors become informed by a new causal theory of action.

Notice that this combination of both more constrained and more general inferences is just what we predict with the formation of a new theory. The new theory, like the earlier empirical generalizations, leads to a particular pattern of predictions. This pattern, however, is quite different from the earlier pattern. The theory allows new predictions not allowed by the earlier theory plus generalizations. Presented with new problems, the 9-month-old can immediately assess that he will succeed when there is spatial contact but will not otherwise.

At the same time, the interpretative effects of the theory may make the infant actually less able to detect real contingencies than she had previously been and more constrained in the patterns she will accept. Bower (1982), following Monnier (1980), reports that infants at 12 months became less willing than earlier to accept an arbitrary, though genuine, connection between action and consequence, such as kicking to break a light beam that causes a visual display. Rovee-Collier (1990) reported some similar results. Likewise, as we have noted already, learning techniques that work well with younger infants become quite ineffective with children of this age.

The new understanding is also reflected in habituation studies, as well as in infant's actions, though the results of these studies are complex and their interpretation is not entirely clear. Suppose that we present an infant with a sequence in which an object influences another object without making spatiotemporal contact with the object. Leslie found that 7-month-old infants dishabituated in one particular context of this kind, a "launching event" in which one stylized object made contact with another and led to the movement of the other object. Notice that this type of understanding of causal structure, like the early under- standing of objects, seems very much bound up in an account of objects moving on trajectories (Leslie, 1982; Leslie & Keeble, 1987).

However, there is no evidence as yet for such effects at ages younger than 7 months. Moreover, this type of effect also seems to be very much limited to this particular, narrow perceptual setting. Oakes and Cohen (1995), using more naturalistic stimuli, found such effects for 10-month-olds but not for 7-month-olds. Similarly, 10-month-olds but not 7-month-olds generalized this finding to a wider range of settings, for example, a context in which an object moved in a slightly different trajectory after the launching. Oakes and Cohen's findings are more in line with the findings from infants' active behaviors.

The discrepancy is similar to the discrepancy we saw in the case of object permanence. In a habituation paradigm, we can find some relatively early signs of an understanding of spatial causality in rather restricted contexts that deal with object movements and trajectories. However, this information is only put to use in action, and in the habituation paradigm is only generalized to wider cases, somewhat later in development. The same range of alternative explanations apply. Leslie's results may reflect a completely encapsulated module. In fact, there is a tradition going back to the work of Michotte (1962) suggesting that there is this sort of encapsulated perceptual notion of causality, which is not the same as the notion of causality that governs action. Alternatively, the representations of such a module may be redescribed to form an initial theory that can be generalized and used in action. Finally, Leslie's results may reflect an empirical generalization that the infants form about a particularly salient type of causal event. The devel- opment of the theory allows infants to make appropriate predictions across a much wider range of events, as suggested by Oakes and Cohen's findings, and enables them to put the information to use in active prob- lem solving. Overall, the findings suggest that there is a switch to a new view of causality toward the end of the first year. Children's under- standing of the relations between their actions and the events that follow those actions becomes much more sophisticated.

Interactions with persons

Almost all discussions of children's understanding of causality have focused on a very narrow range of causal situations. Piaget's (1952, 1954) account of causal understanding and most other accounts have stressed the way in which actions are used to manipulate physical objects. Indeed, in discussions of children's understanding of causality it is often taken for granted that mechanical, physical causality is what is at issue. But there is no reason to suppose that these are the only or even most important cases of causation in the child's world. In a broader sense, children understand causality whenever they appreciate the relations among events and can use those relations to make predictions and take effective actions. Even the very early contingency learning involves some appreciation of causality in this broad sense.

Moreover, in the child's world, some of the most important types of causal structure are not mechanical. In practice, actions have psychological consequences as well as physical ones, and there are deep and interesting differences in the causal structure of actions on objects and actions on people. "Action at a distance" is the rule rather than the exception in psychological causality. We influence others by talking, pointing, gesturing, and generally communicating. Only in the most extreme situations would we attempt to causally affect others by direct spatial contact. In contrast, all the types of physical causality with which children are likely to be acquainted involve spatiotemporal chains of contact between objects.

Indeed, we might argue that much of what is typically called "magical" or "animistic" thought in children and in various societies, including our own, involves simply the misapplication of psychological causality to physical phenomena (see Boyer, 1994). As we saw in chapter 2, some kinds of magical thinking really do seem to be irrational. But much magic involves a perfectly sensible overextension of the principles of psychological causality to complex physical objects. Magicians typically say things, dress up, prepare special foods, and wave their hands about to influence complex events in the world. But then, so do we all. In fact, this is most of what we do most of the time. The fact that we spend considerable time selecting particular garments (well, at least one of us does), preparing and consuming particular foods, and producing particular patterns of words and gestures is utterly rational, given that our aim is to influence the actions of other people. Such procedures are, in fact, far more likely to have the appropriate causal consequences than, for example, lifting or pushing other people or manipulating them with physical tools, techniques that tend to be rather counterproductive. The mistake in magical thinking is in selecting precisely the right domain to influence, and often, without higher-level knowledge of the causal structure of domains, the guess that psychological causality will apply is quite rational. After all, if you can talk someone into a red-hot fury, why not talk them into a serious illness? If you can talk them into bed, why not talk them into becoming pregnant?

There is some evidence that at about 9 months infants begin to make theoretical advances in the realm of psychological causality that are similar to their new understanding of physical causality. We saw that infants distinguish people and objects at an early age. However, there is evidence that at this early stage they do not yet differentiate between the kinds of actions that affect people and those that affect objects. Notice that the infant's very early appreciation of contingency applies equally well to physical and psychological causality. In both cases there will often be temporal and structural parallels between the baby's actions and their effects in the world. At least some of the "magical procedures" demonstrated in various experiments include elements of psychological as well as physical causality. For example, infants smile and coo at objects in contingency experiments (Watson, 1972). This has been taken by some as a sign that smiling is not "really" social and by others that there is a mastery smile as well as a social smile (Bower, 1982; Watson, 1972). It may also be, however, that infants are genuinely attempting to use psychologically effective procedures to bring about physical effects. If, in early infancy, they understand the effects of actions only in terms of temporal contingency and structural parallelism, they may not differentiate psychological and physical contingencies. Both physical and psychological consequences of actions may have both physical and psychological features. However, the idea that contingencies are constrained by temporal contiguity applies only to physical causality.

At around 9 months, in contrast, infants begin to produce communicative intentional behaviors. At the same time that infants begin to try to influence objects by producing behaviors that obey the rules of spatial contact, they also begin to try to influence people by producing particular gestures and vocalizations. For example, infants begin to use pointing gestures to direct their mothers' attention to objects, or pick-me-up gestures to be picked up (Bates et al., 1979; Lock, 1980; Trevarthen & Hubley, 1978; Tomasello, Kruger & Ratner, 1993). Again, these communicative gestures are used in a theorylike way that is both productive and constrained. They are exclusively addressed to other people and not objects, and they can be modified or intensified if, for example, there is no response from the other (Bates et al., 1979).

These communicative behaviors also suggest that the spatial contact rule is not some general problem-solving strategy, and that the developments in means-ends problem-solving at 9 months are not merely the result of an increase in information-processing or strategic or motor capacity. Infants correctly assume that quite a different set of causal principles will apply to people. The infant has developed quite different, in fact in some ways opposing, accounts of the causal structure of the physical and psychological domains.

Watson (1979) has suggested that there are important differences in the contingent nature of infants' interactions with objects and with people. Most significant, the actions of others are, quite generally, only partially and probabilistically contingent on our own actions, while the responses of objects are much more reliably correlated with our own actions. The empirical generalizations infants accumulate in the preceding period license a general theoretical distinction between physical and psychological causality. The babies' accounts of these two types of causality are complementary, however, and there is some evidence that their emergence is developmentally linked.

The self and the other
So far we have been talking about changes in infants' understanding of the consequences of actions at 9 months. We can return now to the infants' understanding of the parallels between their own actions and internal states and those of others. The kinds of internal states that infants will attribute to others change as their understanding of causality changes.

Like the infant's theory of bodily movements, the infant's theory of consequences seems to apply both to his own actions and to those of others. That is, as soon as the infant shows an understanding of his own causal relations to objects and persons, he apparently assumes that other people's causal relations to objects and persons are similar. Imitation is again a dramatic example of this. By 9 months, though not before, infants will imitate another person's novel actions on objects that lead to a particular consequence, as well as imitating simple bodily actions. Suppose that you show a 14-month-old a novel action with an interesting outcome, like touching a box with your forehead to make it light up, without letting them act on the object themselves. If you present them with the same object after a substantial delay, a week or more, they will immediately touch the box with their own foreheads (Meltzoff, 1988a, 1995b).

This suggests that the underlying theory of spatiotemporal contact is applied to the actions of others and the child's own actions simultaneously. Infants will immediately, without an intervening period of trial and error, make the generalization that if the perceived actions of another caused a certain result, their own actions will cause a similar result. This is true even though they may never have produced such an action before and even though their own actions may be structurally quite different from the actions of others. Contra Piaget, 9-month-olds even make such predictions when there is a 24-hour delay between their observation of the other's action and their own actions (Meltzoff, 1988b).

While the matter has not been systematically studied, infants' ability to learn the rather arbitrary communicative gestures and vocalizations of early language implies a similar ability to generalize notions of psychological causality and to productively imitate the actions of others in order to produce intentional consequences.

It is striking that infants will not imitate these kinds of object-directed behaviors earlier, though they will imitate simple bodily actions. Notice that if imitation were simply a kind of mindless instinctive repetition, infants could, in principle, move their heads forward as easily as they could stick out their tongues. Instead, however, infants' imitative acts seem to be deeply caught up in their theory of action. Where the action makes sense theoretically, they imitate; where the action does not, they do not. This suggests that the theory has interpretive effects. The initial theory makes the link between the actions of the self and those of the other, but it fails to extend this link to more complex cases in which actions have causal consequences on objects.

In addition to this active evidence from imitation studies, there is also habituation evidence for a developing understanding of the actions of others. In a series of experiments Gergely et al. (1994, 1995) presented 9-to-12-month-old infants with two circles and the infants were then habituated to a scene in which one of the circles jumped over a barrier and went toward the other circle. Then they were presented with one of two scenes in which the barrier no longer separated the two actors. In one scene the actor moved directly toward the other circle; in the other it reproduced its earlier leap. Interestingly, 9-month-olds, though not 6-month-olds, dishabituated to the second scene. In other words, in the habituation paradigm 9-month-old infants seemed to attribute some understanding of goal-directed behavior to others as well as themselves, whereas 6-month-olds did not. In Gergeley's terms, as well as behaving in a rational way themselves, infants seemed to assume that others would also behave in a rational way.

These behaviors imply that the infants generalize their account of the consequences of actions to other people. They also imply that by the end of the first year the infant has a rather different and richer conception of the internal states that cause movements than the newborn infant did. The 9-month-old infant seems to think that actions are directed toward objects in a goal-directed way, rather than simply conceiving of them as bodily movements per se.

A number of writers have remarked on this characteristic of the 9-month-old's theory, which is also manifested in mind-to-world states in behaviors like joint attention. Indeed, it has led some writers to suggest that 9-month-olds not only attribute internal mental states to others but attribute intentional states to them as well (Wellman, 1990; Baron-Cohen, 1995). If these states are intentional, however, they are so in a rather different way than the more sophisticated states of desire and belief that children attribute later in development. Nothing in the 9-month-old's behavior suggests that they think internal states are separable from action, let alone think that these states are representational.

The Eighteen-Month-Old's Theory

Actions on objects

While the theory that the infant develops at around 9 months is dramatically superior to the earlier theory, it is still incomplete in many respects. The fundamental idea in the 9-month-old child's theory of action is that there are two separate domains, people and objects, and that the first set of entities is susceptible to communicative acts while the second is subject to actions that involve spatial contact.

This theory enables the infant to produce much more constrained and accurate predictions than the earlier theory. However, it will lead to incorrect predictions in cases where the particular characteristics or underlying features of an object play a role in its causal properties. For example, suppose the infant now sees an object out of reach and is presented with a rake with which to reach the object. While a 6-month-old might simply wave the rake at random, a 1-year-old, in contrast, will typically use the rake to make some sort of contact with the object. The 1-year-old's theory tells him that only actions that involve the right sort of spatial relation to the object will be effective. The trouble is that merely making spatial contact will not solve the problem in this case: the toy will come no closer. Such an attempt, in fact, constitutes counterevidence for the spatial-contact theory. The infant makes contact, but no appropriate result emerges. Instead, the infant must adapt his actions to the particular features of the object, often nonobvious underlying features.

There are a number of similar cases reported in the literature. Here are two more that we have particularly explored: We show infants a long necklace that must be inserted bead by bead into a bottle with a small opening. Or we show them a post on which stacking rings are to be placed and one taped-over ring (Gopnik & Meltzoff, 1984, 1986a; Piaget, 1952, 1954; Uzgiris & Hunt, 1975, 1987). In both these cases, making predictions strictly on the basis of spatiotemporal contact will lead to some incorrect predictions. The infants scrunch the necklace into a ball and try to put it directly in the bottle or, perhaps most strikingly, repeatedly try to put the solid ring directly on the post.

Such counterevidence may be dealt with in several ways. In some cases the children continue to interpret the counterevidence in terms of the original theory. The children persist, with some consistency, with the inappropriate prediction, even in the face of the evidence. Strikingly, 12- and 15-month-olds seem quite resistant to learning this set of contingencies, much more than we would assume, given, say, their competencies as very young infants. This is consistent, however, with the notion that they have replaced a set of predictions based on simple temporal and structural parallels with a more constrained theory.

With repeated trials, some infants may learn a particular rule for dealing with the specific case. They develop an additional ad hoc empirical generalization to deal with the counterevidence. Piaget (1952, 1954) described these behaviors in terms of trial-and-error learning. Again, however, it seems that the issue has less to do with a type of problem-solving than with a type of problem. Infants do demonstrate trial-and-error learning in other contexts much earlier: we can think of some of the early contingency learning in just such a way. They do not demonstrate trial-and-error learning in situations covered by their theory. For example, at 12 to 15 months infants immediately and insightfully recognize that the rake must make some sort of contact with the object. Trial-and-error problem solving, we would argue, accompanies the accumulation and exercise of particular empirical generalizations.

By 18 months, in contrast, infants do make the correct predictions. On the first trial they will place the necklace in the bottle in the correct position, adjust the rake so that it captures the object correctly, and avoid the solid ring. They demonstrate such behaviors whether or not they have been presented with the problem earlier and whether or not they have made attempts at a solution. Notice that it is difficult to explain the emergence of these behaviors in terms of some sort of motor competence, since younger children can sometimes learn to effectively produce exactly the same actions after a period of trial and error. There are many other instances of this sort of immediate problem solving at this age.

Piaget (1952) christened this development "insight" and conceived of it as a new, general problem-solving strategy replacing an earlier trial-and-error strategy. This does not, however, capture the real difference between the younger and older infants, just as describing the 9-month-old's developments in terms of the emergence of goal-directed behavior doesn't capture the essential point.

We would argue that insightful problem-solving in a domain, like deduction, is a consequence, in fact the most characteristic consequence, of developing a theory of that domain. "Deduction" and "insight" are terms for capturing the way that theories allow new explanations and predictions. Indeed, these very terms are those we would characteristically use to describe the benefits of theory formation in science. On this view, deduction and insight are not new general skills or strategies that emerge at 18 months. Rather, Piaget pointed to specific instances of these abilities in important domains in which infants had developed a new theoretical understanding.

In this particular case the infants' discovery seems to involve an understanding of how the specific properties of objects lead to particular consequences. It represents a considerable advance over the earlier spatiotemporal-contact theory, with its inaccurate predictions. The infant can now make predictions about the effects of actions on objects that take the particular properties of those objects into account. These predictions, across a wide range of instances not covered by the previous theory, lead to the appearance, indeed to the reality, of insight. Note that there is a close correlation in performance on the three tasks—the rake, the necklace, and the ring—in spite of the many differences in the information-processing and motor requirements of the tasks and their very different perceptual features.

Notice also that in these cases the infant is making not only incomplete predictions but actively incorrect ones as well. For adults, the correct inference in these cases seems intuitively compelling in an almost Kantian way. After all, an adult is no more likely to have seen the particular problems of the necklace and the ring than the child. But the correct solution to those problems leaps out at us adults immediately. Strictly from the point of view of adult phenomenology, these inferences would seem to be as good candidates for modularity as any. Yet the developmental evidence suggests that quite different predictions are equally compelling for 1-year-olds. Infants seem to have a qualitatively different account of action than adults.

Interactions with persons

We have some reason to believe that there are equally deep changes in the infant's understanding of psychological causality at this point. As we have suggested, part of the infant's development at 9 months is understanding the different causal structure of action on others and on objects: objects are influenced by contact, while people are influenced by communication. At 18 months, the infant's discovery of the recalcitrance of objects is accompanied by their parallel discovery of the (rather different) recalcitrance of persons.

We mentioned earlier that the contingency patterns of communication are less regular than those of object causality. Presumably, even young infants note that their communicative efforts are sometimes ineffective. Yet 9-month-old infants show no signs of understanding why their attempts to act on others are ineffective or, indeed, when the attempts of others to act on them will be. Either such infants interact with some expectation of mutual causal consequences, or they simply fail to interact at all and concentrate their attention on objects instead.

In contrast, by 18 months or so infants begin to explore the causal regularities of at least one distinctive group of failures to influence other people. These failures occur when there is conflict between yourself and another person. If the other person's desires conflict with yours, then all your attempts to communicate will have precisely the opposite of their intended consequence. The more clearly you signal your desire for the lamp cord, the lipstick, the cookie on the high shelf, the more adamantly will the other act to ensure that the desire is not fulfilled. To the 9-month-old, this must seem not only like counterevidence to the theory but practically paradoxical. By 18 months, however, infants seem to explore these regularities consistently and indeed to have formulated some consistent theoretical story about them. These infants will systematically set up situations in which their own desires conflict with those of others and explore the consequences of these conflicts. They reach for the lamp cord not in spite of Mom's prohibition but rather because of it. (This period is technically called "the terrible twos" among one experienced school of infant observers. The British term "bloody-mindedness" also seems to capture the idea. Interestingly, it is just the cold-bloodedly experimental nature of these behaviors that makes them so difficult to deal with. A 12-month-old who crawls determinedly toward the lamp cord until he is dragged away kicking and screaming is one thing; an 18-month-old who looks you straight in the eye as he slowly and deliberately moves his hand toward the lamp cord is quite another.)

The terrible twos are a compelling naturalistic phenomenon, but we also want to explore children's understanding of desire conflicts more systematically. We know that young two-year-olds appreciate something about the diversity and possible conflict of desires (Bartsch & Wellman, 1995; Wellman & Woolley, 1990). These experiments, however, are limited by the verbal abilities of the children. In the lab of one of us, Repacholi has demonstrated just such a developing appreciation of desire conflicts at about 18 months using a nonverbal method (Repacholi, 1996; Repacholi & Gopnik, in press). In her studies the infants are presented with a plate of raw broccoli and a plate of goldfish crackers. Even Berkeley babies prefer the crackers. The experimenter indicates her preference for one object or another by producing a particular emotional expression (disgust or pleasure). The experimenter then reaches her hands out to the infant and asks the infant to give her (unspecified) food. In a control condition the experimenter reverses her reactions. Even when the preference differed from their own desire, 18-month-old infants consistently gave the experimenter the food for which she had expressed a preference. They gave her broccoli when she had previously expressed a desire for the broccoli and crackers when she expressed a desire for crackers, despite their own unalterable conviction that broccoli is yucky. In contrast, 14-month-olds did not make these predictions. Instead, they always gave the experimenter crackers, their own preference, regardless of her desires. In this systematic experiment, as in the terrible-twos anecdotes, these infants also seem to show a new appreciation of the differences and conflicts among desires at about 18 months and of the consequences of these conflicts for emotion and action.

The self and the other
As in the earlier examples, there is evidence that infants apply their new theory of action to other people as well as to themselves. First, as soon as they understand particular causal schemas, infants assume that the schemas apply to witnessed actions as well as to executed ones. Just as 9-month-olds begin to imitate simple actions on objects, so 18-month-olds begin to imitate more complex kinds of goal-directed actions. Before 18 months, for example, infants will not imitate the correct action with the necklace or the rake. Instead, they will produce the incorrect version of the action, as if the demonstration was simply one of their own earlier trials. After 18 months, however, infants will immediately imitate such complex goal-directed actions, even if they have never performed those actions themselves.

Moreover, 18-month-olds will read through failed attempts to accomplish particular goals. When they see such a failure, they infer the nature of the other's goal and the nature of the object properties involved in the goal. In an experiment, one of us presented infants with another person who attempted and failed three times in different ways to accomplish a goal (Meltzoff, 1995a). The other person might try to use a stick to press a button on the top of a box but each time have the stick slip off the box. Or the person might make three unsuccessful attempts to pull apart two attached blocks. When infants were subsequently presented with such an event, they themselves immediately and successfully used the stick to push the button or pulled apart the blocks.

Moreover, the infants did not react in the same way when a mechanical device operated on the blocks in precisely the same way as the person. They did not use the behavior of the device as a clue to the kind of behavior they themselves should produce. They appeared yet again to have made a distinction between psychological goal-directed agents, like themselves, and mere mechanical objects.

These experiments demonstrate that at 18 months infants can read a complex goal from failed attempts, attempts that contradict the spatio-temporal contact theory, as well as from successful ones. They seem to recognize the property of the object that led to the failure and to infer the particular correct solution.

These examples again confirm our earlier claim that infants immediately apply their theory of action to the actions of both themselves and others. This relation, however, seems to run both ways. If infants cannot conceptualize an event theoretically, they fail to do so for both themselves and others. Thus, as well as providing evidence that theoretical predictions apply to both the self and others, these imitation results with older children again suggest an interpretive effect of the theory.

Moreover, the imitation results suggest a change in the kinds of internal states that the infants attribute to others. In the failed-attempt experiment the infant seems able to abstract away from particular bodily movements. All three different failed movements seem to be treated as the causal consequences of the same underlying mental state, the same goal. Notice that this is quite different from the newborn's ability to relate kinesthetic sensations or motor plans to actions. According to that representational system, all three failed attempts would be correlated with quite different internal states. It is even different from the 9-month-old's notion that actions are directed at objects and have consistent effects on them. The effects of the action on the object are different in each failed attempt. In this case, for the first time the infant seems to understand that quite different explicit bodily movements, with different consequences, may be indications of the same underlying internal mental state.

Other Evidence for the Theory Theory

We have suggested that there are important changes in children's predictions about actions and interpretations of actions at 18 months. Moreover, just as with the concept of objects, we can see signs of dynamic processes of theory change in this period. For instance, there is consistent experimentation in these domains between 12 and 18 months. Piaget (1952) described what he called "experiments in order to see" in this period. In these experiments, infants systematically explored and manipulated the effects of their actions on objects with varying properties. In these experimental contexts infants carefully graded their actions in relation to the object's properties. They would systematically explore the effects of the same action on objects with slightly different properties or the effects of slightly different actions on the same objects. Such experimentation all takes place within the context of the spatial-contact theory. Indeed, this theory allows such experimentation to take place and is quite different from the more arbitrary exploration of contingency we see in younger infants. Bloom (1993) and Lifter and Bloom (1989) also describe systematically observed changes in the spontaneous object play of infants of this age. Similarly, Reddy (1991) describes what she calls "teasing" and "mucking about" behaviors in infants from about 10 to 18 months old. These behaviors are like the "experiments in order to see," but they involve people rather than objects. In these activities infants explore the effect of communicating one intention and performing another, or they systematically experiment with the link between intention and action.

Finally, we see much the same affective behavior in these contexts that we see in our studies of object-permanence problems. Again, notice that often there is no obvious functional reward for solving these problems. The necklace task is a particularly striking demonstration in this regard. Placing the necklace in the bottle correctly, bead by bead, requires considerable patience, particularly by 18-month-old standards. Moreover, there is no reward in so doing: the necklace is a much more desirable toy than the bottle, and the baby relinquishes it by placing it in the bottle. And yet not only do the infants do the task, but they ask to repeat it over many trials. Similarly, the testing behaviors of "terrible twos" seem affectively paradoxical. Why would the baby deliberately do something that he knows will produce a dramatically negative reaction in his mother? The theory theory makes more sense of these phenomena. Like scientists, babies sometimes prefer truth to love.

In our longitudinal studies of the rake, necklace, and ring tasks, we also see the same changes in affect over time that we see in object-permanence problems. Initially, children repeatedly produce the incorrect solution with happy insouciance. They go through an intermediate period in which they show mixed behavior (such as trying to place the necklace in the bottle successfully the first time and unsuccessfully the next) and considerable misery interspersed with pleasure at the solution. A particularly interesting behavior comes when children who have insightfully solved the task actually refer back to their earlier incorrect predictions. For example, children may hold the solid ring up close to the post without putting it on and then not just avoid it but dramatically throw it to the far side of the room. Or they may hold the solid ring up to the post and say "no" repeatedly. Eventually, the children approach these tasks routinely as an adult would, without the implication that their successful attempts at a solution are worthy of particular comment.

A final point to mention about these results is that in our studies, as in those of others, there is little or no correlation between children's performance on these means-ends "insight" tasks and their performance on object-permanence tasks, although on average the two types of development both occur at about 18 months. Children may do well on these tasks and poorly on the object permanence tasks or vice versa. There are, however, correlations among the three types of means-ends tasks. The results do not support the idea of a very general cognitive-stage change underlying the change in all these areas. Rather, each conceptual domain appears to develop largely independently of the other domains (see also Uzgiris & Hunt, 1975, 1987).

Semantic Development: "No," "Uh-oh," and "There"

We saw that the changes in problem solving that result from the 18-month-old's development of the object theory were closely accompanied by the development of language that concerned precisely the central notions of the theory. Much the same is true of the child's understanding of actions. Consistently and across languages, some of the child's earliest words refer to the success and failure of children's goal-directed actions. In American English children typically use "uh-oh" to express failure and a variety of words, including "there" and "yeah," to express success. (The British children we first studied used "oh dear" and, memorably, "oh bugger" to talk about failure; Korean speakers use "twaetta.") Like "gone" and other relational words, these terms have been relatively neglected in the literature, and for much the same reason. They do not neatly fit semantic analyses of the adult language. Like

Table 5.1
Typical uses of success and failure expressions by nine 12-to-24-month-old children

Nature of situation	Term	Situation
Failure	"Oh dear."	Unable to fit a large top on a small box.
	"Oh dear."	Putting a block on a slab that is already full of blocks, child pushes off one block.
	"Oh dear."	A nut that the child is trying to take off his work-bench sticks.
	"Oh dear."	Places a beaker on a tower of beakers, and it falls down.
	"Oh dear."	Pushes a flap on the tape recorder, and it pops up again.
	"Oh dear."	A toy falls off the shelf.
	"Oh dear."	Holds up a broken toy.
	"No."	Tries to put a jigsaw puzzle piece in the wrong space.
	"No."	Tries to put a beaker on a tower of beakers, and it falls down.
Success	"There."	Puts a block on a slab already full of blocks without pushing off blocks already on the slab.
	"There."	Places beaker on top of a tower of beakers, and it does not fall down.
	"There."	Slides a car down to the end of a ramp.
	"Done it."	Correctly gets a piece into a jigsaw puzzle.
	"Good."	Puts a block into the right slot of the puzzle mailbox.

"gone," however, these words are extremely common in early vocabularies (Fenson et al., 1994). In our cross-sectional studies about 50 percent of 18-month-olds produced such words. In our longitudinal studies nearly all the children produced such words by the time they were 24 months old.

In the same study we described earlier we looked systematically at young children's spontaneous uses of these expressions. Table 5.1 shows some typical uses. Again notice that these terms cover a wide array of events with very different superficial perceptual characteristics. Note also that the vast majority of these contexts involve cases in which it is an intrinsic underlying feature of the object that causes the failure. For example, the most frequent uses of failure terms, like "oh dear," came when infants tried to fit a piece into a wrong hole or space or tried to build towers and the towers tumbled down. Notice also that in some cases the contexts did not even involve an action on the part of the child. In some cases infants seemed to have "standing orders," long-term goals, or preferences, and they used failure words when these preferences were violated.

These words also had the same affective quality as the uses of "gone." It is striking, given the content of the terms, that the children did not express unhappiness when they said "uh-oh" or "no." Indeed some of the most frequent cases of failure words came when infants deliberately failed, as it were. In these contexts the infants set up experimental situations in which they explored the effects of object properties on their plans. For example, one child deliberately and systematically placed puzzle pieces in the wrong space, saying "no" each time.

Just as in the case of "gone," the child's success and failure words are not simply associated with a single "script" or perceptual feature. Indeed, "uh-oh," like "gone," does not so much pick out an event as pick out the absence of an event. Instead, these words encode a concept closely related to the theoretical developments at 18 months. Just as children use "gone" to generalize across both visible and invisible displacements, so children generalize across failures caused by lack of contact with an object and failures caused by underlying properties of the object. At this point children begin to understand how the underlying properties of objects can lead to the success or failure of plans. This generalization is also encoded in their language.

As with "gone" and object-problem solving, we have found the same close and specific empirical relationship between the development of 18-month-old's use of success and failure words and their development of relevant problem-solving abilities (Gopnik & Meltzoff, 1984, 1986a). Just as in the case of "gone," children develop success and failure words within a few weeks of developing the ability to solve tasks like those of the rake, the necklace, and the ring. As in the case of "gone," these relations are very specific: success and failure words are not related to object-permanence developments that on average take place at the same time, and "gone" is not related to the development of these means-ends abilities. In fact, the relations between specific semantic and cognitive developments in the same domain are much stronger than those between cognitive developments in different domains or semantic developments in different domains. The relations are not the result of some broader relation between language and cognition. Also, as in the case of "gone," the emergence of success and failure words accompanies rather than follows the cognitive theory change. The terms for success and failure emerge just at the time that the child begins to solve the problems insightfully. The linguistic markers and the nonlinguistic behaviors emerge in concert with one another and are highly correlated.

The same morals also apply. Our linguistic data come from observations of children's spontaneous language in the home. The specific relation between this language and the child's problem solving in the laboratory strongly suggests that both developments tap some underlying and quite wide-reaching conceptual change. Only such a change could be responsible for common developments in both areas. This is itself prima facie evidence that the behavioral developments indicate conceptual changes.

It is also interesting to note that at about the same stage in their development children also typically produce a word, usually "no" in English, when they mark clashes between their desires and those of others. In fact, these uses of "no" are practically diagnostic of the terrible twos. These uses of "no" are not correlated to means-ends problem solving. However, they may well be related to the child's changing understanding of psychological causality. We are currently exploring this possibility.

Later Developments: From Actions to Desires

As in the case of the object theory, the 18-month-old's theory of action is still limited in many respects. In the adult theory, we can and often do talk about the representational relations between desires and the world, without even thinking about action at all. This does not seem to be true for these very young children. In particular, we have little evidence that at 18 months infants conceive of actions as being the consequence of a prior mental state that represents desirable events.

In fact, it is not clear at all at this point that children completely divorce desires, plans, and intentions from actions. Their understanding of action is not "mentalistic" in a sense that involves a conception of desires or intentions as mental entities separate from the actions they lead to. Even when children abstract across different actions, as in the "failed attempt" experiments, they still treat intentions as states linked to some action or other (Meltzoff, 1995a). The early conception of desire and intention seems to be more like what Searle (1983) calls "intention in action" than like a notion of prior intention. "Intentions in action" capture the adult sense that some behaviors may be intentional even if they do not involve articulated prior mental states.

At the same time, the infant's conception of action is also not "physicalistic." The infant does not simply identify actions with particular bodily movements. Rather, infants seem to understand something about the goal-directed character of actions.

Instead of distinguishing between mental states and physical ones, as adults and older children do, infants seem to distinguish between persons, whom they conceive of as combinations of bodies and minds, and objects. In particular, they distinguish between actions, which are intentional and goal-directed, and mere object movements, which are not. This distinction cuts across the distinction between physical and mental entities in the adult theory of mind. Infants seem to treat ideas like success and failure as simple relational notions that connect the actions of a person and events in the world, rather than connecting prior mental states, actions, and events. Infants do not linguistically refer to cases in which desires or intentions are completely divorced from actions, nor do they show an understanding of such cases in their behavior.

We saw how, in the case of object appearances, infants elaborate their account of vision into a genuinely mentalistic account of perception and later of belief. We know that by $2\frac{1}{2}$ years or so infants will have elaborated this initial theory of intentional action into a genuinely mentalistic account of desire. These young children know, for example, that we try to get what we want, that we are disappointed if we want something and don't get it but happy if we do get it, and that there may be mismatches between what we want and what others want (Astington & Gopnik, 1991; Wellman, 1990; Bartsch & Wellman, 1995; Wellman & Woolley, 1990; Yuill, 1984). More significant, these children talk about desires without actions. By $2\frac{1}{2}$ or so they also show some signs of appreciating the notion of a prior desire or intention. That is, they seem to conceive of desires as genuinely mental states, prior to and independent from actions, directed at states of affairs in the world, and satisfied or not satisfied by those states of affairs (Wellman, 1990; Bartsch & Wellman, 1995; Wellman & Woolley, 1990).

There is, however, some evidence that other aspects of desire and intention are only understood later. For example, only by around 3 or 4 do children appreciate the fact that desires may change with satiation, that intentions mediate between desires and actions, and that desires may be different in different people as a consequence of misrepresentation (Astington & Gopnik, 1991; Gopnik & Slaughter, 1991).

The evidence suggests that children's initial understanding of desire is nonrepresentational, a "drive" theory of sorts (Wellman, 1990). The satisfaction relation between desires and their objects is nonrepresentational, it is "wanting" *tout court*, rather than "wanting that." The early understanding of desire is in this respect much like the early understanding of perception: "seeing" rather than "seeing that." There is also evidence, however, that representational aspects of desire, like representational aspects of perception, are understood earlier than similar aspects of belief. It seems that an understanding of the representational character of desire, like a similar understanding of the representational character of perception, underpins the child's acquisition of a more general representational account of belief (Astington & Gopnik, 1991; Gopnik & Slaughter, 1991).

In the case of perception, the perspective-taking experiments we described earlier provide direct evidence for intermediate theories that bridge the gap between the theories of the 18-month-olds and those of the $2\frac{1}{2}$-year-olds. We have no direct cognitive evidence for intermediate conceptions that link the understanding of goal-directed action at 18 months and the more elaborated understanding of desires as mental states at $2\frac{1}{2}$. It seems plausible, however, that continuing processes of theory formation and change bridge these two developmental periods. For example, formulating the 18-month-old's theory will give children access to evidence relevant to a mentalistic conception of action. Cases of failure provide evidence for a distinction between a prior mental state and the action itself. To explain the difference between failures and similar events that are not failures, we need to begin to develop a notion of mental states that are divorced from action. Similarly, to understand how different people can have different attitudes toward the same object, we may need to develop a more mentalistic concept of desire.

Later Semantic Developments: "Want"

We saw that changes in the children's understanding of perception are accompanied by changes in the way they use "gone" and "see." We have some suggestive evidence from natural-language data about the bridge between infancy and early childhood. At around 21 to 24 months children begin to use the explicitly mentalistic term "want" to talk about their desires. The term consistently appears after the early success/failure expressions (Bartsch & Wellman, 1995). The developmental sequence is quite similar to how "see" replaces "gone." In both cases terms that refer to relations between people and objects are replaced by terms that refer straightforwardly to mental states. By around $2\frac{1}{2}$ "want" seems to be used to refer also to children's prior desires and their unfulfilled desires. This suggests a linguistic parallel to the cognitive shift from a relational to a genuinely mentalistic account of action.

Conclusion

In sum, we suggest that there is a parallel between infants' development of an understanding of actions and their development of an understanding of appearances. The parallel is not, however, a structural parallel, as in Piaget's theory, so much as a parallel in the kinds of cognitive processes that lead to changes in both areas. In both cases an initial, innately given theory provides abstract representations and enables predictions. Yet in both cases this initial theory is limited in its application and makes incorrect predictions. Later the theory is replaced by a more generally applicable theory that deals with cases not explained or predicted by the earlier theory. But the new theory also leads to new incorrect predictions, such as the 12-month-old's erroneous prediction that the solid ring will go on the post. The onset of the new theory is also marked by a new pattern of both generality and constraint on predictions. Eventually this theory is replaced by yet another, more generally applicable theory. And so on. In both cases we can see interpretive effects in which the infant misinterprets or ignores counterevidence, such as the infant's failure to imitate actions she does not understand. In both cases we see evidence for the new theory not only in problem solving but also in language. Words that encode concepts central to the theory emerge at about the same time as the new predictions that the theory allows. As the theory changes, so does the child's language.

The construction of both the object theory and the action theory also involve typical dynamic processes. In both cases infants accumulate ad hoc empirical generalizations, like the one that says "The mobile will move when I kick my foot and the striped crib liner is present" or the one that says "The object will be at place *A*, where it appeared before." These empirical generalizations deal with cases where the theory makes no predictions or where its predictions are falsified. In both cases there seems to be extensive and appropriate experimentation just before the new theory emerges. Both cases show the same affective patterns and the same changes in affect over time. In all these respects the child's developing cognitive structures look like theories.

Again, we have no direct evidence that it is in fact changes in evidence that lead to the theory changes in these young children. A crucial prediction of the theory theory is that altering the child's evidential base could alter, delay, or accelerate the acquisition of the theory. As we will see in chapter 7, we do, however, have indirect evidence that making particular kinds of evidence salient, by encoding them linguistically, can delay or accelerate the theory. Children learning languages that particularly clearly and saliently mark plans are accelerated in their nonlinguistic problem solving. Again, this suggests that the developmental process is genuinely theoretical. Changing the weight of the evidence can change the pattern of cognitive development.

6

The Child's Theory of Kinds

So far we have looked at two aspects of children's understanding of the mind and the world: their understanding of object appearances and their understanding of action. In this chapter we will turn to children's understanding of object kinds. The theory theory has proved to be particularly useful in describing young children's understanding of object categories. It suggests that children categorize many objects in terms of an underlying notion of kinds (Gelman & Wellman, 1991; Keil, 1989; Soja, Carey & Spelke, 1991). In this chapter we will try to trace our understanding of object kinds back to infancy.

The Adult Theory

Our adult understanding of object categories has been the focus of extensive psychological research and philosophical discussion. Early views, both in psychology and philosophy, assumed that we could understand categories in terms of properties. Our conception of an object category was really a conception of a collection of properties or features of objects. These same properties or features could be recombined to form new categories.

In the mid 1970s this picture was overturned by simultaneous though independent attacks in psychology and philosophy. In psychology, Rosch et al.'s experiments showed that adults did not typically categorize objects in terms of lists of properties. Rather, adult categories showed a "prototype" structure, with central exemplars and graded structure around those exemplars. Our category of birds, rather than being specified by a set of defining features (flies, lays eggs, has wings, etc.), turned out to consist of a set of central examples of birds (robins, bluebirds) and then with decreasing acceptability, a set of other birds (ostriches, penguins, toy birds, and so on), all with different features in common with the central exemplars. Moreover, Rosch argued, on psychological grounds, that a particular level of object categorization, the basic level, is fundamental. The basic level is the level with maximum intracategory similarity and intercategory difference. Other types of subordinate and superordinate categories are derived from the basic level (Rosch & Mervis, 1975; Rosch et al., 1976).

In philosophy, at about the same time, Putnam (1975) argued vigorously against the conception of object categories as lists of properties, though from a rather different angle (similar arguments also were articulated by Kripke [1980]). While Putnam's work was overtly philosophical, it was also psychological in that in his arguments he appealed to our common intuitions about category membership. One way of thinking of Putnam's work is as an explication of our ordinary folk theory of the meaning of certain object names. In this regard it is not terribly different from Rosch's work. Putnam considered cases where there were quite radical changes in our beliefs about the properties of objects, such as cases of scientific theory change. Our intuition in these cases is that the category membership of the object and, not incidentally, the name of the object remain constant, even though the properties we associate with the object may be completely different.

Putnam suggested that we understand the world in terms of what he called "natural kinds" and that this drives our intuitions about naming and categorizing.[1] Our everyday notion of natural kinds includes some very general ontological claims about the world. In particular, adults tend to think of natural kinds in terms of some kind of shared "essence." The essence of an object is some underlying unobserved quality that is causally responsible both for the observed properties of the object and for other properties of the object that may emerge only in the future. Essences lead to particular properties of objects and also allow predictions about future properties of the object and about the object's causal powers. Moreover, adults assume that all the natural objects in the world can be divided into kinds of this sort.

The adult account also includes some very general epistemological claims. We seem to believe, for example, that we might be ignorant or mistaken about which properties characterize object categories. If our theories of the object changed, we could also change our views about which properties were relevant to our identification of the object's essence. Finally, the account also includes some semantic claims. Most notably, the adult intuition is that names typically pick out these essences. We'll call this background theory, this general account of natural kinds, the Putnam framework.

Moreover, as a consequence of the Putnam framework, particular category judgments typically reflect the subject's particular theories about the nature of objects. We might say that our understanding of object kinds is doubly theory-dependent. We have a general account of what kinds are like, in particular, that they maintain their essence independently of our theories about them. And we also use our current theories to determine, at a particular moment, which category a particular object before us belongs to. In the remainder of this chapter we will be concerned primarily with the development of the first sort of general background theory; we will trace the origins of the Putnam framework. It is this second sense of the theory-dependent nature of categories, however, that has been the focus of most of the attention in the recent literature on adult categorization.

Recent work in categorization (e.g., Murphy & Medin, 1985; Rips, 1989) is a kind of unification of Rosch's and Putnam's views. This recent work suggests that many, though perhaps not all, ordinary adult categories are deeply theory-dependent. That is, at any given time adults decide which object to place in which category on the basis of their particular theory of the world. One characteristic of theories, recall, is that they make ontological commitments, commitments about how the world can best be carved at its joints. Many natural basic-level categories in adults reflect these basic theoretical commitments.

For example, our understanding of animal natural kinds reflects our "folk biology." We believe that a cat that is painted to look exactly like a skunk would still be a cat, not a skunk, and should still be called "cat" rather than "skunk" (see Keil, 1989). Animal-category membership is determined by such things as internal structure, breeding compatibility, and so on, and ultimately (given our acceptance of the current scientific theory) by DNA. As we might expect, if they are specified by theories, adult category judgments seem strongly influenced by the causal powers and propensities of objects, rather than by their more superficial perceptual features.

The more general Putnam framework is a precondition for this kind of theory-dependent category judgment. We might think of the Putnam framework as a sort of metatheory about the nature of particular theories, about their changes and differences, and about their relation to the world.

How do Rosch's findings fit in this picture? The prototype structure of ordinary concepts might be, at least in part, a consequence of their underlying theoretical nature. In applying a theory to a particular object, we are forced to rely on our perceptual experience of the object, that is, we are forced to rely on evidence. If, for example, I want to know whether something is a black hole, I will have to rely on the evidence of my telescope. However, the evidence will not constitute or be the criterion for the application of the category. There is no list of phenomena observed in a telescope that defines "black hole"; it is defined by the astronomer's theory. Instead, different patterns of evidence have to be weighed in a probabilistic way to infer the underlying causal structure, and this might give rise to prototype structure. When we have a rich theory of objects, the theory will heavily influence which types of evidence we consider to be important. Interestingly, however, if we know rather little about a set of objects, if our specific theory of them is relatively impoverished, a "basic level" prototype-based categorization does provide a good first-pass guess at their underlying causal structure.

In the rest of this chapter we will be concerned with the nature and origins of the general background knowledge of object kinds that drives the intuitions Putnam and Rosch discovered. Are these intuitions themselves theoretical? Putnam's intuitions pretty clearly pass the conjuror test. Events that violate the intuitions are magical. Along with disappearances and mentalist feats, another of the conjuror's stock-in-trade tricks is, of course, mysterious transformations. In such transformations an object of one kind unexpectedly manifests some of the properties of an object of another kind: the rabbit turns into a hat or the hat into a rabbit. Such events not only surprise us but violate our deep ontological convictions. The Putnam framework suggests that properties are linked by some underlying causal regularity. Our explanation for these magical events is that the conjuror has somehow replaced one kind of object with another; properties can't simply leap around from object to object.

Moreover, while the Putnam framework is deeply rooted, it also seems to be defeasible, just as other commonsense theories are both deeply rooted and defeasible. Can we conceive of a world that violated this framework? As with earlier examples, science already presents us with such worlds. Putnam's arguments have generated a great deal of philosophical unease. Much of this perturbation comes from the tension between the commonsense intuitions Putnam discusses and the assumptions of scientific physics and psychology. Contemporary science disavows essences. Indeed, objects and kinds themselves play little role in the best contemporary theories of physics. Similarly, the epistemological and semantic views implicit in the Putnam framework conflict with many of the assumptions of contemporary psychology and cognitive science, particularly the assumption that meanings and concepts can be defined in terms of representations in individual brains. If Putnam's intuitions were correct, then, for example, if two people lived in universes with different underlying causal structures, they could say exactly the same thing and have all the same beliefs and yet mean quite different things (see Stich, 1983; Block, 1986). Philosophers and psychologists are reluctant to accept this, and this also suggests that Putnam's intuitions might be defeasible.

Once again, the more concrete *Star Trek* cases are relevant. Take two more of the *Star Trek* premises. The holodeck reproduces all the superficial perceptual features of an object through a computer program that generates holograms. The replicator produces molecular duplicates of objects by using a kind of recipe. Are the objects that these processes produce real examples of their kinds or not? Is the holodeck Prof. Moriarty a person in view of his deviant causal origin but also his perfect match with the perceptual features of his kind? Again, the very fact that we can consider these questions hints at the defeasibility of our natural-kind intuitions. Our central thesis, once again, is that children who lived in a *Star Trek* world would develop a *Star Trek* theory of natural kinds.

Just as in the case of object appearances and actions, we want to suggest that our intuitions about object kinds constitute a theory. They include claims about the abstract underlying entities, kinds, or essences that underlie the empirical regularities of property clusters. The abstract entities are related to one another in ways that cohere, lead to ontological commitments, and generate predictions, explanations, and interpretations.

Categories and Kinds

What is the history of the Putnam framework? If parts of it are defeasible, are parts of it also developed? What is the initial state on which the framework is built? In answering these questions about categorization, we face a special conceptual problem not so clearly presented in the other areas of research we have considered so far. We have suggested that our understanding of object kinds is itself a sort of theoretical understanding. However, in both the philosophical and psychological traditions there is a very different sense of categorization that does not include any of this elaborate theoretical apparatus. Categorization can simply reduce to something like perceptual generalization. Thus if an animal or infant shows the capacity to discriminate between objects and yet generalizes across them, we may say that the animal or infant categorizes. In this sense, practically any living organism, and many nonliving systems, can be deemed to categorize. Moreover, this sense of categorization motivates the traditional picture of categories as lists of perceptual features.

The question is, What is the relation between this very simple and basic kind of categorization and the complex and abstract kind of categorization reflected in the Putnam framework? This question becomes particularly acute when we start to consider the developmental research. We know that by the preschool period, children seem to have some elements of the Putnam framework. But the literature on infancy has almost always been concerned with the simpler and more general sense of categorization. When are we tapping a genuine part of the Putnam framework, and when are we simply tapping capacities for discrimination and generalization?

The problem is exacerbated by the fact that we are eternally cursed in psychology with either too few studies, as in the case of the infant's understanding of action, or, as in the current case of categorization, rather too many. A multitude of different studies have investigated different types of categorization. Several different techniques employing different measures of categorization have been used, and each technique involves different types of cognitive demands. Moreover, within each type of task, different levels of categorizing may be distinguished, and different types of objects may be presented. We need to plow through these distinctions to make sense of the evidence.

First, consider the different measures of categorization behavior. Infants may demonstrate categorization abilities in the broad sense (1) by the amount of time that they look at particular stimuli, as in habituation or preferential-looking paradigms, (2) by their behavior in conditioning or learning experiments, (3) by touching objects in one category before they touch those in another, (4) by actively sorting objects into groups, or (5) by naming objects. Each of these measures has benefits and drawbacks and each may assess rather different aspects of the understanding of categories.

Habituation and preferential looking and to some extent conditioning do not require complex motor abilities. However, they are not spontaneous, and they may train the child to detect the relevant category within the course of the study itself. Moreover, discrimination and generalization in such paradigms seem to tap the simpler sense of categorization rather than the more complex and abstract notion of kinds.

In other studies, infants are presented with a mixed array of objects, and the experimenters record whether they touch different types of objects and the order in which they do so. This sort of serial touching is spontaneous, but it may merely reflect preferences for one type of object over another rather than genuine categorization (see Sugarman, 1983, for discussion). Children may simply be interested in only one type of object and so only touch those objects. Certain types of linguistic behaviors have a similar disadvantage. If an infant simply shows comprehension of a name, we do not know whether such behavior is merely an association between the name and the object or genuinely reflects the assumptions of adult naming.

Sorting objects, spontaneously placing objects of one type into one location and those of another type in another location, intuitively appears to be one of the most convincing indices of spontaneous categorization. In fact, sorting was long taken to be the sine qua non of categorization. However, it is not clear that sorting objects necessarily implies a notion of kinds. Moreover, such behaviors are more motorically demanding than simpler serial touching or habituation, and their absence in early infancy might reflect motor constraints rather than cognitive limitations.

In addition, children may display different levels of categorization. It is particularly useful to distinguish between cases in which children merely need to pick out a single category from an array and those in which a mixed array of objects is exhaustively grouped into a number of categories. Habituation and preferential-looking studies have involved the recognition of only a single category at a time. Indeed, it is difficult to see how these studies could do otherwise. However, with more active measures there is evidence that 15-to-18-month-olds will place all the objects in an array into groups—a behavior we have called "exhaustive categorization." Exhaustive categorization seems to require a different and more sophisticated concept of categorization than distinguishing a single group of objects. Rather than simply seeing that a particular object belongs or doesn't belong with others, it implies that the child realizes there may be many different object categories and makes different responses to each one.

Finally, the degree and scope of variation within a category has been different in different studies. Usually we think of categorization as involving the ability to place together objects that have some perceptually salient variation among themselves. Habituation, preferential-looking, and conditioning studies have typically used such categories with a wide variety of variations. In contrast, studies of serial touching and spontaneous sorting in infancy originally almost all used stimuli that were identical. For example, four identical clay balls might be mixed with four identical plastic pill boxes in an array. Investigators have begun to explore different kinds of intracategory variation in these paradigms only quite recently.

So another dimension that varies in different studies, and often covaries with the measure of categorization employed in a study, is whether the children are presented with objects with internal variation, particularly the kind of variation we find in adult natural-kind categories. Because of this range of possibilities, it is perhaps not surprising that the developmental picture is rather complex. However, in spite of this empirical complexity, there seem to be some general, wide-ranging shifts in infant's understanding of object categories.

The Initial Theory

The same innate representations that form the basis for the child's theory of object appearances seem to be necessary presuppositions for the child's account of object kinds. Putnam's conception of kinds requires a prior conception of objects. As we have seen, the notion of coherent objects moving in a three-dimensional space seems to be innately given.

Equally, there is extensive evidence in the habituation and preferential-looking paradigms that from very early in development, indeed from birth, infants make perceptual discriminations and generalizations.

These include discriminations and generalizations about a wide range of perceptual features, such as shape and color, that are likely to be relevant to category membership (see e.g., Bornstein, 1981; Bornstein, Kessen & Weiskopf, 1976; Caron, Caron & Carlson, 1979; Cohen, Gelber & Lazar, 1971). Moreover, even very young infants can show some capacity to abstract features away from specific instances. For example, well within the first 4 to 6 months of life, infants' can generalize across changes in color and orientation (see, e.g., Cohen et al., 1971; Fagan, 1976).

Moreover, Rovee-Collier and her colleagues have shown equally striking perceptual discrimination and generalization using a more active learning measure. As we saw earlier, infants trained to respond in a certain way to make a mobile move will generalize that response to other similar mobiles (Greco, Hayne & Rovee-Collier, 1990; Hayne, Rovee-Collier & Perris, 1987; Rovee-Collier, 1990). Kuhl (1979, 1983) has done work with similar techniques that shows generalization across perceptually salient variations in the domain of speech categories.

There is also some interesting and suggestive evidence that very young infants have to learn to integrate information about the movement of objects and information about the perceptual features of objects. This is an important development for the understanding of object appearances, but it is even more important in developing an account of object kinds. In chapter 4 we discussed the fact that infants initially seem to take place and common movement, rather than features of any sort, as the criteria for object identity. They can make fairly elaborate inferences about objects' locations and trajectories, even extending to such things as the projection of invisible trajectories or the fact that an object cannot occupy the same space as another object. As we saw, there is at least some evidence that infants do not initially treat perceptual features, such as shape and color, as criterial for object identity in the same way. Very young infants are disrupted more by changes in the trajectory of an object than by changes in its features. Even infants in the second year of life do not consistently use features to individuate objects (Xu and Carey, in press). It is difficult to see how an infant with this conception of the object could even be in the ball park of understanding kinds. That is, if the infant doesn't believe that individual objects maintain their features across time, it is difficult to see how he could believe that they are instances of kinds that produce such features.

Eventually, however, the infant is bound to notice that perceptual features co-occur in interesting ways with place and movement. Most of the time objects will maintain their features across places and trajectories, and most of the time objects with different places and trajectories will have different features. Infants should be able to collect empirical generalizations about these co-occurrences of features and locations. As we saw, this sort of observation seems to lead to an important change. Infants do begin to pay attention to perceptual features in their judgments of object identity, and this plays an important role in changing their theory of object appearances.

Two types of phenomena will still be problematic for the infant's otherwise elegant theoretical unification of movements and features. First, as we saw, cases of invisible displacement will be problematic. In these cases the displaced object, though maintaining identical features, appears to fail to follow the rules of object movement. But in addition, cases of multiple instances of the same kind, particularly multiple instances of featurally identical or nearly identical objects, are equally disturbing. Multiple instances of very similar objects are fairly common in the infant's world: consider the contents of your average toy box or, for that matter, the leaves, pebbles, and sticks that might have been Pleistocene playthings. In invisible displacements, paying attention to features tells you that there is a single object; paying attention to movements tells you that there are multiple objects. In the case of multiple instances of the same kind of thing, place and movement tell you that the objects are different, but feature analysis tells you they are the same. The fundamental theory of place and movement should tell the infant that these are multiple objects. Yet at the same time the infant is using feature similarity as a mark of object identity, and feature similarity predicts a single object. Which prediction is correct? The only way of making complete sense of both features on the one hand and places and movements on the other is by introducing the idea of multiple instances of the same kind of object.

The Nine-Month-Old's Theory

In fact, there is substantial evidence for a new account of object categories toward the end of the first year. By around 9 months of age infants show clear signs of what we will call *single-category grouping* of objects. These infants seem to be able to focus on one category of objects in an array and to distinguish these objects from other objects. They seem to believe that these objects go together.

In habituation and preferential-looking paradigms, for example, 9-month-olds discriminate new extracategory objects from new intra-category objects in ways that suggest prototype-based categories (Cohen & Strauss, 1979; Sherman, 1985; Strauss, 1979; Younger, 1985). More significant, these abilities appear to go beyond simple discrimination and generalization. An infant who is simply generalizing should respond to features rather than to relations among features. However, at 10 months, though not earlier, infants respond to correlated clusters of features that appear in particular objects, and not just to individual features or even averages or sums of features (Younger, 1990, 1992; Younger & Cohen, 1983, 1986). Such patterns of correlation among features are typically a key to underlying causal structure in objects. In particular, Roberts, using a habituation paradigm, has shown that 9-month-olds can recognize basic-level prototype-based categories of objects, which exhibit just this sort of correlated structure (Roberts, 1988; Roberts & Horowitz, 1986). These are the categories that correspond to kinds for adults. There is no convincing evidence that infants can do this much before this point.

At about 9 months infants also begin to demonstrate categorization in a more spontaneous and active way. The same developments that appear in looking-time paradigms also appear in infants' actions. When the objects within each category do not vary from one another, 9-month-olds begin to serially touch all the objects of one kind without touching the objects of another kind (Starkey, 1981). Mandler and Bauer (1988) have demonstrated such behaviors in 12-month-olds who are presented with objects with some intracategory variation. In our lab, we have demonstrated such behaviors in infants who are presented with prototype-based basic-level "kindlike" categories (for example, a wide variety of rocks of different shapes, colors, and textures contrasted with a wide variety of rings, also of different shapes, colors, and textures). Moreover, by about 12 months infants who are presented with two groups of objects without intracategory variation, say four identical boxes and four identical balls, will spontaneously begin to place all the objects of one kind into a single pile, while ignoring the objects of the other kind (Langer, 1982; Gopnik & Meltzoff, 1987; Nelson, 1973; Ricciutti, 1965; Starkey, 1981; Sugarman, 1983).

As we mentioned above, this sort of spontaneous sorting seems like particularly compelling evidence of "real" categorization. It is interesting to think about why this is so. One reason that sorting seems to be a particularly convincing demonstration of categorization is precisely because the sorting responses, placing objects in one particular location rather than another, are in some ways so arbitrary and so removed from any immediate reward. In cases of simple habituation or conditioning, the fact that the infant generalizes a response from one stimulus to another or discriminates between the two stimuli seems tied to the functional qualities of the response. The infant becomes bored by one stimulus and responds with recovered interest to a novel stimulus, or the infant is rewarded for a response and produces similar responses to similar stimuli. Even serial-touching behavior might be interpreted in this way in terms of intrinsic preferences for some features rather than others.

In contrast, the only function of sorting for the infant seems precisely to be to work out the categorical structure of the world. Categorizing, in these cases, is its own reward. The situation is analogous to the difference between operant conditioning and the more "experimental" behaviors that suggest that infants are exploring contingencies. These behaviors seem to have a purely cognitive motivation. They are among the clearest indications that the infant is actively working out a cognitive problem. Some kinds of naming also have this purely experimental and cognitive quality, as we will see below.

There is yet another potentially compelling reason for treating sorting as a powerful index of categorization. Why would infants choose this arbitrary response, in particular? Why on earth would infants suddenly begin to place objects with particular features in a single spatial location? One possibility may be that infants are interpreting the kinds theory in terms of the earlier place and movement theory. The idea of a kind is the idea of a spatially distributed ontological entity. The essence of one object is the same as that of another object of the same kind, even though they are located in different places in space. Sorting maps this spatially distributed ontological entity onto the simpler ontology of places and movements. By placing similar objects in similar places, both infants and adults may express their sense of the objects' underlying identity. We might draw an analogy to some scientific cases. For example, consider the role of Feynman diagrams in our understanding of quantum dynamics. The great conceptual advance of these diagrams is to place a strikingly unintuitive set of concepts in a framework that is much closer to our intuitive concept of space. Similarly, putting objects of the same kind in the same place may give infants an intuitive feel for their identity.

Still other behaviors relevant to kinds emerge in late infancy. Part of the adult Putnam framework is the idea that the essence of an object not only predicts its currently perceived properties but also predicts its future properties. The Putnam framework allows us to make inductive inferences about objects. Baldwin, Markman, and Melartin (1993) found behaviors that seem to suggest some such inductive ability in 9-month-old infants. In their experiments 9-month-olds were presented with an object that produced an odd and unexpected property, such as a can that made a mooing sound when it was turned. Infants were then exposed to a perceptually similar object. The infants attempted to reproduce the earlier feature and showed distinctive exploratory behaviors when the object was disabled so that the new feature was not produced. Interestingly, similar behaviors are also found in 14-month-olds, even when the infants did not themselves originally produce the unexpected property but rather saw it produced by someone else (Barnat, Klein & Meltzoff, 1996). Madole, Oakes, and Cohen (1993) found that infants in an object-examining task paid attention to the function as well as the form of an object at 14 months, though not at 10 months. The functional properties they studied were unexpected novel properties of objects, like rolling or rattling.

Finally, at least some infants begin to produce names for particular objects at about 1 year (by "names" we mean all early nouns, including both proper names like "John" and common names like "dog"). Some of these early names are actually not very indicative of categorizing. For example, some early names may only occur in well-defined scripts or in particular social contexts. But among these early names there are also some that seem to function much like adult names. They are used across a wide variety of pragmatic contexts to indicate objects in a particular category. Such genuinely cognitive uses of names are among the earliest uses to occur and could do so well before 18 months (Gopnik, 1988b; Harris et al., 1988, Mervis et al., 1992).

It is interesting to consider the range of objects categorized by such names. A large number of studies indicate that many of the infant's very early names have a prototype-based structure rather than referring to particular features (Bowerman, 1978; Kuczaj, 1982). Indeed, the death of feature theories of names in infant cognition paralleled the death of such theories in accounts of adult cognition. However, the detailed prototype structure of early names is often quite different from that of the same adult lexical items. The classic instances of this are overgeneralizations, such as the infant who calls all quadripeds "dog" or all men "Daddy" (Clark, 1974). Finer observation, however, suggests that infants' early names are not so much consistently broader than adults' names as they are simply different. Early names are likely to be simultaneously over- and undergeneralized.

Mervis, who has done extensive studies of this period, uses the notion of "child-basic" categories to describe early meanings (Mervis, 1987; Mervis & Bertrand, 1993). She suggests that even children's very early names already instantiate the theoretical distinctions to which they are committed. An elegant example of this in somewhat older children is the fact that many children use "money" exclusively to refer to small round objects like coins, and not to refer to paper money, in spite of quite explicit feedback from adults. The amalgamation of bills and coins, and even credit cards and stock coupons, into a single category and the exclusion of other objects obviously depend on an adult theoretical "folk economics." This concept is incoherent to children, and they replace it with one that fits their own theoretical preconceptions. Moreover, it is not that the children categorize perceptually and the adults categorize theoretically. Rather, children make incorrect inferences about coins and bills that reflect theoretical differences. For example, young children frequently treat getting change as a profit-making enterprise. In return for a worthless piece of paper, the purchaser receives both the purchase and lots of money besides.

There is evidence for these child-basic categories even among very early words. Mervis provides extensive examples of such early categories, both under- and overextending the adult categories, and also suggests that the categories are similar across different children and across normally developing children and children with Down's syndrome (Mervis et al., 1992).

We might see Mervis's discovery of child-basic categories as analogous to the work on adults by Murphy and Medin (1985). In both cases, if we carefully examine the ways that people use names, we find no universal set of features associated with a name. Rather, both older and younger people use names to encode the categories that are ontologically central in their particular theory of the world. As their theories change, so do their conceptions of what is ontologically central.

Taken together, these behaviors suggest some sort of change at the end of the first year in the infant's theory of kinds. Such infants begin to pay attention to the correlational structure of features, they show primitive inductive and predictive behaviors, such as assuming that similar forms will lead to similar functions, and they notice when correlations among features are not maintained. They show a recognition of prototype-based basic-level categories in their habituation behavior and slightly later in their serial touching and sorting behaviors. In their spontaneous naming, they group objects together in a way that is different from the groupings they hear in the language of the adults around them and that does not seem to be based on simple combinations of perceptual features. Rather, these early names reflect child-basic prototype-based organizations particularly relevant to the child's underlying conception of the "joints" of the world around her.

These behaviors are quite different from the simpler sorts of generalization and discrimination we see in younger infants. Of course, these behaviors do not necessarily imply the full richness of an essentialist theory of kinds. But the behaviors are at least suggestive of an account of object categories that goes beyond a superficial inventory of features. By 9 to 12 months infants seem to have the capacity to pay attention to the correlational structure of features in a category, to predict future properties of objects on the basis of current properties, to produce prototype categories, and to indicate categories by producing behaviors, like spatial sorting and naming, that have no immediate functional reward. In adults, we would think of similar behaviors as indicating at least a deeper, more Putnamian understanding of kinds than simple perceptual generalization.

We suggest, at least as a tentative hypothesis, that by the end of the first year infants have the conception that there are common ontological properties, kinds, distributed across enduring stable objects, and that they do not have this conception before this point. They may also see these properties as underlying and as responsible for, but not identical with, clusters of perceptual properties of objects. An interesting test of this hypothesis would be to extend Baldwin and Markman's (1989) paradigm to more genuinely causal properties of objects. For example, suppose that we demonstrate to infants that perceptually identical objects have some consistently different causal effects on other objects. Will the infants take this information into account in their sorting and naming of the objects? If they do, this would suggest that the infants do indeed understand object kinds in terms of causal propensities. Clearly, however, sorting out precisely what conception of kinds these infants have awaits further research.

It is also interesting that these new capacities are plausibly a consequence of two dynamic processes that we commonly see in theory change: experimentation and the extension of a model already developed for other purposes. At 7 months infants characteristically show a strikingly general pattern of object exploration. Every object that comes within the infant's reach is explored, everything the infant can see is seen, and infants perform actions on objects, like mouthing and throwing them, that characteristically lead to the discovery of new features. As Piaget (1952, 1954) noted, however, these behaviors are not systematically coordinated with the particular properties of objects. Instead, the infants' explorations of object features seem to take the form of what scientists would call a fishing expedition. Yet the information from these fishing expeditions may very well be put to use eventually in detecting the higher-order correlation patterns understood by 9-to-12-month-olds.

As for model extension, infants may integrate the notion of features with their notion of object identity provided by their earlier theory of places and trajectories. In fact, we might think of the initial place and trajectory theory of object identity as providing a sort of model for the ontological structure of the natural-kinds theory, just as it also provides a model for the infant's account of invisible trajectories.

The Eighteen-Month-Old's Theory

As in our other examples, while the 18-month-old infant's theory begins to approach the adult theory, it is still different from that theory in important ways. All of the behaviors we have discussed so far involve identifying a *single* category of objects, knowing that one object belongs with a group of others. Infants initially appear to restrict this account to particular categories. They behave in these ways when the similarities between objects are made particularly salient by external circumstance. In some cases the experimenter makes the category structure particularly salient. This is obviously true in the habituation and preferential-looking studies. In these studies the experimenter sequentially presents infants with a salient set of objects from one category and studies their response to a new object. It is also true in induction studies. In other studies the infant's own interests seem to make one particular category salient. Early category names are notoriously likely to refer to a few common and important object kinds in the child's environment, such as dogs, balls, and bottles (Clark, 1974; Nelson, 1973; Nelson & Lucariello, 1985). Similarly, in early serial touching or sorting, infants commonly focus on only one kind of preferred object to the exclusion of other objects.

For adults, in contrast, the account of kinds is not restricted to a particular class of salient objects. On the contrary, it is part of our deepest conviction that all natural kinds belong in some category or other. One way of thinking of the project of a natural science like chemistry or biology is precisely as an attempt to specify the natural kind of everything. In fact, only exceptional objects, like artifacts, are immune from this sort of investigation, and even in such cases we make kind judgments on other bases. We suggest that, as in other examples of theory change, the notion of kind membership begins as an adjunct, as a kind of auxiliary hypothesis, to the more conceptually basic theory of object identity based on place and movement. It is designed to deal with such exceptional cases as clear collections of similar objects. At 18 months, however, the relation is reversed. The theory of kinds now takes over from the earlier theory. Rather than using a kinds account to deal with occasional cases of featural similarity among different objects, the infant begins to assume that all objects will belong to some kind or other.

Several developments at about 18 months support this idea. In particular, only between 15 and 21 months do children begin to exhaustively sort objects into different categories. Children of this age begin to touch all the objects in one group, then all those in another—what we will call "exhaustive serial touching"—when the objects in each group are identical (Gopnik & Meltzoff, 1987; Langer, 1982; Nelson, 1973; Ricciutti, 1965; Starkey, 1981; Sugarman, 1983). Mandler and Bauer (1988) found some exhaustive serial touching in arrays of objects with basic-level variation in 15-month-olds, but more in 20-month-olds. We found such behaviors in a majority of 18-month-olds, though none at all in 12-month-olds.

Moreover, starting at about 18 months, but not before, children first begin to sort all the objects in an array into two spatially distinct groups.

At this point they can demonstrate exhaustive sorting when the objects do not have intracategory variation (Gopnik & Meltzoff, 1987; Langer, 1982; Nelson, 1973; Ricciutti, 1965; Sugarman, 1983). This exhaustive-sorting behavior clearly indicates that the child can hold both categories in mind at the same time and differentiate between them. In addition, it suggests that the child is motivated to place all the objects in an array into categories, not just the preferred or salient ones. Moreover, we have demonstrated that 18-month-olds will also sort objects that have basic-level variation within a category (Gopnik & Meltzoff, 1992, 1993). We tested 18-month-old children on categorization tasks, using both identical objects within each category, as in the earlier experiments, and objects with prototype basic-level variation (e.g., four toy horses of different shapes and breeds, combined with four pencils of different shapes, colors, and sizes, or our previous example of rocks and rings). When the stimulus properties were controlled for, there was no significant difference between the levels of sorting of the identical objects and objects varied at the basic level.

In these studies we demonstrated, for the first time, that 18-month-old children do indeed exhaustively and spontaneously sort varied objects into categories when the categories are at the basic-level. This finding contradicts the widely held view that such abilities develop rather late. It is worth pausing for a moment to consider why this view has been prevalent. Earlier studies, inspired by feature theories of categories, presented older children with objects that varied on many dimensions, a set of artificial objects of different shapes and colors, for example (Vygotsky, 1962). Presented with such arrays, children often sorted "complexively," placing, say, a red circle next to a red square, next to a blue square, and so on. Similarly, children presented with a mixed array of artifacts might sort objects into "thematic" categories, placing all the objects that belong in the kitchen together in one category. Notice that neither of these tasks, however, really tests children's understanding of kinds. Rather, they test children's capacity to understand properties of objects, or to understand a balance between thematic and kind organization, both of which are appropriate for artifacts.

By using objects that exemplify the basic-level variation of natural kinds, we can show exhaustive categorization even in very young children. The details of the infants' behavior in the course of sorting are quite interesting. For example, children in our studies would place objects in alternate categories, taking a pencil and putting it in one of the experimenter's hands, then taking a horse and placing it in the other hand, and so on, rather than simply grouping one set of objects and then another. Children also often showed interesting hesitant behavior. For example, a child might place a pencil just above the "horse" hand for a moment, hesitate and then rapidly move it to the "pencil" hand. Some children showed even more exhaustive sorting than we expected. In one sorting task, the top of one of the pencils broke off just before the objects were presented, one little girl not only sorted the horses and three intact pencils into the experimenter's hands, she also reached for her mother's hand and made a separate location for the broken pencil.

Notice that there is no question that the 12- and 15-month-old children who did not exhaustively sort these objects could easily discriminate the groups of objects perceptually. Indeed, we chose objects that were very easy to discriminate perceptually. Nor was there any question that the 15-month-olds could perform the same actions as the older children. Some 15-month-olds given our task would sunnily place objects in our hands in mixed bundles. The change in sorting behavior at 18 months is difficult to explain in terms of some simple increase in perceptual or motor capacities. We suggest that a new part of the Putnam framework, a new aspect of the general theory of object kinds, is put in place at this point.

Again, however, the current evidence is suggestive rather than definitive. In particular, the crucial notion behind kind membership has to do with the underlying causal properties of objects and how they support inductions. Ideally, we would want to show that the changes in sorting we have described are paralleled by changes in the range of inductive inferences children will generate. We are currently working on studies of this kind.

Other Evidence for the Theory Theory

We saw some dynamic processes involved in the transition from the initial-state theory of objects to the 9-month-old conception of object kinds. We can point to some similar processes in the later transition from the 9-month-old's notion that some objects belong in kinds to the 18-month-old's notion that all objects belong in kinds. Earlier we mentioned Piaget's "experiments in order to see" that emerge at this stage in the child's understanding of action. These experiments also indicate a new and rather different exploration of objects than the early fishing expeditions. At 1 year infants systematically vary their actions on objects in a way that respects the particular underlying features of those objects. These experiments are well placed to pick out underlying causal structures and to demonstrate that all objects have this sort of structure.

Moreover, it might be argued that the very spontaneous sorting behaviors we see in the lab are themselves experimental. The object-permanence and means-ends tasks do have a certain functional motivation—there are problems to be solved—though as we have noted, children in our studies often treated these tasks in an experimental way. The spontaneous sorting task might be constructed in a parallel way, perhaps by rewarding children for correct sorts. But in our version of the task, there is no such functional motive. The children's manipulation of the objects reflects a purely cognitive interest. As we suggested, these experimental behaviors may change as the child's understanding of kinds changes.

Dynamic processes of theory change also often seem to involve expanding an idea only marginally present in the earlier theory or adopting an explanatory scheme from elsewhere. We suggested earlier that there is this sort of reversal in the development of the concept of objects. Infants begin by explaining exceptional disappearances in terms of object movements, and they end by explaining all disappearances in terms of object movements. In the present case as well, the idea of object kinds, which initially only seems to be invoked for particularly salient cases of common features, might be generalized at 18 months to include all objects, even those whose kind membership is far from obvious on the surface.

We can also imagine that there might be a useful interaction at this point between the child's understanding of actions and her understanding of kinds. We saw that the solution to the paradoxes and failed predictions of the 12-month-old's theory of action depended on the idea of underlying causal properties of the object. These failures may provide an important source of collateral data for the child's understanding of kinds. Similarly, the new conception of kinds seems to contribute to the infant's advanced understanding of action and causality.

We should note, however, that there is relatively little correlation between exhaustive sorting and means-ends development. There may be interactions between the two domains, either because advances in one area provide data for theory change in another area or because one theory pirates a conceptual advance in the other area for its own use. However, the understanding of kinds appears to be a separate domain with it own theoretical structure.

Semantic Development: The Naming Spurt

As in the previous domains, the new theory is not only exemplified in the children's behavior but is also apparent in their language. The relational words like "gone" and "uh-oh" that we discussed earlier have been rather neglected, not to say snubbed, in the literature on early semantic development. In contrast, early names have been the favorite children of many students of early language, and there is an extensive literature on their acquisition. By 12 months or even earlier, infants are often capable of using names to pick out particular categories of salient objects. At around 18 months, however, there is typically a striking change in the children's naming behavior. Children suddenly produce a large number of new names, a behavior that has been called "the naming insight," the "vocabulary spurt," or most graphically, "the naming explosion" (Bates et al., 1979; Bloom, 1973; Corrigan, 1978; Goldfield & Reznick, 1990; Reznick & Goldfield, 1992). The clearest index of this change is a sudden marked increase in the child's vocabulary. But the linguistic change is actually more specific than that. For one thing, the increase in vocabulary consists almost entirely of object names (Goldfield & Reznick, 1990). For another the vocabulary increase is often accompanied by a near obsession with naming.

For example, children of this age also often develop an expression like "Whatsat?" which they use to request names for objects. Typically, children of this age may also point to every object in the room, giving it a name or asking for a name for it. Finally, children this age show a strikingly increased capacity to learn new names. In particular, at this point, though not before, they show clear evidence of what has been called, "mutual exclusivity," "lexical gap filling," or the "new name, new category" principle (Mervis & Bertrand, 1994; Clark, 1987; Markman, 1989). Given an array of familiar named objects, an unfamiliar object, and a new unfamiliar name, they immediately assume that the name refers to the new object category and learn the new name. All this suggests a new understanding of names. More than one commentator on this phenomenon has pointed out that it's as if the child discovers that every object, not just salient or significant objects, has a name.

There is an obvious conceptual link between this discovery and the claim we have made that at this point the child recognizes that all objects belong in natural-kind categories. We might say that both the ontological and semantic parts of the Putnam framework are discovered at the same time. At the same time that the child demonstrates in her exhaustive sorting behavior that she thinks every object kind should go in a particular spatial location, she also demonstrates that every object kind should have a name.

Moreover, naming, particularly the naming we see in the naming explosion, like sorting, involves an arbitrary marking of object-kind membership. When 18-month-old children learn names, they are not simply exploiting some particular well-established association between the word and some object property. Instead, these infants seem to assume that every distinctive kind of thing will have a distinctive name and that the name will apply to other instances of the kind. Later on in their development, by $2\frac{1}{2}$ or so, naming seems to take over as the most significant marker of category membership, as it does for adults. Children as young as $2\frac{1}{2}$ will override perceptual-feature information in favor of treating a common name as a marker of common kinds (Gelman & Markman, 1986; Gelman & Coley, 1990). Moreover, there is strong evidence that by $2\frac{1}{2}$ many, if not most, of the child's names in fact encode kinds (Gelman & Wellman, 1991; Soja, Carey & Spelke, 1991).

We have also discovered strong and specific empirical links between the naming spurt and the development of exhaustive sorting. These links are very similar to the links we discovered earlier between "gone" and object permanence and between success and failure words and means-ends abilities. In a longitudinal study we found that children consistently developed a naming spurt within a few weeks of the time they demonstrated exhaustive sorting behavior in the lab (Gopnik & Meltzoff, 1987). In two later follow-up studies we confirmed this result cross-sectionally and also found a similar specific link with basic-level exhaustive sorting (Gopnik & Meltzoff, 1992). Mervis and Bertrand (1994) replicated this result and also found an additional specific link between both the naming spurt and exhaustive sorting and "fast mapping" abilities. As in our earlier studies, the semantic developments were *not* related to other cognitive developments. In particular, the naming spurt was not correlated with the development of means–ends abilities, although the average age of emergence of these two developments was quite similar. And again, the relations between semantic and cognitive developments within the domain are stronger than those between cognitive developments across domains.

The same morals as in the earlier studies apply. To be correlated in this way, the cognitive abilities and semantic abilities must tap some common conceptual change. In this case the point is perhaps even more important linguistically than cognitively. We really needed the relations to language to demonstrate the conceptual character of the cognitive developments in the earlier cases. In the case of the naming spurt, however, most theoretical accounts have explicitly denied that the linguistic phenomenon indexes such a conceptual change. Instead, a wide variety of specifically linguistic accounts of the spurt have been offered. Various investigators have related the naming spurt to a general difference between "referential" and "expressive" learning styles (Nelson, 1975), a new level of formal linguistic ability (McShane, 1980), the activation of a purely linguistic constraint (Markman, 1989), or a phonological reorganization (Vihman, 1993). The close relations between the spurt and an entirely nonlinguistic sorting ability suggests that this picture is at least incomplete. The naming spurt appears to be a linguistic phenomenon tightly tied to a particular set of conceptual problems. These problems concern the way in which superficial perceptual features are indicators of deeper underlying kinds.

Later Developments

The links between the development of sorting at 18 months and the later understanding of kinds at $2\frac{1}{2}$ are still only partly understood. We do know, however, that there are extensive changes both in children's sorting behavior (Sugarman, 1983) and in their naming throughout this period. One important development may be appreciating the fact that there are other levels of sorting than the level of kinds and that objects can simultaneously belong to many different categories at once. There is some evidence that children initially have some difficulty with this idea and only later develop a nested hierarchy of different levels of categorization (Callanan, 1985; Markman, 1989).

Moreover, we mentioned earlier findings that 2- and 3-year-olds will sort "thematically" or "complexively." Typically, these types of sorting have been seen as earlier or more primitive than the sort of kind sorting we see at 18 months. Ironically, however, just the opposite may be true. That is, the development of these abilities later in childhood may indicate a new attention to modes of categorization that do not respect object-kind structure. These might include paying attention to subordinate properties, such as color, or recognizing the socially constructed character of artifacts.

Moreover, there is evidence that even at $2\frac{1}{2}$ or 3 the child's notion of kinds is still quite different from the adult notion. These children do seem to assume that common objects will share a common underlying causal structure and that names indicate kinds. However, they do not yet have some of the other assumptions of the adult framework, for example, the assumption that one defers to scientific experts in determining kind membership (Keil, 1989). Theory-of-mind research suggests that they may also not have the conception of theory and belief change that supports the epistemological assumptions of the Putnam framework until about 4 or 5 (Gopnik & Astington, 1988).

Conclusion

As in earlier chapters, we have suggested that the child's understanding of kinds changes in ways that can be construed as theory changes. The case of categorization, however, emphasizes a slightly different aspect of theory formation than the other two domains we have studied. In all three domains the new theory allows predictions and interpretations. In all three domains the theory also makes ontological commitments: it postulates abstract entities not simply specified by superficial perceptual features. In our discussion of the other two domains, however, the emphasis was on the child's predictions and interpretations. Of course, changes in children's understanding of kinds also have consequences for prediction. We can see this in the induction studies in which children predict new features of the object on the basis of their kind membership. But in general, in this chapter we have been more deeply involved in tapping the theory's ontological commitments, the way it carves nature at its joints.

Initially, infants seem to believe that the world's joints are determined by spatial factors like places and movements. By around nine months, however, the infant seems to recognize that some spatially discrete objects in the world are nevertheless linked by some common underlying structure. This underlying spatially distributed entity is manifested in the correlations of features across time. It is possible that this underlying structure involves some sort of primitive notion of a causal essence, though this has still not been demonstrated empirically. This idea is manifested in infant's spontaneous sorting and in their language, as well as in other behaviors.

By 18 months both these indices of ontology look rather different than they did earlier. At this time, both in sorting and in naming, children show a very general conviction that *all* objects have these common underlying structures. All objects can be and should be sorted into kinds. If the kind of an object is not immediately visible, there is a simple expedient for discovering it: ask its name. Similarly, if a new name appears, the infant assumes that it refers to some as yet unnamed and ununderstood kind. The idea of kind that underwrites these abilities is highly abstract, clearly much more abstract than mere perceptual discrimination and generalization. As in the other domains, we can see a linked sequence of different conceptions of object kinds in development. Each of these conceptions is quite different from the adult conception. Moreover, as in the other domains, we can see dynamic processes of experimentation in the period when these changes take place.

The theory theory proposes that the motivation for these changes comes from the infants' observations of the behavior of objects. It is the result of evidence. Yet again, we have no direct experimental support for this claim. However, in this case, as with children's understanding of action, it appears that making particular kinds of evidence linguistically salient can accelerate the development of the nonlinguistic conceptual change. As we will see in the next chapter, exposing children to many instances of object naming seems to lead to changes in the development of their sorting behavior. Again, this suggests that relevant evidence, rather than theory-independent maturational or information-processing changes, is responsible for the changes in the children's understanding of the world.

III

Theories and Language

So far we have been discussing the theoretical structure that underlies both problem-solving and much of language in infancy. We provided detailed descriptions of three domains—the child's understanding of object appearances, of actions, and of kinds—in which there seem to be important theorylike changes in infancy and early childhood. We have emphasized the fact that by 18 months both linguistic and nonlinguistic behaviors indicate common conceptual changes in many important domains of development. Moreover, these two kinds of behaviors are empirically closely related to one another. All this indicates that changing theories underlie both semantic and cognitive development.

In this chapter and the next, however, we want to consider the relation between language and cognition from a rather different standpoint. Rather than seeing how developments in both these areas indicate a common underlying theory change, we want to consider how language might be causally related to theory change. The question is a specialized version of a more general set of questions about the relationship between language and thought. While this is one of the oldest, most complex, and most ferociously debated issues in philosophy and psychology, there are surprisingly few empirical results that tell on it.

7

Language and Thought

One possible relation between language and thought is that structural features of language, such as the ability to use words or to combine words into strings, might be related to similar structural cognitive abilities. A number of investigators have explored this possibility with little positive result (Piaget, 1962; Sinclair, 1970; Bates et al., 1979; Fischer & Corrigan, 1981). There is little evidence suggesting that structural features of language, general or specific, are connected to structural features of cognition.

A second, rather different way in which language and cognition could be related concerns the content of language and thought, the relationship between semantic development and conceptual development. How is the development of words or other linguistic structures that encode certain types of concepts related to the development of the concepts themselves? These are the relations that we have explored, and here there is strong and consistent evidence for relations between language and cognition. These relations are, however, rather different from the relations proposed by many accounts of language and thought in the past.

Prerequisites

Several different views of the relation between semantic and conceptual development have been advanced in the literature. The classical Piagetian view is that conceptual development precedes semantic development. Children must first develop concepts and only then can develop linguistic forms that encode them (Piaget, 1962). This view also dominated early psycholinguistic thinking about this relationship (Clark, 1974; Slobin, 1973).

In spite of the ideological divides between Chomskyans and Piagetians, versions of the prerequisites view have also been common in broadly Chomskyan accounts of semantic development. These neo-Chomskyan views differ from the classical Piagetian views in two important respects. First, they tend to see cognitive structure itself as innate rather than constructed or developed. Second and more significant, they see cognition as a necessary but not sufficient condition for semantic development. On this view, merely having a cognitive representation of the world does not determine one's semantic representations. Further rules or other constraints are necessary to determine which aspects of the cognitive representation should be encoded linguistically.

For example, Pinker (1989) argues that children have innate cognitive representations of situations and events. They also have equally innate syntactic structures. The child learns the semantic structure of his particular language by linking the cognitive representations of relevant contexts to the relevant syntactic structures—a process Pinker calls "semantic bootstrapping." Similarly, Landau and Jackendoff (1993) suggest that semantic structures encode innate and universal representations determined by the perceptual system.

Perhaps the most influential view of this sort in the literature on lexical acquisition comes from the work of Markman and her colleagues. Markman (1987, 1989) has proposed that there are quite general linguistic constraints on children's interpretations of early words. These constraints influence, even determine, children's decisions about which concepts those words encode. The constraints, moreover, ensure that the child's decisions will be very similar to adult decisions. For example, children assume that nouns refer to whole objects rather than to object parts or stages. While Markman is herself agnostic about the source of these constraints, the implication of much of her work is that they are not directly the result of conceptual development itself, nor are they the result of particular patterns in the input to the child. Instead, they are a consequence of the child's specifically linguistic knowledge.

Constraints are necessary because of the classic riddle of induction proposed by Quine (1960), among others. In principle, a word used in a particular context could refer to any of an infinite variety of aspects of that context, and yet the child must eventually converge on the adult meaning. Specifically linguistic constraints could limit the child's hypotheses about possible meanings. The analogy is to the way that syntactic constraints in Chomskyan theory ensure that the child considers only a limited range of the infinite variety of possible grammars and quickly converges on the adult grammar.[1]

Interactions

Semantic and conceptual development may also be related in another way, classically associated with Whorf (1956) and Vygotsky (1962). Semantic development may actually facilitate and modify conceptual development. Linguistic information may restructure our nonlinguistic knowledge. Recently this interactionist view has been experiencing something of a revival. After decades of obloquy, even Whorf has begun to be approvingly cited in the literature.

One Whorfian version of the interactionist view may be found in recent work investigating crosslinguistic effects on semantic development. In particular, Bowerman (1980, 1989), Choi and Bowerman (1991), Slobin (1982, 1985), and Levinson (1994) suggest that the specific structure of particular languages might strongly influence both semantic and conceptual development. Different languages carve up the world in different ways, making certain semantic distinctions obligatory and others optional or marking certain distinctions with clear morphological variations while others can only be expressed by complex and indirect means. In Korean, for example, there is no standard linguistic distinction between placing an object in a container and on a surface, a distinction English speakers code with "in" and "on." Korean spatial terms do, however, morphologically distinguish between "tight fit" spatial relationships (a finger in a ring, a picture on a wall) and "loose fit" relationships (a piece of fruit in a bowl, an object leaning on the wall). This distinction cross-cuts the in/on distinction in English (Choi & Bowerman, 1991). Similarly, in some Mayan languages all spatial terms mark absolute distinctions (like English "north" and "south" or "upwind" and "downwind") rather than marking spatial relations between objects and the speaker (like English "left" and "right") (Levinson, 1994).

These differences among particular languages might influence children's semantic development: they might influence which conceptual distinctions children find easy or difficult to encode. More powerfully, they might also influence the child's and the adult's conceptual distinctions themselves, drawing attention to particular similarities and differences encoded in a particular language. Berman and Slobin (1994) point out, for example, that crosslinguistic differences affect which elements are included in a narrative of the same event, and Choi and Bowerman (1991) have stressed the different ways the same continuous spatial event can be subdivided in different languages. Levinson (1994) has actually shown some differences in recall and spatial-problem solving between speakers of Mayan and Dutch that seem to reflect the differences between the two languages. A number of other recent crosslinguistic studies have made suggestions of this kind (Shatz, 1991; Sera, Reittinger & Castillo-Pintado, 1991; Waxman, 1991; Weist, Wysocka & Lyytinen, 1991).

A second version of the interactionist position, the one more closely associated with Vygotsky rather than Whorf, is that the distinctive linguistic patterns that adults use in their interactions with infants, rather than the distinctive syntactic and lexical structure of particular languages, might influence semantic and conceptual structure. There is evidence supporting this. For example, Callanan (1985) and Mervis (1987; Mervis & Bertrand, 1993) have suggested that particular features of the adult use of category names might lead the child to develop new types of language and categorization. Moreover, Nelson, Hampson, and Shaw (1993) and Goldfield (1986) have shown correlations between details of maternal linguistic style and children's early semantics. Mervis (1987; Mervis et al., 1992) has charted interactions between input and semantic structure in case studies.

The guiding force in this case is not the acquisition of language in general or even a specific language in particular but rather exposure to the particular kind of language used by significant adults. In fact, Mervis (1987), Nelson et al. (1993), and Callanan (1985) argue that there are interactions between this input and cognitive development. In its purest Vygotskyan form, this theoretical view might suggest that both semantic and cognitive development are simply a consequence of the child's attempt to match adult behavior, and so to become a member of the social community.

Most of the empirical work supporting both the prerequisites view and the interactionist view has involved children who already have acquired much linguistic knowledge. Moreover, rather surprisingly, almost all of the studies investigating relations between language and thought have inferred the child's cognitive structures from the child's linguistic behavior itself. Very few studies have directly and systematically examined the impact of language on significant nonlinguistic cognitive developments or vice versa.

A Theory-Theory View

Our empirical studies suggest a relation between semantic and cognitive development that is rather different from either of these interactionist views, though it includes elements of both. In our studies semantic and cognitive developments emerge simultaneously; neither type of development appears to precede the other. Our results suggest a bidirectional interaction between conceptual and semantic development. Earlier cognitive developments may not only serve as a prerequisite for semantic developments, as the classic Piagetian and neo-Chomskyan models suggest, but actually motivate semantic developments. Children are actively engaged in solving particular conceptual problems at particular times, and the child's attention is drawn to words relevant to those problems. At the same time, children are actively engaged in solving the problem of language itself. In Annette Karmiloff-Smith's (1979) phrase, they treat language as a problem space. Children may be drawn to investigate a particular linguistic pattern because of its relevance to particular cognitive problems. But discovering the nature of that linguistic pattern may also help children to solve those problems and direct their attention to new ones.

The theory theory provides a very helpful model for this kind of relation between language and thought. Indeed, this is why we were drawn to it in the first place! We can think of the child's acquisition of at least some early words as being analogous to a physics student, or perhaps a Kuhnian "normal" scientist, hearing about a new theoretical possibility from a scientific innovator. Consider the acquisition of scientific terms like "entropy" in these circumstances. Developing an understanding of such words and the ability to use them appropriately is one sign, often the most relevant sign, of theory formation.

Considering the acquisition of "entropy" also may be revealing about the processes that actually lead to theory change in children. We pay attention to words like "entropy" because they are relevant to the scientific problems we are trying to solve. At the same time, learning the words is an important part of learning the concepts. At the simplest level, hearing the same word across a variety of contexts may lead us to see similarities in those contexts that we might not otherwise have considered. Hearing the professor say "entropy" both when she discusses randomness and when she discusses heat may lead us to link these otherwise disparate phenomena, and this linkage itself has implications for other aspects of our understanding of physics.

Neither the prerequisites view nor the interactionist view seem to capture the character of semantic change in science. In such cases we do not say either that conceptual development precedes semantic development or vice versa. It is not simply that we have an innate repertoire of concepts, including that of entropy, and are merely waiting to map the correct term on to that concept. But it is also not the case that we are simply mindlessly matching our linguistic behavior to that of our teacher and that our cognition is shaped accordingly. Rather, the two types of developments, learning the word and learning the related concept, appear to go hand in hand, with each type facilitating the other.

A particular example from the last chapter may help to illustrate the general idea in a very simple way. Imagine a 15-month-old infant who knows that salient and significant objects sometimes are put into groups by others, either linguistically or physically. Such a child may notice, for example, that all objects of a certain kind are called "bottle" and may use this word to refer to these important objects. As she pays more attention to names, she notices that her mother not only uses names to refer to salient or significant objects like bottles but names a wide variety of objects. Looking at a picture book, for example, the mother may name every object on the page, exclaiming "horse" or "umbrella" or "elephant" as each object comes into view. What is the infant to make of this behavior? One thing she could infer is that all objects, salient or not, significant or not, have a name to be discovered (hence the "Whatsat?" behavior so common in this period). This is often described as the central insight of the naming spurt. But the infant might also infer that all objects, salient or not, significant or not, belong in some category or other, that objects in general are divided up into kinds. In dealing with objects, the child may also express this discovery in her sorting behavior, exhaustively placing all the objects in a mixed array into different locations. Her nonlinguistic behavior would parallel how she (and her mother) linguistically place all the different objects into different categories. Of course, we might expect that in the case of most concepts the process will be much more complex than this relatively simple generalization, as it is in the case of entropy. Many words will be linked to one another in a coherent, theoretical way, and appreciating these links is part of understanding the theory.

Similarly, we have suggested that children who hear a word like "gone" applied to a wide variety of perceptually disparate object disappearances may be helped to make the generalization that all disappearances, no matter what their perceptual character, involve the same underlying relations of objects and space. This generalization is relevant to the ability to deduce the location of objects that disappear in unfamiliar or mysterious ways, the highest-level object-permanence ability (Gopnik, 1984b). Finally, children who hear the same word, say "uh-oh," applied to the myriad cases in which a plan fails may be helped to generalize about the structure of plans. This may play a role in their ability to solve means–ends tasks (Gopnik, 1982).

In all these cases children can take advantage of these linguistic signals only if they see them as relevant to the specific problems they are trying to solve; if, to adapt Vygotsky's phrase, they occur in the children's "zone of proximal development." Moreover, children do not simply match the meanings of "gone" and "uh-oh" that they hear in the adult language. Rather, they use these words to encode the conceptual structures they are themselves developing at the moment, the structures that are central to their theories.

On this view, linguistic knowledge might interact with cognitive development. However, the nature of the interaction would itself depend on the child's previous cognitive achievements and present cognitive problems. Semantic and conceptual development genuinely proceed in tandem, with each area of development facilitating the other, and they are closely intertwined in this way from the very beginnings of language. This seems to capture precisely the relation between semantic and conceptual development, and the balance between purely cognitive and social factors, in scientific theory change.

Methodological Issues: Specificity and Correlation

How can we test these different models of the interaction between language and thought? So far in this book we have outlined a number of specific empirical relations between language and thought in infancy. In this chapter we will report crosslinguistic studies and studies of individual differences in input that suggest that linguistic information may itself influence cognitive development. We will begin by addressing some methodological points relevant to all these studies. Investigating relations between language and cognition in this early period raises particular methodological issues. Such studies largely rely on correlational methods, since we are unable to randomly assign children to one of several linguistic or cognitive paths. Like other investigators, we began our research by looking for correlated patterns of development in language and nonlinguistic problem solving. There are, however, notorious problems associated with this method. They involve the inference of underlying causes from correlational data. The most significant problem is the possibility of hidden third factors—particularly such general developmental factors as increasing intelligence, motor ability, or general processing capacity—that may be responsible for apparent relations between linguistic and cognitive developments. Early studies that looked for very general structural correlations between measures of overall cognitive skill and such linguistic measures as mean length of utterance or vocabulary size foundered on precisely these problems. Once general factors like age and general intelligence are controlled for, little relation between cognition and language remains (see Corrigan, 1978; Bloom, Lifter & Broughton, 1985). It is possible to experimentally control for some of these general variables, such as age, as we have done in our cross-sectional studies. But most of these possible hidden variables are not amenable to such controls. Fortunately, the fact that cognitive development is domain-specific helps point to a solution.

Theory change and the semantic changes associated with it are specific to the particular domain being investigated, unlike across-the-board structural changes. As we have seen, our empirical work, like much recent work in cognitive development, suggests that cognitive developments in different domains may be quite independent of one another. Milestones of development in different domains—such as the understanding of object appearances, actions, and kinds that are reflected in our object-permanence, means-ends, and classification tasks—appear on average at about the same age but are nevertheless relatively independent of each other in particular children.

On average, children acquire these abilities at about 18 months—a fact that led Piaget to group them as a single "stage change." In one of our longitudinal studies (Gopnik & Meltzoff, 1987), for example, the average age of development of the highest-levels of object permanence, means-ends ability, and sorting were 521, 522, and 524 days respectively (approximately 17 months). In another cross-sectional study of 18-month-olds 56, 50, and 53 percent of the children passed each of these tasks (Gopnik & Meltzoff, 1992).

However, a more detailed look at the data suggests that this concordance may be misleading. For individual children, there may be gaps of several months between developments in one area and another. Moreover, there is no evidence for any significant correlation between performance in one domain and performance in the others. In these same studies there were no significant correlations among the ages of acquisition of achievements in the three domains. Children who accomplish one milestone relatively early may be relatively late in developing another (see also Uzgiris & Hunt, 1975, 1987). Similarly, in the cross-sectional studies there were no correlations among performances in the three domains. The detailed pattern of development suggests that there is no single conceptual change underlying all these problem-solving changes.

This very empirical fact implies a methodological strategy that can be particularly helpful for resolving classical problems about the interpretation of correlational data. This independence and domain-specificity enables us to deal with the effects of hidden variables in a different way. We can compare the variables under investigation with measures in other cognitive and linguistic domains. We can compare an individual child's achievements in one domain to this individual child's achievements in another domain, using each child as his or her own control, as it were.

For example, as we saw, categorization is closely correlated to the naming spurt. This relation, in and of itself, might be due to many different factors. In particular, more intelligent children might also be more verbal. However, if naming is not related to other developments, such as the emergence of means-ends abilities, then this suggests that some more substantive and specific link is involved. Means-ends abilities are clearly no more intrinsically difficult or easy than categorizing, and they emerge, on average, at about the same time. This argument is particularly compelling when the other cognitive measures are themselves related to other types of linguistic measures, such as the emergence of relational words. As we suggested above, the very fact that, say, means-ends abilities are related to language suggests that they are valid measures of *some* cognitive abilities, just not the ones related to the particular semantic domain of naming.

A similar logic applies to the various studies we have designed to test the interactions between linguistic input and cognition. In these studies we compared the cognitive development of children who have different linguistic input, either because they are learning different languages or because their mothers have different individual speech styles. For example, as we will see, we found that Korean speakers are delayed in both naming and categorization compared with English speakers. Such crosslinguistic differences, like other crosslinguistic differences in the literature, might have many explanations. These children might be less motivated, subject to different cultural conventions regarding display, and so on. However, if these children are also *advanced* in both verb learning and means-ends development, these general explanations seem far less likely. This pattern would instead suggest one very specific relation between naming and categorization and another between verbs and means-ends understanding.

Again, the same logic applies to studies of individual differences. If children whose mothers use more nouns are the ones who categorize at younger ages, this might reflect many general relations between the two variables. For example, talkative mothers might just have brighter babies. But if noun input is not related to other cognitive developments and other input variables such as the number of verbs are not related to categorizing, these findings gain force. In general, then, we have employed a two-pronged strategy for detecting causal relations between language and cognition. First we compared the linguistic and cognitive developments that we hypothesize may be related, but also, and just as significant, we compared these developments to other concurrent linguistic and cognitive developments. The logic of this method is similar to the logic that seeks "double dissociations" in cognitive neuroscience.

Developmental Relations between Language and Cognition

As we described above, our earliest studies looked at the relations between relational words like "gone" and "uh-oh" and relevant cognitive developments: object-permanence and means-ends developments.

More recently we have examined the relations between children's spontaneous categorization and their development of a naming spurt. In a series of intensive longitudinal studies, we recorded children's spontaneous language development in detail, using both a maternal questionnaire and video recordings, and we also recorded children's performance on a variety of nonlinguistic cognitive tasks. The studies were double-blind, with linguistic and cognitive behavior recorded independently.

We observed a relation between the development of words for disappearance, like "gone," and the development of high-level object-permanence abilities—a finding also replicated in other studies (Corrigan, 1978; Gopnik, 1982, 1984b; Gopnik & Meltzoff, 1984; McCune-Nicolich, 1981; Tomasello & Farrar, 1984, 1986). Within a week or two of the time children showed the highest-level object-search behaviors in the lab, their mothers, quite independently, recorded that they had begun to say words like "allgone."

We also observed an independent relation between words encoding success and failure, such as "there" and "uh-oh," and the development of means-ends abilities, in particular the ability to solve certain problems with "insight," immediately, and without a period of trial and error (Gopnik & Meltzoff, 1984, 1986a). Again within a week or two of our first observation of these behaviors in the lab, mothers independently reported the emergence of these words.

Finally, we observed a relation between "the naming spurt" and children's spontaneous classification, in particular, the ability to exhaustively sort objects into many categories, a finding since replicated by Mervis and Bertrand (Gopnik & Meltzoff, 1987, 1992; Mervis & Bertrand, 1994). In addition, we have replicated and confirmed all these longitudinal studies with data from cross-sectional studies with a larger number of subjects (Gopnik & Meltzoff, 1986a, 1992).

We discussed each of these findings in detail in the relevant chapters, but now we want to consider the relations among them. All three of these specific relations between semantic and cognitive developments have some similar characteristics. All three take place on average at about the same time, around 18 months. All three involve particular semantic developments, the development of words with specific types of meanings, rather than involving structural developments, such as the ability to use words or combine them. Most significant, in all three cases the linguistic developments and the nonlinguistic cognitive abilities appear to emerge at about the same time, within a few weeks of one another in our longitudinal studies. Indeed, in the case of the first two relations, the two developments can appear in either order. Sometimes the cognitive achievement emerges just before the word but sometimes the word emerges just before the cognitive achievement.[2]

Yet the three conceptual domains—knowledge about disappearance, knowledge about means-ends relations, and knowledge about object categories—are strikingly independent of each other. Some individual children acquire "gone" and related nonlinguistic object-permanence abilities months before they acquire success/failure words and related means-ends abilities. Other children reverse this pattern. Moreover, while there are strong relations between the ages at which the semantic developments emerge and those at which the related cognitive developments emerge, cross-relations do not hold: object permanence is not linked to success/failure words, and means-ends development is not linked to disappearance words. The same pattern holds for means-ends development and the naming spurt.[3] Specifically, there are relatively small temporal gaps between the related cognitive and semantic developments in longitudinal studies. Individual children begin to say the words and develop the related abilities at about the same time. There are much larger gaps between the unrelated developments.

There are also strong statistical correlations between the ages at which the children acquire the related abilities but little correlation between the age of acquisition of the unrelated abilities. Individual children are likely to acquire "gone" early if they develop object permanence early, but there is no such relation between "gone" and means-ends abilities. Similarly, in cross-sectional studies, 18-month-olds who solve object-permanence tasks are more likely to say "gone" than children who do not solve these tasks. They are not more likely to say "uh-oh." Conversely, 18-month-olds who solve means-ends tasks are not more likely to say "gone" than children who do not (Gopnik & Meltzoff, 1986a).

Rather than being the result of some more general relation between linguistic and cognitive abilities, these relations appear to involve quite specific links between particular conceptual developments and related semantic developments. These results are among very few empirical demonstrations of a close and specific relation between language and nonlinguistic cognition in this period (or any other). As we argued earlier, the results strongly suggest that a conceptual change underlies both types of development.

Notice that the temporal patterns provide additional evidence for a causal relation between language and cognition that is stronger than the correlational evidence. If we only had the correlational evidence, it might be that some earlier linguistic or cognitive development was responsible for the later developments, and the apparent relation between the specific cognitive and linguistic developments at 18 months was due to these earlier relations. Of course, this would still imply that there were specific links between cognitive and linguistic developments, but they might not be the links we have identified. However, the fact that the two developments emerge at almost the same time would be difficult to explain on this view.

These findings don't fit neatly with either of the classical pictures of the relations between language and thought: 18-month-olds do not simply encode every aspect of their cognitive representation of a context, nor do they encode those aspects of their cognitive representations that are most primitive and fundamental. They also do not encode the aspects of cognitive representation that most closely match the meanings expressed in the adult language, as neo-Chomskyan views would suggest. Rather, they choose to encode the concepts that are at the frontiers of their cognitive development, the concepts in their "zone of proximal development."

In fact, there are interesting parallels between the kinds of cognitive developments that are most likely to be in the "zone" at 15 to 21 months and the kinds of concepts expressed most frequently in early language. As we have seen, object appearances, actions, and kinds, as well as spatial relations, are all areas of great cognitive significance to children of this age. These are also the notions most likely to be encoded in early language.

Theories and Constraints

The picture that emerges from this research is also rather different from "constraint" views, at least if those views are considered as a neo-Chomskyan mechanism for semantic development rather than as a useful description of certain regularities in semantic development. Children do not simply converge on those representations that are most like the representations of the adult language. Instead, these very early words appear to encode a very selected set of concepts at the cutting edge of the child's cognitive development. These are the most significant concepts in the children's currently constructed theories.

We would argue that theory change itself is the source of some of the most powerful constraints on the child's semantics at this stage of development. We can see semantic constraints as a special case of the interpretive effects of theories. We argued above, on quite independent cognitive grounds, that such interpretive effects are one of the most significant characteristics of theories. Theories dictate which pieces of evidence will be considered relevant or salient, and they impose a particular kind of ontological classification on the world. Theories themselves provide strong constraints on induction. Indeed, this is one of their most useful features. These constraints, rather than being fixed, however, are themselves revisable in the light of further evidence. These effects of theories plausibly, indeed almost certainly, influence the interpretation of words, as well as the interpretation of nonlinguistic evidence. Empirically, Markman's constraints look much more like these interpretive effects than like the strong constraints of syntactic theory.

For example, all three of Markman's most well-established constraints (the assumption that names encode whole objects, the assumption that they encode taxonomic object categories, and the assumption that there is only one name per object kind) are closely related to the child's developing conception of kinds, as Markman (1989) herself notes. These constraints are imposed by the most important conceptual advances of this period, just as an interest in and knowledge of physics will constrain your acquisition of words like "entropy."

There has always been something a bit odd about Markman's constraints because, of course, as Markman (1992) herself has recognized, they are not actually constraints at all in the way that, say, syntactic or phonological constraints are constraints. In fact, none of Markman's constraints are true of the adult language. There is something paradoxical about the idea that using these constraints will solve Quine's (1960) induction problem. Eventually, after all, the child will have to discover that not all names do encode whole objects or taxonomic categories, that names can encode many things. On the constraint view, children should be faced with Quine's problem all over again when they are forced to override constraints. On the theory theory, however, constraints are a starting set of assumptions about the likely meanings of early words, assumptions that are later revised in the light of further evidence. The empirical demonstration of close links between language and cognitive development suggests that these assumptions are motivated at least as much by cognitive concerns as by purely linguistic evidence.

The debate in the literature between Markman and her opponents (see, e.g., Golinkoff, Mervis & Hirsh-Pasek, 1994; Nelson, 1988; Bloom, 1993) is reminiscent of the broader and more general debate between rationalist and empiricist approaches to cognitive development. The opponents point to several sources of data that might inform the children's hypotheses about early meanings (notably, maternal input). Markman points to the underdetermination of semantic hypotheses by these data. The theory theory might help to resolve this debate. Theories constrain hypotheses and allow only limited varieties of induction, the phenomena that Markman points to in support of constraints. At the same time theories are revisable in the light of evidence and show a distinctive developmental trajectory—precisely the empirical points raised by Nelson, Golinkoff et al., and Bloom.

This theory-theory interpretation of constraints becomes even more plausible when we consider early relational words, rather than just early names. As we have seen, there is just as much uniformity in children's use of these words as there is in their use of names. Children consistently choose to encode concepts of disappearance, success and failure, in their early language. In a sense, their interpretation of early words like "uh-oh" or "gone" is even more constrained than their interpretation of early names. Not only do they choose a subset of the possible meanings of these words; they also choose a set of meanings that has rather little overlap with the adult meanings. In fact, these children seem to pick up words and phrases that are quite peripheral in the adult language. Children in our studies sometimes derived a success or failure word from one salient use of the term. One little girl, for example, used "come off" for all cases of failure. Bowerman (1978, 1980) reports many examples along similar lines from her diary studies of her own children.

The phenomenon of constraint is as clear and strong for relational words as for names. In a way, it is stronger: children not only give words a particular meaning; they find a word to assign that meaning to, even when there is no such word in the adult language. The linguistic interpretation of constraint seems highly implausible in these cases. In the case of names, we might see early constraints as at least a bridge to the crucial meanings in the adult language, even if they do not match the adult meanings. In the case of relational words, however, it is very hard to see how this could be true. Our more cognitive interpretation of the constraints, on the other hand, accounts for the development of both names and relational words and also accounts for the close empirical relations between linguistic and cognitive developments in this period.

Crosslinguistic Studies

The results of our empirical studies strongly suggest that cognitive development interacts with semantic development. We can repeat the arguments we made when discussing noncognitive interpretations of changes in problem solving. The only way to account for the strong and specific relations between the linguistic and cognitive developments at 18 months is to assume some common cause for both developments, a cause not connected to other linguistic and cognitive developments at the same period. The most plausible candidate for such a cause is some common underlying conceptual change responsible for both changes in language and changes in behavior. But what are the determinants of that conceptual change itself? We discussed some of the purely cognitive factors—counterevidence, experimentation, and the like—in earlier chapters. Could linguistic input itself be a factor in theory change?

The fact that in our longitudinal studies the semantic and conceptual developments occurred in close temporal concert suggests that the interaction might go in both directions. The changes in problem solving occurred at about the same time as the linked linguistic changes, and sometimes the linguistic changes preceded the behavioral changes. This temporal pattern raised the possibility that language is causally implicated in the conceptual change. Moreover, some studies suggest that providing infants with linguistic (or nonlinguistic) labels for objects in the laboratory makes them more likely to categorize those objects (Baldwin & Moses, 1994; Roberts & Jacob, 1991; Waxman, 1991). Neither of these findings by itself demonstrates, however, that language is implicated in the kinds of theory changes we have described here.

How can we test the interactionist hypothesis that language may restructure and influence cognition further? As always, the crucial experiments are immoral or impossible; we cannot experimentally alter the child's linguistic environment and observe the effects on their problem solving. But we can see whether naturally occurring variations in linguistic input are related to different patterns of cognitive development. As we saw, both Bowerman (1989) and Slobin (1982) have suggested that morphological and syntactic differences in different languages might make certain conceptual distinctions particularly salient. In collaboration with Soonja Choi at San Diego State University, one of us has been investigating the relations between language and cognition in Korean speakers (Gopnik & Choi, 1990, 1995; Choi & Gopnik, 1995; Gopnik, Choi & Baumberger, in press).

English has a highly analytic structure, with relatively little reliance on morphological variation. Moreover, nouns are generally obligatory in English sentences. In contrast, Korean and Japanese, languages with similar structures, have a very rich verb morphology, depend on different verb endings to make important semantic distinctions, and are verb-final. Pragmatic rules in Korean and Japanese allow massive noun ellipsis, particularly in informal conversation where the context is clear and present (Clancy, 1985). Parental speech in these languages, which occurs in precisely such a setting, often consists of highly inflected verbs with few nouns, very much in contrast to North American English parental speech. As we will see, we have found that Korean-speaking mothers consistently used fewer nouns than English-speaking mothers, and Fernald and Morikawa (1993) report a similar pattern for Japanese-speaking mothers. There is also some evidence that there are differences in the very early language of Korean- and Japanese- versus English-speaking children. A number of investigators have noted that Korean- and Japanese-speaking children productively use verb morphology earlier than English-speaking children but use fewer and less varied names (Choi, 1986, 1991; Choi & Gopnik, 1995; Clancy, 1985; Fernald & Morikawa, 1991; Rispoli, 1987; Tanouye, 1979). Au, Dapretto, and Song (1994) did not detect such a difference, but there are a number of methodological reasons for this (see Gopnik, Choi & Baumberger, 1996).

Given the relations between language and cognition in English speakers, we might predict that Korean speakers would be advanced in their understanding of actions, concepts encoded by verbs, and delayed in their understanding of object kinds, concepts encoded by nouns.

Gopnik and Choi (1990) studied the linguistic and cognitive development of 5 Korean-speaking children in an intensive longitudinal study. The results suggested that both the emergence of a naming explosion and the development of exhaustive categorizing were indeed particularly delayed in Korean-speaking children relative to the children in a comparable English-speaking sample. In a second longitudinal study (Gopnik & Choi, 1995; Gopnik, Choi & Baumberger, 1996), we tested a larger sample of Korean-speaking children ($N = 11$). In each testing session, children received both the cognitive tasks that we used in our earlier studies of English-speakers and an extensive language questionnaire specifically designed for Korean. There was a significant difference between the Korean and English speakers' performances on the categorization tasks. The Korean speakers were significantly delayed on this measure in comparison with the English speakers. Similarly, there was a significant difference between Korean and English speakers' development of a naming explosion.

Intriguingly, the opposite pattern held for the development of means–ends abilities and success/failure words. Korean-speaking children were significantly advanced in both these areas of development in comparison with the English speakers.

In a second cross-sectional study, we again compared the cognitive performance of 18 Korean-speaking children and 30 English-speakers (Gopnik, Choi & Baumberger, 1996). The results confirmed those of the longitudinal studies. The Korean speakers were significantly worse on categorizing tasks than the English speakers but significantly better on means–ends tasks.

Moreover, we also collected data comparing the speech of these Korean-speaking mothers to their children and the speech of English-speaking mothers to their children. At the start and end of each testing session in the cross-sectional study, the mothers were asked to play and talk with their children for five minutes in one of two semistructured sessions, either "reading" picture books or playing with a toy house. We then analyzed the mothers' use of nouns and verbs. Korean-speaking mothers consistently used more action words than English-speaking mothers, they used more referential verbs, that is, verbs that refer clearly to actions, and in a pragmatic analysis they also used more activity-oriented utterances than English-speaking mothers. In contrast, English-speaking mothers used more nouns, more referential nouns, and more naming utterances. The specific patterns of relations suggests that these differences in linguistic input may be responsible for the children's different patterns of cognitive development.

Individual-Difference Studies

It is also possible, however, that general cultural differences between the two groups of mothers might be responsible both for the linguistic differences and the cognitive differences among the children. Would we find similar differences within a single culture and language if we compared English-speaking mothers who did or did not use many nouns or many verbs in their speech to their children? We might think of this possibility as more closely related to a Vygotskyan interactive picture. Some previous studies had suggested that maternal input might influence the naming spurt: mothers who used more nouns were more likely to have children with a spurt than mothers who used fewer nouns (Goldfield, 1986; Nelson, Hampson & Shaw, 1993). More crucial from the present point of view, we wanted to explore whether maternal input might be related to cognitive development. Do the mothers of children who categorize use more nouns in their speech to the children, while the mothers of children who solve means-ends tasks use more verbs?

We compared the mothers of 46 children who did or did not sort, or did or did not solve means-ends tasks, in our cross-sectional studies. As we might expect, the two contexts, the books and toy house, elicited different kinds of speech: mothers used significantly more nouns and fewer verbs in the book setting than in the toy setting. As we might also expect, we found significant effects of verbs in the toy setting and significant effects of nouns in the book setting. However, the two types of language were related to cognition in different ways. The mothers of children who succeeded on the means-ends tasks used significantly more verb types overall than mothers of children who did not, and also used significantly more referential verb types. There were no similar effects for categorizing. On the other hand, mothers of children who passed the categorization task tended to use more noun types overall, and more referential noun types in particular, than mothers of children who did not pass the task. But there was no such relation between using nouns and passing means-ends tasks. If anything, the relation went in the opposite direction. Similarly, in the lab of one of us, Baumberger (1995) found that the mothers of children who passed categorization tasks used significantly more object-oriented gestures, while the mothers of children who passed means-ends tasks used significantly more action-oriented gestures. The differences between children of mothers who used many nouns or many verbs looked very much like the differences between Korean- and English-speaking children (Gopnik & Choi, 1995).

This even more directly suggests that the interaction between cognitive and linguistic development in 18-month-olds may go in both directions. Changes in children's linguistic input may lead to variation in their cognitive development. As we described earlier, a child who hears language with many highly directed uses of nouns may come to pay special attention to category problems. A child with a parent who focuses on verbs, in contrast, may focus her attention on actions and events and the relations between them.

Conclusion

The data we have presented here suggest that there are extensive interactions between semantic and cognitive development in infancy. These interactions are well captured by the theory theory. As in learning a scientific theory, conceptual and semantic change seem to go hand in hand. However, we would emphasize, we do not think that all language bears this intimate a relation to conceptual development. Even in the one-word stage, there are some types of words that really do seem to be more closely related to social routines and scripts than to theory changes, words like "hello" and "mama," for example. In empirical studies these early words have turned out to be unrelated to nonlinguistic cognitive developments (Gopnik, 1988b). Similarly, the changes we describe all involve semantic and lexical developments rather than syntactic developments. It is perfectly conceivable, even likely, that the acquisition of syntax involves different processes with different relations to cognition than those we have described here. Nevertheless, a very sizable portion of the child's early language does seem to be tied to theory change in this way.

Moreover, the crosslinguistic and individual-difference studies suggest that aspects of linguistic input can have quite striking effects on conceptual development. Children who hear language relevant to a particular conceptual problem are more likely to solve that problem than children who do not. As we mentioned earlier, this fact tends to support the theory theory over modularity theories. If the conceptual developments we are concerned about were simply the result of maturation or changing information-processing skills, it is extremely difficult to see why they would be influenced by hearing particular types of language relevant to them.

The interactionist findings by themselves are, of course, also compatible with more empiricist or social-constructivist views. Indeed, the classic Whorf/Vygotsky picture is itself a social-constructivist one. Other aspects of the findings, however, like the generality of early words or the lack of fit between the child's semantic structure and that of adults, are less congruent with such views. Our view is that linguistic information is simply one more source of evidence, one more set of representations that the theory-formation system must deal with. It may be a particularly important source of evidence, but in this regard the child is again no different from any modern scientist who relies on the reports of others for almost all of his evidential base.

It is an open question whether there is some more profound social influence on cognition than this, whether, for example, the child actually internalizes the structure of the theory from adults, rather than simply using adult language as an additional source of information. A serious difference between the scientist and the child is that the child can rely on adults to provide reasonably good linguistic information most of the time. It seems very likely that the fact that cultures transmit solutions to problems through language plays a major role in the child's ability to make such extremely rapid cognitive progress. In much the same way, it is much easier to learn about Einstein's theory than to discover it, or perhaps even than to know whether to accept it just after it was formulated. Scientists have much less reason than children to believe that the information they receive from members of their community is reliable, and they likely have to resolve contradictions much more frequently. Indeed, one might argue that a great deal of science consists of deciding who your mother is. The exact relation between this kind of socially provided information and theory change is still very unclear in both cases. We are still largely in the dark about the "social epistemology" of both children and scientists. Crosslinguistic, crosscultural, and individual-difference studies of the sort we have described here may, however, start to illuminate this darkness.

8

The Darwinian Conclusion

For the last four chapters we have been focusing on the empirical details of the theory theory. We have argued that treating cognitive development as theory change gives us a particularly perspicuous way of describing changes in semantic and conceptual structure and the relations between those changes. In this chapter we will pull back again and consider the broader philosophical implications of these empirical facts.

Who's Afraid of Semantic Holism?

The picture of knowledge and meaning that emerges from our empirical work is not much like the pictures that have generally been advanced in cognitive science. It is, however, similar to a picture from quite a different philosophical tradition. In "Two Dogmas of Empiricism" (1961) Quine famously rejects the analytic/synthetic distinction. Quine holds that meanings are deeply interdependent and deeply flexible. Meanings depend on larger theories of the world. Understanding the meaning of a term requires understanding the theory in which the term is embedded. Moreover, there are no central, fixed points at which meanings can be articulated, no analytic sentences true simply by virtue of their meanings. Quine presents few arguments for this view. Instead, he presents a picture. The picture is of "the web of belief," a set of interconnected conceptual strands. According to this metaphor, the peripheral strands are the beliefs that are most easily influenced by the outside world, while the central strands are beliefs, like our fundamental beliefs about space and time, that seem relatively immune from such influences. Quine's point is that even the most central strands of the web are ultimately subject to modification by vibrations at the periphery. As our understanding of the world develops, as we experience more and organize our experience, the interrelations between our cognitive structures will alter in deep respects. This may eventually lead to the revision of what seem to be "analytic" or "conceptual" truths. Moreover, these changes will often not take place sentence by sentence; often the appropriate unit of change will be an entire theory. These changes will be reflected in changes in the meanings of our terms.

Why has Quine's picture been so widely accepted in philosophy in view of the lack of arguments for it? The web of belief is the picture of conceptual and semantic change that emerges from the history of science. It is perhaps difficult to think of Quine as a humble figure, but really his view reflects a kind of instinctive humility in the face of the conceptual achievements of science. We think that knowledge is what the best scientific theories tell us it is and that the language of these theories is meaningful. But this means that in light of the conceptual bizarrerie of the best scientific theories, there is little that we can say a priori about what knowledge or meanings *must*, necessarily, be like. Quine doesn't present his picture as an empirical claim, but it gains its force from empirical facts about the history of conceptual change in science, and Quine does clearly refer to those changes in justifying his view.

Over the past 400 years, as science has developed, the conceptual structures of the best scientific theories have become increasingly remote from our ordinary everyday conceptual structures. At the end of the eighteenth century Kant could still argue that the psychologically basic structures of our ordinary experience of the world were also ontologically basic. He could claim that our experience is necessarily the way it is because the world is necessarily that way (and vice versa). (Indeed, from our present historical perspective it might be said that Kant did not so much argue for this claim as systematically confuse and conflate psychological and ontological questions). In fact, of course, even Newtonian physics is already significantly counterintuitive. Still, it was far from absurd in Kant's time to think that the apparent limitations of our ordinary cognition would also always constrain scientific theorizing. The Kantian view dominated philosophy for the next 100 years.

But Kantian notions could not possibly survive the scientific revolutions of the early twentieth century: relativistic physics and quantum theory. All Kant's plausible candidates for inescapable constraints on the thoughts we could think—the separation of time and space and of matter and energy, for example—had to be abandoned. The unthinkable not only could be thought; it turned out actually to be true.

One fundamental argument we hope to have made in this book is that Quinean conceptual humility should be our reaction not only to the words and thoughts of the great, Einstein and his fellow physicists, but also to the words and thoughts of the small, Allison Bloom (Bloom, 1973) and her fellow 1-year-olds. Indeed, we have suggested that Allison Bloom and Einstein are two ends of a single continuum. The 1-year-old Allison was in the process of constructing a theory of the world around her, a theory whose fundamental constructs were in many respects as far removed from our ordinary view of the world as our ordinary view of the world is removed from Einstein's. Her early vocabulary reflected the fundamental tenets of that theory. "Allgone," "more," "uh-oh," and the rest are terms that are as theoretical as "energy" and "mass." As the theory changed, so her vocabulary changed. To characterize the meaning of her language, it is fundamentally necessary to characterize the changes in her theories.

In development we see the same kinds of phenomena brought about by radical conceptual change that we see in the history of science. As Quine suggests, apparently central aspects of our adult conception of the world are revisable. In fact, we already revised them when we were children. Moreover, these revisions often involve units at the level of a theory. We have argued that children, like scientists, may preserve a theory for some time by introducing ad hoc auxilliary hypotheses and that conceptual changes often have a "revolutionary" character, with one whole theory replacing another. The view of knowledge and language that emerges from the study of theory change in science is also the view that best characterizes young children's knowledge and language.

Another way of putting this is to point out that children's conceptual structures, like the conceptual structures of science, violate many of the most fundamental tenets of our adult theory of the world. Introspectively, it might seem that the central convictions of our adult theory of objects and people are in fact analytic or conceptual, and not the result of empirical experience. For example, to us, as adults, the fact that an invisibly displaced object will be somewhere along the trajectory of its container might seem like a necessary truth. But we have, we hope, shown that throughout infancy and childhood there are cases where children do not make predictions that seem self-evidently true to us adults. Indeed, children often make predictions that seem self-evidently false.

While Quine's picture has dominated views of the nature of meaning in philosophy, it has never been adopted, or even widely recognized, in contemporary cognitive science. On the contrary, many projects of contemporary cognitive science have sought some set of conceptual foundations. In empiricist camps the search has been for perceptual or sensory primitives and rules of combination. In more rationalist camps the search has been for a priori structures that sharply restrict the range of possible thoughts. Both views imply that there are indeed the equivalent of analytic sentences, sentences true simply by virtue of their meanings, that there are necessary and indefeasible conceptual structures. Within cognitive science there has been a revival of the Kantian views, shorn of their metaphysical implications.

But for this neo-Kantian view to work, there must be a sharp divide between the conceptual structures of science and those of ordinary cognition. Ordinary everyday cognition must be governed by fundamentally different mechanisms than scientific cognition. The arguments from development suggest, on the contrary, that the conceptual structure of much of ordinary cognition is simply a way station, a particular snapshot, of a fundamentally dynamic process of theory formation and revision.

In this sense, the theory theory is both a theory of cognitive development and a theory of cognition itself. On the theory view, everyday cognition ought to be considered the "starting state" theory for science, just as the infant's innate theories are the starting state for their later theories. Indeed, everyday cognition, on this view, is simply the theory that most of us most of the time have arrived at when we get too old and stupid to do more theorizing. Or, more optimistically, it is the theory we have arrived at when our period of protected immaturity, our cognitive Eden, has ended and we are forced to take on the serious adult evolutionary chores of feeding, fighting, and reproducing. We might think of our enterprise as scientists as the further revision of the theory by the fortunate, or possibly just childish, few who are given leisure to collect evidence and think about it.

If the conceptual structures of infancy and childhood, of ordinary cognition, and of science are largely continuous, as we have been suggesting in this book, then the psychological Kantianism of much cognitive science becomes less tenable. In fact, the project of finding a certain type of conceptual foundation, whether this is phrased in terms of constraints or in terms of primitives and combinatorial rules, becomes much less plausible. To put it another way, the pervasive failure of such projects in cognitive science becomes more comprehensible.

The literature on concepts in adult cognitive psychology is a good example of this. The project began with a variety of attempts to decompose concepts into primitives or features and combinatorial rules. The current state of the art suggests that the phenomena these accounts were intended to explain, category judgments, in particular, cannot be explained in this way. Rather, these judgments seem to reflect particular, coherent, revisable bodies of knowledge: theories (Murphy & Medin, 1985; Rips, 1989).

There is a reason, however, why Quine's view has not been adopted more widely in cognitive science. There has always been a sense that his view committed you to a kind of skeptical pessimism about the possibility of characterizing human cognition and cognitive change. This is further exacerbated by the fact that other philosophers, particularly Davidson (1980), hold a version of Quine's holism that really does have these skeptical, not to say mystical, implications. Moreover, historically, Quine's view has interacted with a more general skepticism about the possibility of characterizing scientific change in any systematic way. It is true that if there are no mechanisms for cognitive change in science, then Quine's point would hold. But the converse claim does not hold. At least it does not follow from the evidence that Quine presents that there is no mechanism for cognitive change in science.[1]

The conceptual structures that Quine points to, the ones revised in science and in childhood, are conceptual structures of a particular type: they involve substantive claims about the nature of objects, space, and so on. Quine does not provide evidence that basic patterns of scientific inference, and the assumptions about the world that underlie those patterns, have changed with changes in science. Even in relativistic and quantum physics, we still assume that there are consistent relations between theory and evidence, that there is an underlying order to our phenomena, that the future is like the past, that, in a paraphrase of Einstein, God is slick but not mean. If we are right, we also use these patterns of inference and make these assumptions in childhood.

We would again revert to our point about the underdetermination problem. We are not saying that every theory that is logically consistent with the data can be constructed by either scientists or children. There are constraints on the kinds of theories human minds will construct, given a particular pattern of input. We can think of these constraints as embodying implicit assumptions about the way that the world works. The truth of these assumptions is, in some way, guaranteed by evolution. The point is that the constraints we propose when we extend our view of cognition to include scientists and children are very different from those we propose when we simply consider the man in the street. Moreover, they are very different from those that constrain the kinds of perceptions or grammars we construct, given a particular pattern of input.

The combination of innate theories, restricted mechanisms of theory change, and relatively uniform patterns of evidence means that it is possible (though not easy) to characterize the typical succession of different theories in infancy and childhood. In the same way, despite qualitative conceptual change and defeasibility in science, it is possible (though not easy) to characterize the succession of different theories in the history of science.

The same conceptual flexibility that allows us to formulate new theories also allows us to formulate and characterize the qualitatively different theories we have held in the past, as we have attempted to do in this book. In doing so, we need to perform a special kind of meta-theorizing: we must construct theories of theories that are qualitatively different from our own. But again, if we are right about our general cognitive capacities, this task is no more difficult, if also no easier, than other types of scientific theorizing. In principle, we should be able to continue the project that we began in this book and that others have attempted before us. We should be able to chart the typical successive theory changes in children's (and adult's) understanding of the mind and the world.

A Developmental Cognitive Science

Embracing the theory theory, then, need not mean giving up cognitive science. However, the picture of cognition that emerges from the study of children does suggest a fundamental reorientation for cognitive science. One way of describing the hitherto usual projects of cognitive science is that they attempt to give a full account of the representations and rules that underlie our everyday knowledge of the world. (There is a possibly apocryphal story that one famous cognitive scientist proposed that this could be done by getting several platoons of undergraduates to write down everything they knew over two or three summers.) Or if this seems too ambitious a description, cognitive scientists at least propose that they are discovering the basic nature of the representational systems that underlie ordinary cognition. The proposals range from semantic primitives, to metaphors, to features, to constraints, to production systems. The aim of all these accounts is to describe how we get from the input of our sensory systems to the output of our beliefs and actions.

If we are correct, this project, however useful in some ways, is fundamentally misguided in others. At least a large part of our ordinary knowledge of the world has no particular privileged set of representations and rules. Rather, it is the product of a system of theory formation and revision that restructures the very nature of the representational system. This system alters the very relations between representations and input as it gets more input and constructs more representations. We see the system at work most dramatically in childhood and in our endeavors as scientists, but there is no reason to suppose that it is not equally responsible for much of our everyday cognition. On this view, the real explanatory action in cognitive science lies in trying to describe the dynamic mechanisms responsible for conceptual change, as much as in trying to describe our static conceptual structures.

We might draw an analogy to the shift in explanatory strategies in biology that came with Darwin. Before Darwin, the project of biology was to characterize the morphology of all living species. The fact that species changed over time was seen as a peripheral, and probably irremediably mysterious, problem. Darwin turned this picture on its head. Obviously, describing the morphology of existing species was still possible and important, but the explanation for the morphology comes from facts about species change. Moreover, the species extant at any moment are merely a fortuitous subset of all possible species. Similarly, the theory theory might turn explanation in cognitive science on its head. Conceptual change, rather than being a mysterious extra problem, appearing on the last page of textbooks along with consciousness and romantic love, would be a fundamental explanatory mechanism for important areas of cognition. The actual representational system we have at any given moment is only a fortuitous subset of the possible representational systems we could construct.

Also like Darwinian biology, the view we have presented here suggests that explanations in cognitive science will often be historical and contingent. If we want to say why we have a conceptual structure of a particular kind, we will typically not be able to reduce that structure to some set of first principles. Rather, we will need to trace the historical route that led from our innate theories to the theory we currently hold. On this view, all of cognitive science would be developmental.

Computational and Neurological Mechanisms

The last few paragraphs will seem attractive to those who embrace dynamic connectionist computational models of cognition, and dynamic models more generally (see similar arguments in Clark, 1993). We feel a certain attraction to such models ourselves because they hold the promise of the sort of dynamic reorganization that we think is typical of cognitive development. At the same time, however, there is no current computational system we know of, connectionist or serial, algorithmic or dynamic, that is capable of the kinds of reorganization that we see in theory change in development and in science. In particular, connectionist models tend to lack the kind of abstract structure that is characteristic of theories and gives them their predictive and explanatory force. Connectionism seems to fit more naturally with the view we described in terms of empirical generalizations: many connectionist systems seem restricted to a kind of sophisticated pattern matching between perceptual data and internal representations. In fact, many of those who advocate the connectionist view most strongly tend to see cognition as a large network of interacting particular pieces of information, rather than as a coherent lawlike system like a theory. It should be pointed out, however, that this problem is one that many connectionists are keenly conscious of, and a number of connectionists are currently trying to formulate more structured connectionist architectures. The theory theory implies a computational system that combines the capacity for learning and qualitative change of connectionism with the structure and systematicity of classical implementations. Developmental work in psychology might provide computationalists with an additional impetus to develop such systems.

The theory theory might also be related to a rather different line of research that comes out of more classical computational accounts of learning. There is a strong tradition of research that formally considers how systems can make reliable inferences about the world (Kelly, 1996; Osherson, Stob & Weinstein, 1986). In developmental psychology this approach has been almost exclusively applied to problems in syntax. It has been associated with a strongly nativist and modular approach to cognition, most notably in Pinker's (1989) neo-Kantian theory of language acquisition. But there is nothing about the general computational approach that automatically has these implications. The approach simply tries to formally specify what the relations are between particular kinds of evidence and particular kinds of inferences, given particular kinds of learning procedures.

In fact, these techniques have been extensively applied to problems of scientific inference, where a Kantian account is very unlikely to be correct. We have been arguing that the learning procedures of childhood are like the learning procedures of science. If it is possible to formally describe how certain kinds of learning procedures in science lead to reliable knowledge, then those formal descriptions are also likely to apply to cognitive development. To so apply them, however, we would have to be able to specify both the child's theories and the child's evidence with much more precision than we can muster at the moment. (Those who argue against the learnability approach to syntax would say that the same is true of language. Syntax lends itself more easily to formalization than cognition, but this formalization may lead to misleading idealizations of both the input and the resulting linguistic structures.)

Similar remarks apply to the neurological instantiation of the theory theory. Just as modularity theories have adopted evolution and learnability, so they have adopted neuroscience, as if modular systems were intrinsically more suited to the brain than other representational systems. But neither evolution nor neural structure implies modularity. In fact, current neuroscience increasingly emphasizes the plasticity of neural structure and its close relation to experience. In some sense, of course, this has long been the case: we have known about the effects of experience on the brain at least since the 1950s. It is a simple calculation that a few genes could not determine billions of possible neural connections. But recent research has moved even more in the direction of seeing the brain as a dynamic, flexible system, rather than as a set of fixed representational mechanisms. (For one thing, we are now looking at live brains instead of dead ones, and living things in general tend to look more dynamic than dead ones.) As a matter of fact, the brain seems rather well suited to instantiate theories and theory change. This is not too surprising, since, so far as we know, it is the only thing in the world that does.

We hope that in the future, computational and neurological work will suggest how theories and theory change are instantiated in human brains. From our perspective, however, the arguments for the theory theory should be largely independent of such instantiations. Far too often in the past psychologists have been willing to abandon their own autonomous theorizing because of some infatuation with the current account of computation and neurology. We wake up one morning and discover that the account that looked so promising and scientific—S-R connections, Gestaltian field theory, Hebbian cell assemblies—has vanished and we have spent another couple of decades in vain trying to accommodate our psychological theories to it. We think that we should summon our self-esteem and be more standoffish in the future. Any implementations of psychological theories, either computational or neurological, will first depend on properly psychological accounts of psychological phenomena.

After Piaget

The most important benefits of the theory theory lie in its ability to help explain the psychological phenomena of cognitive development. We can return to the debate between Socrates and Piaget that we started with. As we have made clear in this book, the theory that we and others have advanced is, in almost all its details, completely unlike Piaget's theory. Our empirical claims are almost always quite different from Piaget's in important ways. Our theoretical claims as well are quite different from those of Piaget. The theory theory, as we are advancing it here, proposes that there is elaborate, rich, representational structure from birth. We also propose that there are more powerful mechanisms of theory change initially in place than Piaget originally supposed. Our theory does not predict domain-general logical stage changes of the sort that Piaget proposed. Rather, it holds that the child accumulates theories of particular domains and the structure of those theories allows inferences in those domains. Unlike Piaget, we do not propose that action is the central motor in cognitive development. Finally, we propose a rich and powerful causal role for linguistic input. We propose that language change may often lead to conceptual change rather than vice versa. In all these respects, our theory is very different from, indeed, stands in opposition to, Piaget's.

Nevertheless, in a broader sense we and other theory theorists are staking out the same conceptual territory as Piaget. It is probably no coincidence that many of those working in this area come out of a broadly Piagetian tradition and see themselves as Piaget's inheritors. We want to provide an account that is both genuinely cognitive and genuinely developmental. The collapse of Piagetian theory has, we think, left many developmentalists in an uneasy state of conflict between the realities they see in their empirical work and the theoretical positions on offer. The "miracle baby" research of the last 25 years has made the initial resources of infants seem ever more impressive. At the same time, the empiricist projects of, say, traditional behaviorism have seemed ever more bankrupt. Nonetheless, we suspect that most scientists who actually spend their days watching babies and children change are reluctant to accept a full-blooded modular account. Even Spelke et al. (1992), for example, point out that some developmental story must be responsible for infants' learning such highly abstract yet fundamental physical notions as the effects of gravity and inertia. Anyone who has conducted a longitudinal study is bound to be struck by the changes in infants' and children's cognition over time. Anyone who has watched infants and children engaged with the world—testing, experimenting, and exploring—is bound to suspect that these changes are more than just maturational.

The theory theory is, however, more than just a compromise between rationalist and empiricist views. It is a specific position with specific proposals. In particular, our claim that there are innate theories and that infants have innate capacities for theory change is in many ways as powerfully nativist a position as one could have. For us, unlike Piaget, for example, the empiricist side of the theory does not consist of denying or minimizing innate structure. The empiricism we propose is an empiricism of revision rather than reduction, and in this sense it echoes the empiricism of contemporary philosophy of science. What theory theorists are trying to do is to outline the causal relations among existing abstract conceptual structures, input from the outside world, and new abstract conceptual structures. This is not an easy problem, and developmental psychologists have only made a start on it in the last several years. But at least it is a much easier problem than that of trying to reduce abstract conceptual structures to sensory input—the classical problem of empiricists. Postulating innate theories gives us a kind of jump start on the empiricist project.

At the same time, the defeasibility of theories gives us a genuinely conceptual mechanism for development, not merely an accumulation of exogenous developmental facts, like maturation or performance constraints. Rather than explaining away conceptual change, the theory theory gives us a way of talking about conceptual change in a reasonably constrained way. We can even begin to make predictions about the causes and consequences of such change in childhood and in science. It also gives us a way of describing representational systems that are genuinely engaged with the external world. We are still in the process of understanding and specifying those systems more precisely, but the general framework already allows us to make progress in explaining many empirical phenomena in cognitive development.

Sailing in Neurath's Boat

Finally, there is another respect in which we might continue the comparison to Darwin. Part of Darwin's accomplishment was to bring what had seemed rather peripheral, if not despised, sources of information to bear in biological explanation. Certainly in philosophy and largely in adult cognitive science, children have seemed as unlikely a source of central insights as beekeepers, pigeon fanciers, and cottage gardeners seemed to the natural philosophers of Darwin's day. There are thousands of philosophical books about scientists and machines; there are almost none about children.[2] Another part of our aim in this book has been to try to remedy this situation. We want to show why the empirical study of infants and children can offer important solutions to philosophical questions.

Cognitive science is a discipline devoted to answering philosophical questions by naturalistic methods. Socrates' other method, the method of developmental psychology, is one of the most significant and revealing of all. Socrates' question and Augustine's and Piaget's are ultimately scientific questions. We can only uncover children's cognitive structures, and so our own, by a painstaking and painful process of theory formation, experimentation, and revision. These are not questions that can be answered from the armchair, or even the Attic couch.

In this sense, developmental psychologists ought to feel a profound kinship with the children they study, more even than other scientists. We share their mad ransacking of the experimental cupboards, their miserable frowns of puzzlement, their triumphant delight in solutions. We sail in Neurath's boat alongside our subjects, and while it is often a messy, damp, and difficult journey, we could not ask for better company.

Notes

3 Theories, Modules, and Empirical Generalizations

1. It is worth noting that the term "module" is used in quite a different way in cognitive neuroscience, where it seems to mean something like "functional unit." These modules really have nothing in common with modularity in developmental psychology except the word. For example, they include units like "written-letter/ phoneme conversion" that are obviously not intended to be innate. It is also worth noting that some developmentalists have proposed softened versions of modularity and constraints (e.g., Baron-Cohen, 1995; Karmiloff-Smith, 1992; Markman, 1992) in which the idea of indefeasible representations is replaced by much weaker notions such as default assumptions or biases. The trouble is that such softenings make it difficult to see what the claim of modularity or constraint amounts to. In particular, such soft structures and biases might be predicted by almost any account of cognitive development. Soft "modules" or "constraints" may be a convenient way of capturing the fact that our knowledge is roughly divided into pieces or the fact that our previous knowledge affects our interpretations of current input. When these "modules" or "constraints" are specified in detail, they are also often really useful for describing certain developmental phenomena. But the claims must be stronger if they are to constitute an explanatory account of the origins of knowledge.

2. It is interesting to consider whether *all* the static and functional features of theories can also be found in modules. In particular, it seems difficult to see an equivalent of explanation, ontological committment, and counterfactual support in modules. Unfortunately, however, these are also features of theories that may be particularly difficult to test for empirically.

3. Fodor, of course, thinks that the concepts of central knowledge are also innate, but he thinks that these include fundamental concepts of science—quarks and quanta—no less than concepts of common objects and ordinary mental states (Fodor, 1975, 1981). From our perspective, Fodor's arguments for the innateness of central representations, as well as peripheral modular ones, are really a reductio ad absurdum of a certain kind of theory about theory formation. If the type of learning Fodor describes is the only type on offer, then all concepts—including those of quarks, typewriters, and jaguars—will have to be innate. But to us, this simply demonstrates that this type of learning is not the only type of learning involved in science (an idea that has much independent support). If this is not the type of learning involved in

science, then some other type of learning must be involved in science. If there is such an alternative type of learning, it too may be responsible for cognitive development in children.

Interestingly, one interpretation of Fodor's views on the innateness of concepts might simply be that the relations between inputs and central conceptual representations are causal but not algorithmic (see, for example, his discussion of Mill's "mental chemistry" [Fodor, 1981]). Fodor's argument is that there is no syntactic procedure we know of that can get to abstract concepts like those of jaguars and quarks by combining or rearranging the representations of input; there is no algorithm to get from evidential concepts to theoretical ones. There might, however, be nonalgorithmic causal processes that could lead from inputs to abstract theoretical representations.

On this interpretation, Fodor's apparently radical nativist view might indeed be quite compatible with our version of the theory theory, surprising though it seems. We are agnostic about whether the relations between inputs and theoretical representations are algorithmic or not. There are no plausible algorithms on offer, but then there are also no proofs that such algorithms are impossible. If there are no such algorithms, then our view and Fodor's view will be quite similar. But in a sense, this question is beside the present point about modularity. On both Fodor's view and ours, there is an important distinction to be made between peripheral modules and central-belief processes.

4. It is interesting to note that both Bowerman and Karmiloff-Smith support these claims by pointing to developmental phenomena in syntax that are not explicable on standard modularity views. They both, for example, point to U-shaped curves, cases where correct predictions are followed by incorrect predictions, which are then replaced by correct predictions. These cases are notoriously problematic for modularity accounts. Even in the case of syntax, the developmental phenomena sometimes force us to supplement modularity accounts with something more like a theorizing account, particularly later in development.

5. Note, for example, the difference in emphasis and approach between Perner's (1991) account of theory-of-mind development, which hinges on the development of metarepresentation, and Wellman's (1990), which hinges on the particular causal and explanatory structure of the child's theory.

II Evidence for the Theory Theory

1. A last and probably equally important area of language and cognition in late infancy is the child's understanding of spatial relationships, particularly, containment, support, and attachment. However, we won't discuss this domain in this book, partly because we don't have the space but mostly because we don't (yet) have the data. This is an important domain that has not been fully investigated. We're working on it.

4 The Child's Theory of Appearances

1. It is extremely interesting that human beings seem so drawn to just such thought experiments not only in the science-fiction examples we will use but also in myth,

magic, and fantasy of all sorts (notice that this fascination is particularly intense in children and is one we associate with them). We suggest that this fascination is a natural consequence of being theory-forming animals. Imagining and generating alternative conceptual schemes is an intrinsic part of theorizing, and we may like doing it even when it is divorced from its cognitive truth-discovering function, just as cats play at hunting.

6 The Child's Theory of Kinds

1. Both Rosch and Putnam were particularly concerned with one particular type of object category: categories of natural objects like birds, lemons, or trees. Many common names apply to objects of this kind in this way. Of course, there are also categories that really *are* defined by a set of properties in the classical way, for example, the category of even numbers or round, red things. Moreover, some functional and conventional categories, for example, categories of certain artifacts, such as tea-kettles or carburetors, also seem to have a rather different structure than the natural-kind categories. Putnam's and Rosch's intuitions don't apply to them in quite the same way.

7 Language and Thought

1. Quine is ritually cited at the beginning of practically every "constraints" paper. He must hold the record for philosophers. This is rather ironic, however, because, as we will see, the whole point of Quine's work was quite explicitly to reject this obvious Kantian solution. Quine thought the problem was interesting just because the Kantian solution had been shown to be untenable.

2. In the case of categorizing, the naming spurt was consistently recorded either at the same time or just after the appearance of exhaustive categorizing. However, this may reflect a measurement problem: our criterion for the spurt was that the child had acquired ten new names, a criterion that by definition will only be fulfilled sometime after the spurt itself has begun. If we shift our criterion slightly and plausibly and credit the child with a naming spurt in the session before the first session in which ten new names were recorded, the pattern of development is almost identical to that in the other two domains.

3. The relation between object permanence and the spurt is more complex. In one longitudinal study (Gopnik & Meltzoff, 1987) we found a weak relation between these domains. In our cross-sectional studies we did not find a relation between the two developments. By any measure, the relation, if it existed at all, was much weaker than the relation between categorizing and naming.

8 The Darwinian Conclusion

1. Quine's own view is not completely clear on this. Quine did articulate this kind of skepticism elsewhere (Quine, 1960). But he also combined the sensible denial of the analytic/synthetic distinction with a thoroughgoing behaviorism, and it was his

behaviorism that led to his skeptical arguments. We think our view is much like the view Quine would have had if he had hung out with Jean Piaget and Irv Rock instead of Fred Skinner. But, despite some philosophical background, we do not make claims to expertise in great-man exegesis, particularly counterfactual great-man exegesis.

2. It is difficult not to suspect that the prevailing gender of philosophers throughout history has had something to do with this.

References

Aaron, F., Hartshorn, K., Klein, P. J., Ghumman, M., and Rovee-Collier, C. (1994). Developmental changes in the specificity of memory retrieval. Paper presented at the meeting of the International Society for Developmental Psychobiology, Islamorada, Fla., November.

Amabile, T. A., and Rovee-Collier, C. (1991). Contextual variation and memory retrieval at six months. *Child Development* 62 : 1155–1166.

Astington, J. W., and Gopnik, A. (1991). Developing understanding of desire and intention. In A. Whiten (ed.), *Natural theories of mind: evolution, development and simulation of everyday mindreading* (pp. 39–50). Cambridge, Mass.: Basil Blackwell.

Astington, J. W., Harris, P. L., and Olson, D. R. (1988). *Developing theories of mind.* New York: Cambridge University Press.

Atran, S. (1990). *Cognitive foundations of natural history: towards an anthropology of science.* New York: Cambridge University Press.

Au, T. K., Dapretto, M., and Song, Y. K. (1994). Input vs. constraints: early word acquisition in Korean and English. *Journal of Memory and Language* 33 : 567–582.

Bahrick, L. E. (1983). Infants' perception of substance and temporal synchrony in multimodal events. *Infant Behavior and Development* 6 : 429–451.

Bai, D. L., and Bertenthal, B. I. (1992). Locomotor status and the development of spatial search skills. *Child Development* 63 : 215–226.

Baillargeon, R. (1986). Representing the existence and the location of hidden objects: object permanence in 6- and 8-month-old infants. *Cognition* 23 : 21–41.

Baillargeon, R. (1987a). Object permanence in $3\frac{1}{2}$- and $4\frac{1}{2}$-month-old infants. *Developmental Psychology* 23 : 655–664.

Baillargeon, R. (1987b). Young infants' reasoning about the physical and spatial properties of a hidden object. *Cognitive Development* 2 : 179–200.

Baillargeon, R. (1991). Reasoning about the height and location of a hidden object in 4.5- and 6.5-month-old infants. *Cognition* 38 : 13–42.

Baillargeon, R. (1993). The object concept revisited: new directions in the investigation of infants' physical knowledge. In C. Granrud (ed.), *Visual perception and cognition in infancy* (pp. 265–315). Hillsdale, N.J.: Erlbaum.

Baillargeon, R., and DeVos, J. (1991). Object permanence in young infants: further evidence. *Child Development* 62 : 1227–1246.

Baillargeon, R., and Graber, M. (1987). Where's the rabbit? 5.5-month-old infants' representation of the height of a hidden object. *Cognitive Development* 2 : 375–392.

Baillargeon, R., Spelke, E. S., and Wasserman, S. (1985). Object permanence in five-month-old infants. *Cognition* 20 : 191–208.

Baldwin, D., and Markman, E. (1989). Establishing word-object relations: a first step. *Child Development* 60 : 381–398.

Baldwin, D. A., Markman, E. M., and Melartin, R. L. (1993). Infants' ability to draw inferences about nonobvious object properties: evidence from exploratory play. *Child Development* 64 : 711–728.

Baldwin, D. A., and Moses, L. J. (1994). Early understanding of referential intent and attentional focus: evidence from language and emotion. In C. Lewis and P. Mitchell (eds.), *Children's early understanding of mind: origins and development* (pp. 133–156). Hillsdale, N.J.: Erlbaum.

Barkow, J., Cosmides, L., and Tooby, J. (eds.) (1992). *The adapted mind: evolutionary psychology and the generation of culture*. New York: Oxford University Press.

Barnat, S. B., Klein, P. J., and Meltzoff, A. N. (1996). Deferred imitation across changes in context and object: memory and generalization in 14-month-old infants. *Infant Behavior and Development* 19 : 243–253.

Baron-Cohen, S. (1995). *Mindblindness: an essay on autism and theory of mind*. Cambridge: MIT Press.

Bartsch, K., and Wellman, H. M. (1995). *Children talk about the mind*. New York: Oxford University Press.

Bates, E., Benigni, L., Bretherton, I., Camaioni, L., and Volterra, V. (1979). *The emergence of symbols: cognition-communication in infancy*. New York: Academic Press.

Bates, E., and Elman, J. L. (1993). Connectionism and the study of change. In M. J. Johnson (ed.), *Brain development and cognition: a reader*. Oxford: Blackwell.

Baumberger, T. (1995). Word, gesture, and concept: relations between maternal language and pointing and 18-months-old's categorization. Paper presented at the Society for Research in Child Development, Indianaopolis, Ind.

Bennett, P., and Harvey, P. (1985). Brain size, development, and metabolism in birds and mammals. *Journal of Zoology* 207 : 491–509.

Berman, R., and Slobin, D. (1994). *Relating events in narrative: a crosslinguistic developmental study*. Hillsdale, N.J.: Erlbaum.

Bertenthal, B. I., Campos, J. J., and Kermoian, R. (1994). An epigenetic perspective on the development of self-produced locomotion and its consequences. *Current Directions in Psychological Science* 3 : 140–145.

Bickerton, D. (1981). *The roots of language*. Ann Arbor: Karoma.

Block, N. (1986). Advertisement for a semantics for psychology. In P. French, T. Uehling, and H. Wettstein (eds.), *Studies in the philosophy of mind*, Midwest Studies in Philosophy (no. 10, pp. 615–678). Minneapolis: University of Minnesota Press.

Bloom, L. (1973). *One word at a time: the use of single word utterances before syntax.* The Hague: Mouton.

Bloom, L. (1993). *The transition from infancy to language: acquiring the power of expression.* New York: Cambridge University Press.

Bloom, L., Lifter, K., and Broughton, J. (1985). The convergence of early cognition and language in the second year of life: problems in conceptualization and measurement. In M. D. Barrett (ed.), *Children's single-word speech* (pp. 149–181). New York: Wiley.

Bornstein, M. H. (1981). Two kinds of perceptual organization near the beginning of life. In W. A. Collins (ed.), *Aspects of the development of competence,* The Minnesota Symposia on Child Psychology (no. 14, pp. 39–92). Hillsdale, N.J.: Lawrence Erlbaum.

Bornstein, M. H., Kessen, W., and Weiskopf, S. (1976). The categories of hue in infancy. *Science* 191 : 201–202.

Borovsky, D., and Rovee-Collier, C. (1990). Contextual constraints on memory retrieval at six months. *Child Development* 61 : 1569–1583.

Bower, T. G. R. (1965). The determinants of perceptual unity in infancy. *Psychonomic Science* 3 : 323–324.

Bower, T. G. R. (1982). *Development in infancy* (2nd ed.). San Francisco: W. H. Freeman.

Bower, T. G. R. (1989). *The rational infant: learning in infancy.* San Francisco: W. H. Freeman.

Bower, T. G. R., Broughton, J. M., and Moore, M. K. (1970). Demonstration of intention in the reaching behaviour of neonate humans. *Nature* 228 : 679–681.

Bower, T. G. R., Broughton, J. M., and Moore, M. K. (1971). Development of the object concept as manifested in changes in the tracking behavior of infants between 7 and 20 weeks of age. *Journal of Experimental Child Psychology* 11 : 182–193.

Bower, T. G. R., and Wishart, J. G. (1972). The effects of motor skill on object permanence. *Cognition* 1 : 165–172.

Bowerman, M. (1978). The acquisition of word meaning: an investigation into some current conflicts. In N. Waterson and C. Snow (eds.), *The development of communication* (pp. 263–287). Chichester: Wiley.

Bowerman, M. (1980). The structure and origin of semantic categories in the language-learning child. In M. L. Foster and S. H. Brandes (eds.), *Symbol as sense: new approaches to the analysis of meaning* (pp. 277–299). New York: Academic Press.

Bowerman, M. (1982). Reorganization processes in lexical and syntactic development. In E. Wanner and L. R. Gleitman (eds.), *Language acquisition: the state of the art.* Cambridge: Cambridge University Press.

Bowerman, M. (1989). Learning a semantic system: what role do cognitive predispositions play? In M. Rice and R. L. Schiefelbusch (eds.), *The teachability of language* (pp. 133–169). Baltimore: Paul Brookes Publishing Co.

Boyer, P. (1994). Cognitive constraints on cultural representations: natural ontologies and religious ideas. In L. A. Hrischfeld and S. A. Gelman (eds.), *Mapping the mind: domain specificity in cognition and culture* (pp. 391–411). New York: Cambridge University Press.

Brazelton, T. B., and Tronick, E. (1980). Preverbal communication between mothers and infants. In D. R. Olson (ed.), *The social foundations of language and thought* (pp. 299–315). New York: Norton.

Bremner, J. G. (1978). Egocentric versus allocentric coding in nine-month-old infants: factors influencing the choice of code. *Development Psychology* 14 : 346–355.

Bruner, J. S. (1974). Nature and uses of immaturity. In K. J. Connelly and J. S. Bruner (eds.), *The growth of competence* (pp. 11–48). New York: Academic Press.

Bruner, J. S. (1975). From communication to language—a psychological perspective. *Cognition* 3 : 255–287.

Bruner, J. S. (1983). *Child's talk: learning to use language*. New York: Norton.

Bruner, J. S. (1990). *Acts of meaning*. Cambridge: Harvard University Press.

Bryant, P. E., Jones, P., Claxton, V., and Perkins, G. M. (1972). Recognition of shapes across modalities by infants. *Nature* 240 : 303–304.

Bullock, M., and Gelman, R. (1979). Preschool children's assumptions about cause and effect: temporal ordering. *Child Development* 50 : 89–96.

Butterworth, G. (1977). Object disappearance and error in Piaget's stage IV task. *Journal of Experimental Child Psychology* 23 : 391–401.

Butterworth, G. (1991). The ontogeny and phylogeny of joint visual attention. In A. Whiten (ed.), *Natural theories of mind: evolution, development and simulation of everyday mindreading* (pp. 223–232). Cambridge, Mass.: Basil Blackwell.

Butterworth, G., and Hopkins, B. (1988). Hand-mouth coordination in the newborn baby. *British Journal of Developmental Psychology* 6 : 303–314.

Butterworth, G., and Jarrett, N. (1982). Piaget's stage 4 error: background to the problem. *British Journal of Psychology* 73 : 175–185.

Callanan, M. (1985). How parents label objects for young children: the role of input in the acquisition of category hierarchies. *Child Development* 56 : 508–523.

Campos, J. J., and Stenberg, C. R. (1981). Perception, appraisal, and emotion: the onset of social referencing. In M. E. Lamb and L. R. Sherrod (eds.), *Infant social cognition: empirical and theoretical considerations* (pp. 273–314). Hillsdale, N.J.: Erlbaum.

Carey, S. (1985). *Conceptual change in childhood*. Cambridge: MIT Press.

Carey, S. (1988). Conceptual differences between children and adults. *Mind and Language* 3 : 167–181.

Caron, A. J., Caron, R. F., and Antell, S. E. (1988). Infant understanding of containment: an affordance perceived or a relationship conceived? *Developmental Psychology* 24 (5) : 620–627.

Caron, A. J., Caron, R. F., and Carlson, V. R. (1979). Infant perception of the invariant shape of objects varying in slant. *Child Development* 50 : 716–721.

Cartwright, N. (1989). *Nature's capacities and their measurement.* New York: Oxford University Press.

Case, R. (1985). *Intellectual development: birth to adulthood.* Orlando: Academic Press.

Chi, M. T. H., Glaser, R., and Rees, E. (1982). Expertise in problem solving. In R. J. Sternberg (ed.), *Advances in the psychology of human intelligence* (pp. 7–75). Hillsdale, N.J.: Erlbaum.

Choi, S. (1986). A pragmatic analysis of sentence ending morphemes in Korean children. Paper presented at the the the meeting of the Linguistic Society of America, New York, December.

Choi, S. (1991). Early aquisition of epistemic meanings in Korean: a study of sentence-ending suffixes in the spontaneous speech of three children. *First Language* 11 : 93–119.

Choi, S., and Bowerman, M. (1991). Learning to express motion events in English and Korean: the influence of language-specific lexicalization patterns. *Cognition* 41 : 83–121.

Choi, S., and Gopnik, A. (1995). Early acquisition of verbs in Korean: a cross-linguistic study. *Journal of Child Language.*

Chomsky, N. (1980). *Rules and representations.* New York: Columbia University Press.

Chomsky, N. (1986). *Knowledge of language: its nature, origins, and use.* New York: Praeger.

Chomsky, N. (1992). Language and interpretation: philosophical reflections and empirical inquiry. In J. Earman (ed.), *Inference, explanation, and other frustrations.* Berkeley: University of California Press.

Churchland, P. M. (1984). *Matter and consciousness: a contemporary introduction to the philosophy of mind.* Cambridge: MIT Press.

Clancy, P. (1985). The acquisition of Japanese. In D. Slobin (ed.), *The cross-linguistic study of language acquisition.* Hillsdale, N.J.: Erlbaum.

Clark, A. (1993). *Associative engines: connectionism, concepts, and representational change.* Cambridge: MIT Press.

Clark, E. V. (1974). Some aspects of the conceptual basis for first language acquisition. In R. L. Schiefelbusch and L. L. Lloyd (eds.), *Language perspectives—acquisition, retardation, and intervention* (pp. 105–128). Baltimore: University Park Press.

Clark, E. V. (1987). The principle of contrast: a constraint on language acquisition. In B. MacWhinney (ed.), *Mechanisms of language acquisition* (pp. 1–33). Hillsdale, N.J.: Erlbaum.

Clifton, R. K., Rochat, P., Litovsky, R. Y., and Perris, E. E. (1991). Object representation guides infants' reaching in the dark. *Journal of Experimental Psychology: Human Perception and Performance* 17 : 323–329.

Cohen, L. B. (1995). How solid is infants' understanding of solidity? Paper presented at the meeting of the Society for Research in Child Development, Indianapolis, Ind., March.

Cohen, L. B., Gelber, E. R., and Lazar, M. A. (1971). Infant habituation and generalization to differing degrees of stimulus novelty. *Journal of Experimental Child Psychology* 11 : 379–389.

Cohen, L. B., and Strauss, M. S. (1979). Concept acquisition in the human infant. *Child Development* 50 : 419–424.

Corrigan, R. (1978). Language development as related to stage 6 object permanence development. *Journal of Child Language* 5 : 173–189.

Davidson, D. (1980). *Essays on action and events.* New York: Oxford University Press.

De Boysson-Bardies, B., de Schonen, S., Jusczyk, P., McNeilage, P., and Morton, J. (1993). *Developmental neurocognition: speech and face processing in the first year of life.* Dordrecht, Netherlands: Kluwer Academic Publishers.

DeValois, R. L., and DeValois, K. K. (1988). *Spatial vision.* New York: Oxford University Press.

Diamond, A. (1985). Development of the ability to use recall to guide action, as indicated by infants' performance on $A\overline{B}$. *Child Development* 56 : 868–883.

Diamond, A. (1990). *The development and neural bases of higher cognitive functions.* Annals of the New York Academy of Sciences, no. 608. New York: New York Academy of Sciences.

Donaldson, M. (1978). *Children's minds.* New York: W. W. Norton and Co.

Ekman, P., Levenson, R. W., and Friesen, W. V. (1983). Autonomic nervous system activity distinguishes among emotions. *Science* 221 : 1208–1210.

Fagan, J. F., III (1976). Infants' recognition of invariant features of faces. *Child Development* 47 : 627–638.

Fenson, L., Dale, P. S., Reznick, J. S., Bates, E., Thal, D., and Pethick, S. J. (1994). *Variability in early communicative development.* Monographs of the Society for Research in Child Development, vol. 59, no. 5. Chicago: Society for Research in Child Development.

Fernald, A., and Morikawa, H. (1991). How mothers talk about objects in Japanese and English. Unpublished manuscript.

Fernald, A., and Morikawa, H. (1993). Common themes and cultural variations in Japanese and American mothers' speech to infants. *Child Development* 64 : 637–656.

Feyerabend, P. K. (1975). *Against method.* New York: Verso.

Fischer, K. W. (1980). A theory of cognitive development: the control and construction of hierarchies of skills. *Psychological Review* 87 : 477–531.

Fischer, K. W., and Corrigan, R. (1981). A skill approach to language development. In R. E. Stark (ed.), *Language behavior in infancy and early childhood* (pp. 245–273). Elsevier: North Holland.

Flavell, J. (1982). On cognitive development. *Child Development* 53 : 1–10.

Flavell, J. H., Everett, B. A., Croft, K., and Flavell, E. R. (1981). Young children's knowledge about visual perception: further evidence for the Level 1–Level 2 distinction. *Developmental Psychology* 17 : 99–103.

Flavell, J. H., Green, F. L., and Flavell, E. R. (1995). *Young children's knowledge about thinking.* Monographs of the Society for Research in Child Development, vol. 60, no. 1. Chicago: Society for Research in Child Development.

Fodor, J. A. (1975). *The language of thought.* New York: Thomas Y. Crowell.

Fodor, J. A. (1981). *Representations: philosophical essays of the foundations of cognitive science.* Cambridge: MIT Press.

Fodor, J. A. (1983). *Modularity of mind: an essay on faculty psychology.* Cambridge: MIT Press.

Fodor, J. A. (1992). A theory of the child's theory of mind. *Cognition* 44 : 283–296.

Gallistel, C. R. (1990). *The organization of learning.* Cambridge: MIT Press.

Gelman, S. A., and Coley, J. D. (1990). The importance of knowing a dodo is a bird: categories and inferences in 2-year-old children. *Developmental Psychology* 26 : 796–804.

Gelman, S. A., and Markman, E. (1986). Categories and induction in young children. *Cognition* 23 : 183–209.

Gelman, S. A., and Wellman, H. M. (1991). Insides and essence: early understandings of the non-obvious. *Cognition* 38 : 213–244.

Gentner, D. (1982). Why nouns are learned before verbs: linguistic relativity versus natural partitioning. In S. A. Kuczaj (ed.), *Language development,* vol. 2, *Language, thought, and culture* (pp. 301–304). Hillsdale, N.J.: Erlbaum.

Gergely, G., Csibra, G., Bíró, S., and Koós, O. (1994). The comprehension of intentional action in infancy. Paper presented at the meeting of the International Conference on Infant Studies, Paris, June.

Gergely, G., Nádasdy, Z., Csibra, G., and Bíró, S. (1995). Taking intentional stance at 12 months of age. *Cognition* 56 : 165–193.

Giere, R. N. (ed.) (1992). *Cognitive models of science.* Minneapolis: University of Minnesota.

Glymour, C. (1980). *Theory and evidence.* Princeton: Princeton University Press.

Glymour, C., Scheines, R., Spirtes, P., and Kelly, K. (1987). *Discovering causal structure: artificial intelligence, philosophy of science, and statistical modeling.* New York: Academic Press.

Goldfield, B. A. (1986). Referential and expressive language: a study of two mother-child dyads. *First Language* 6 : 119–131.

Goldfield, B. A., and Reznick, J. S. (1990). Early lexical acquisition: rate, content, and the vocabulary spurt. *Journal of Child Language* 17 : 171–183.

Goldman, A. (1986). *Epistemology and cognition.* Cambridge: Harvard University Press.

Golinkoff, R., Mervis, C. B., and Hirsch-Pasek, K. (1994). Early object labels: the case for a developmental lexical principles framework. *Journal of Child Language* 21 : 125–155.

Gopnik, A. (1980). The development of non-nominal expressions in 12–24 month old children. Unpublished doctoral dissertation, Oxford University, Oxford, England.

Gopnik, A. (1982). Words and plans: early language and the development of intelligent action. *Journal of Child Language* 9 : 303–318.

Gopnik, A. (1984a). The acquisition of *gone* and the development of the object concept. *Journal of Child Language* 11 : 273–292.

Gopnik, A. (1984b). Conceptual and semantic change in scientists and children: why there are no semantic universals. *Linguistics* 20 : 163–179.

Gopnik, A. (1988a). Conceptual and semantic development as theory change: the case of object permanence. *Mind and Language* 3 : 197–216.

Gopnik, A. (1988b). Three types of early words: the emergence of social words, names, and cognitive-relational words in the one-word stage and their relation to cognitive development. *First Language* 8 : 49–69.

Gopnik, A. (1993a). How we know our minds: the illusion of first-person knowledge of intentionality. *Behavioral and Brain Sciences* 16 : 1–14.

Gopnik, A. (1993b). The psychopsychology of the fringe. *Consciousness and Cognition: An International Journal* 2 : 109–113.

Gopnik, A., and Astington, J. W. (1988). Children's understanding of representational change and its relation to the understanding of false belief and appearance-reality distinction. *Child Development* 59 : 26–37.

Gopnik, A., and Choi, S. (1990). Do linguistic differences lead to cognitive differences? A cross-linguistic study of semantic and cognitive development. *First Language* 10 : 199–215.

Gopnik, A., and Choi, S. (1995). Names, relational words, and cognitive development in English and Korean speakers: nouns not always learned before verbs. In M. Tomasello and W. E. Merriman (eds.), *Beyond names for things: young children's acquisition of verbs.* Hillsdale, N.J.: Erlbaum.

Gopnik, A., Choi, S., and Baumberger, T. (1996). Cross-linguistic differences in early semantic and cognitive development. *Cognitive Development* 11, no. 2: 197–227.

Gopnik, A., and Meltzoff, A. N. (1984). Semantic and cognitive development in 15- to 21-month-old children. *Journal of Child Language* 11 : 495–513.

Gopnik, A., and Meltzoff, A. N. (1986a). Relations between semantic and cognitive development in the one-word stage: the specificity hypothesis. *Child Development* 57 : 1040–1053.

Gopnik, A., and Meltzoff, A. N. (1986b). Words, plans, things, and locations: interactions between semantic and cognitive development in the one-word stage. In S. A.

Kuczaj and M. D. Barrett (eds.), *The development of word meaning: progress in cognitive development research* (pp. 199–223). New York: Springer-Verlag.

Gopnik, A., and Meltzoff, A. N. (1987). The development of categorization in the second year and its relation to other cognitive and linguistic developments. *Child Development* 58 : 1523–1531.

Gopnik, A., and Meltzoff, A. N. (1992). Categorization and naming: basic-level sorting in eighteen-month-olds and its relation to language. *Child Development* 63 : 1091–1103.

Gopnik, A., and Meltzoff, A. N. (1993). Words and thoughts in infancy. In L. P. Lipsitt and C. K. Rovee-Collier (eds.), *Advances in infancy research* (vol. 8, pp. 217–249). Norwood, N.J.: Ablex.

Gopnik, A., and Meltzoff, A. N. (1994). Minds, bodies, and persons: young children's understanding of the self and others as reflected in imitation and theory of mind research. In S. T. Parker, R. W. Mitchell, and M. L. Boccia (eds.), *Self-awareness in animals and humans* (pp. 166–186). New York: Cambridge University Press.

Gopnik, A., Meltzoff, A. N., Esterly, J., and Rubenstein, J. (1995). Young children's understanding of visual perspective-taking. Paper presented at the First Annual Theory of Mind Conference, Eugene, Oregon, February.

Gopnik, A., and Slaughter, V. (1991). Young childrens' understanding of changes in their mental states. *Child Development* 62 : 98–110.

Gopnik, A., Slaughter, V., and Meltzoff, A. (1994). Changing your views: how understanding visual perception can lead to a new theory of the mind. In C. Lewis and P. Mitchell (eds.), *Children's early understanding of mind: origins and development* (pp. 157–181). Hillsdale, N.J.: Erlbaum.

Gopnik, A., and Wellman, H. M. (1992). Why the child's theory of mind really is a theory. *Mind and Language* 7 : 145–171.

Gopnik, A., and Wellman, H. M. (1994). The theory theory. In L. A. Hirschfeld and S. A. Gelman (eds.), *Mapping the mind: domain specificity in cognition and culture* (pp. 257–293). New York: Cambridge University Press.

Gratch, G. (1982). Responses to hidden persons and things by 5-, 9-, and 16-month-old infants in a visual tracking situation. *Developmental Psychology* 18 : 232–237.

Greco, C., Hayne, H., and Rovee-Collier, C. (1990). Roles of function, reminding, and variability in categorization by 3-month-old infants. *Journal of Experimental Psychology: Learning, Memory, and Cognition* 16 : 617–633.

Haake, R. J., and Somerville, S. C. (1985). Development of logical search skills in infancy. *Developmental Psychology* 21 : 176–186.

Harris, M., Barrett, M., Jones, D., and Brookes, S. (1988). Linguistic input and early word meaning. *Journal of Child Language* 15 : 77–94.

Harris, P. (1987). The development of search. In P. Salapatek and L. Cohen (eds.), *Handbook of infant perception* (vol. 2, pp. 155–207). New York: Academic Press.

Harris, P. (1991). The work of the imagination. In A. Whiten (ed.), *Natural theories of mind: evolution, development, and simulation of everyday mindreading* (pp. 283–304). Cambridge, Mass.: Basil Blackwell.

Hayne, H., Rovee-Collier, C., and Perris, E. E. (1987). Categorization and memory retrieval by three-month-olds. *Child Development* 58 : 750–767.

Hempel, C. G. (1965). *Aspects of scientific explanation and other essays in the philosophy of science.* New York: Free Press.

Hobson, P. (1993). *Autism and the development of mind.* Hillsdale, N.J.: Erlbaum.

Hofsten, C. von (1980). Predictive reaching for moving objects by human infants. *Journal of Experimental Child Psychology* 30 : 369–382.

Hofsten, C. von (1982). Eye-hand coordination in the newborn. *Developmental Psychology* 18 : 450–461.

Hofsten, C. von, and Lindhagen, K. (1979). Observations on the development of reaching for moving objects. *Journal of Experimental Child Psychology* 28 : 158–173.

Hofsten, C. von, Spelke, E., Feng, Q., and Vishton, P. (1994). Infant's predictive head turning and reaching for fully visible and occluded objects. Paper presented at the Ninth International Conference on Infant Studies, Paris, June.

Hood, B., and Willatts, P. (1986). Reaching in the dark to an object's remembered position: evidence for object permanence in 5-month-old infants. *British Journal of Developmental Psychology* 4 : 57–65.

Jackendoff, R. S. (1983). *Semantics and cognition.* Cambridge: MIT Press.

Johnson, S. P., and Aslin, R. N. (1995). Perception of object unity in 2-month-old infants. *Developmental Psychology* 31 : 739–745.

Kahneman, D., Slovic, P., and Tversky, A. (1982). *Judgment under uncertainty: heuristics and biases.* New York: Cambridge University Press.

Karmiloff-Smith, A. (1979). *A functional approach to child language: a study of determiners and reference.* New York: Cambridge University Press.

Karmiloff-Smith, A. (1988). The child is a theoretician, not an inductivist. *Mind and Language* 3 : 183–195.

Karmiloff-Smith, A. (1992). *Beyond modularity: a developmental perspective on cognitive science.* Cambridge: MIT press.

Karmiloff-Smith, A., and Inhelder, B. (1974). If you want to get ahead, get a theory. *Cognition* 3 : 195–212.

Kaye, K., and Fogel, A. (1980). The temporal structure of face-to-face communication between mothers and infants. *Developmental Psychology* 16 : 454–464.

Keil, F. C. (1987). Conceptual development and category structure. In U. Neisser (ed.), *Concepts and conceptual development: ecological and intellectual factors in categorization* (pp. 175–200). Cambridge: Cambridge University Press.

Keil, F. C. (1989). *Concepts, kinds, and cognitive development.* Cambridge: MIT Press.

Kellman, P. J., and Spelke, E. S. (1983). Perception of partly occluded objects in infancy. *Cognitive Psychology* 15 : 483–524.

Kellman, P. J., Spelke, E. S., and Short, K. R. (1986). Infant perception of object unity from translatory motion in depth and vertical translation. *Child Development* 57 : 72–86.

Kelly, K. (1996). *The logic of reliable inquiry.* Oxford: Oxford University Press.

Kepler, Johannes (1992). *New astronomy.* Cambridge: Cambridge University Press. First published in 1609 as *Astronomia nova.*

Kermoian, R., and Campos, J. J. (1988). Locomotor experience: a facilitator of spatial cognitive development. *Child Development* 59 : 908–917.

Kitcher, P. (1993). *The advancement of science: science without legend, objectivity without illusions.* Oxford: Oxford University Press.

Kitcher, P., and Salmon, W. C. (eds.) (1989). *Scientific explanation.* Minneapolis: University of Minnesota Press.

Kornblith, H. (ed.) (1985). *Naturalizing epistemology.* Cambridge: MIT Press.

Kripke, S. A. (1980). *Naming and necessity.* Cambridge: Harvard University Press.

Kuczaj, S. A. (1982). Acquisition of word meaning in the context of the development of the semantic system. In C. J. Brainerd and M. Pressley (eds.), *Verbal processes in children: progress in cognitive development research* (pp. 95–123). New York: Springer-Verlag.

Kuhl, P. K. (1979). Speech perception in early infancy: perceptual constancy for spectrally dissimilar vowel categories. *Journal of the Acoustical Society of America* 66 : 1668–1679.

Kuhl, P. K. (1983). Perception of auditory equivalence classes for speech in early infancy. *Infant Behavior and Development* 6 : 263–285.

Kuhl, P. K., and Meltzoff, A. N. (1982). The bimodal perception of speech in infancy. *Science* 218 : 1138–1141.

Kuhl, P. K., and Meltzoff, A. N. (1984). The intermodal representation of speech in infants. *Infant Behavior and Development* 7 : 361–381.

Kuhn, T. S. (1962). *The structure of scientific revolutions.* Chicago: University of Chicago Press.

Kuhn, T. S. (1977). *The essential tension.* Chicago: University of Chicago Press.

Lakatos, I. (1970). Falsification and the methodology of scientific research programmes. In I. Lakatos and A. Musgrave (eds.), *Criticism and the growth of knowledge* (pp. 91–195). Cambridge: Cambridge University Press.

Lakoff, G. (1987). *Women, fire, and dangerous things.* Chicago: University of Chicago Press.

Landau, B., and Jackendoff, R. (1993). "What" and "where" in spatial language and spatial cognition. *Behavioral and Brain Sciences* 16 : 217–265.

Langer, J. (1982). From prerepresentational to representational cognition. In G. E. Forman (ed.), *Action and thought: from sensorimotor schemes to symbolic operations* (pp. 37–63). New York: Academic Press.

Langley, P., Simon, H. A., Bradshaw, G., and Zytkow, J. (1987). *Scientific discovery.* Cambridge: MIT Press.

Laudan, L. (1977). *Progress and its problems: towards a theory of scientific growth.* Berkeley: University of California Press.

LeCompte, G. K., and Gratch, G. (1972). Violation of a rule as a method of diagnosing infants' levels of object concept. *Child Development* 43 : 385–396.

Lempers, J. D., Flavell, E. R., and Flavell, J. H. (1977). *The development in very young children of tacit knowledge concerning visual perception.* Genetic Psychology Monographs no. 95. Provincetown, Mass.: Journal Press.

Leslie, A. M. (1982). The perception of causality in infants. *Perception* 11 : 173–186.

Leslie, A. M. (1988). Some implications of pretense for mechanisms underlying the child's theory of mind. In J. W. Astington, P. L. Harris, and D. R. Olson (eds.), *Developing theories of mind* (pp. 19–46). New York: Cambridge University Press.

Leslie, A. M., and Keeble, S. (1987). Do six-month-old infants perceive causality? *Cognition* 25 : 265–288.

Leslie, A. M., and Roth, D. (1993). What autism teaches us about metarepresentation. In S. Baron-Cohen, H. Tager-Flusberg, and D. J. Cohen (eds.), *Understanding other minds: perspectives from autism* (pp. 83–111). New York: Oxford University Press.

Levi, I. (1980). *The enterprise of knowledge: an essay on knowledge, credal probability, and chance.* Cambridge: MIT Press.

Levinson, S. C. (1994). Vision, shape, and linguistic description: Tzeltal body part terminology and object description. *Linguistics* 32 : 791–885.

Lifter, K., and Bloom, L. (1989). Object knowledge and the emergence of language. *Infant Behavior and Development* 12 : 395–423.

Lipsitt, L. P. (1990). Learning processes in the human newborn: sensitization, habituation, and classical conditioning. In A. Diamond (ed.), *The development and neural bases of higher cognitive functions,* Annals of the New York Academy of Sciences, (no. 608, pp. 113–127). New York: New York Academy of Sciences.

Lock, A. (1980). *The guided reinvention of language.* New York: Academic Press.

Madole, K. L., Oakes, L. M., and Cohen, L. B. (1993). Developmental changes in infants' attention to function and form-function correlations. *Cognitive Development* 8 : 189–209.

Mandler, J. M., and Bauer, P. J. (1988). The cradle of categorization: is the basic level basic? *Cognitive Development* 3 : 247–264.

Marcus, G. F., Pinker, S., Ullman, M. H., Rosen, T. J., and Xu, F. (1992). *Overregularization in language acquisition.* Monographs of the Society for Research in Child Development vol. 57, no. 4. Chicago: Society for Research in Child Development.

Markman, E. M. (1987). How children constrain the possible meanings of words. In U. Neisser (ed.), *Concepts and conceptual development: ecological and intellectual factors in categorization* (pp. 255–287). New York: Cambridge University Press.

Markman, E. M. (1989). *Categorization and naming in children: problems of induction.* Cambridge: MIT Press.

Markman, E. M. (1992). Constraints on word learning: speculations about their nature, origins, and domain specificity. In M. R. Gunnar and M. Maratsos (eds.), *Modularity and constraints in language and cognition.* Minnesota Symposia on Child Psychology (no. 25, pp. 59–101). Hillsdale, N.J.: Erlbaum.

Marr, D. (1982). *Vision: a computational investigation into the human representation and processing of visual information.* San Francisco: W. H. Freeman.

McCune-Nicolich, L. (1981). The cognitive bases of relational words in the single word period. *Journal of Child Language* 8 : 15–34.

McShane, J. (1980). *Learning to talk.* New York: Cambridge University Press.

Meltzoff, A. N. (1988a). Infant imitation after a 1-week delay: long-term memory for novel acts and multiple stimuli. *Developmental Psychology* 24 : 470–476.

Meltzoff, A. N. (1988b). Infant imitation and memory: nine-month-olds in immediate and deferred tests. *Child Development* 59 : 217–225.

Meltzoff, A. N. (1990). Towards a developmental cognitive science: the implications of cross-modal matching and imitation for the development of representation and memory in infancy. In A. Diamond (ed.), *The development and neural bases of higher cognitive functions,* Annals of the New York Academy of Sciences (no. 608, pp. 1–31). New York: New York Academy of Sciences.

Meltzoff, A. N. (1993). Molyneux's babies: cross-modal perception, imitation, and the mind of the preverbal infant. In N. Eilan, R. McCarthy, and B. Brewer (eds.), *Spatial representation: problems in philosophy and psychology* (pp. 219–235). Cambridge, Mass.: Blackwell.

Meltzoff, A. N. (1995a). Understanding the intentions of others: re-enactment of intended acts by 18-month-old children. *Developmental Psychology* 31 : 838–850.

Meltzoff, A. N. (1995b). What infant memory tells us about infantile amnesia: long-term recall and deferred imitation. *Journal of Experimental Child Psychology* 59 : 497–515.

Meltzoff, A. N., and Borton, R. W. (1979). Intermodal matching by human neonates. *Nature* 282 : 403–404.

Meltzoff, A. N., and Gopnik, A. (1993). The role of imitation in understanding persons and developing a theory of mind. In S. Baron-Cohen, H. Tager-Flusberg, and D. J. Cohen (eds.), *Understanding other minds: perspectives from autism* (pp. 335–366). New York: Oxford University Press.

Meltzoff, A. N., and Kuhl, P. K. (1994). Faces and speech: intermodal processing of biologically-relevant signals in infants and adults. In D. J. Lewkowicz and R. Lickliter (eds.), *The development of intersensory perception: comparative perspectives* (pp. 335–369). Hillsdale, N.J.: Erlbaum.

Meltzoff, A. N., and Moore, M. K. (1977). Imitation of facial and manual gestures by human neonates. *Science* 198 : 75–78.

Meltzoff, A. N., and Moore, M. K. (1983). Newborn infants imitate adult facial gestures. *Child Development* 54 : 702–709.

Meltzoff, A. N., and Moore, M. K. (1989). Imitation in newborn infants: exploring the range of gestures imitated and the underlying mechanisms. *Developmental Psychology* 25 : 954–962.

Meltzoff, A. N., and Moore, M. K. (1992). Early imitation within a functional framework: the importance of person identity, movement, and development. *Infant Behavior and Development* 15 : 479–505.

Meltzoff, A. N., and Moore, M. K. (1993). Why faces are special to infants—On connecting the attraction of faces and infants' ability for imitation and cross-modal processing. In B. de Boysson-Bardies, S. de Schonen, P. Jusczyk, P. McNeilage, and J. Morton (eds.), *Developmental neurocognition: speech and face processing in the first year of life* (pp. 211–225). Dordrecht, Netherlands: Kluwer Academic Publishers.

Meltzoff, A. N., and Moore, M. K. (1994). Imitation, memory, and the representation of persons. *Infant Behavior and Development* 17 : 83–99.

Meltzoff, A. N., and Moore, M. K. (1995a). A theory of the role of imitation in the emergence of self. In P. Rochat (ed.), *The self in early infancy: theory and research* (pp. 73–93). Amsterdam: North-Holland-Elsevier Science Publishers.

Meltzoff, A. N., and Moore, M. K. (1995b). Infants' understanding of people and things: from body imitation to folk psychology. In J. Bermúdez, A. J. Marcel, and N. Eilan (eds.), *The body and the self* (pp. 43–69). Cambridge: MIT Press.

Mervis, C. B. (1987). Child-basic object categories and early lexical development. In U. Neisser (ed.), *Concepts and conceptual development: ecological and intellectual factors in categorization* (pp. 201–234). New York: Cambridge University Press.

Mervis, C. B., and Bertrand, J. (1993). Acquisition of early object labels: the roles of operating principles and input. In A. P. Kaiser and D. B. Gray (eds.), *Enhancing children's communication: research foundations for intervention* (pp. 287–316). Baltimore: Brookes.

Mervis, C. B., and Bertrand, J. (1994). Acqustion of the novel name-nameless category principle. *Child Development* 65 : 1646–1662.

Mervis, C. B., Mervis, C. A., Johnson, K. E., and Bertrand, J. (1992). Studying early lexical development: the value of the systematic diary method. *Advances in Infancy Research* 7 : 291–378.

Michotte, A. (1962). *Causalité, permanence et réalité phénoménales.* Louvain: Publications Universitaires.

Monnier, C. M. (1980). *La genèse de l'éxperimentation: l'exploration d'objets nouveaux par bébés.* Genève: Imprimerie Nationale.

Moore, M. K. (1975). Object permanence and object identity: a stage-developmental model. Paper presented at the meeting of the Society for Research in Child Development, Denver, April.

Moore, M. K., Borton, R., and Darby, B. L. (1978). Visual tracking in young infants: evidence for object identity or object permanence? *Journal of Experimental Child Psychology* 25 : 183–198.

Moore, M. K., and Meltzoff, A. N. (1978). Object permanence, imitation, and language development in infancy: toward a neo-Piagetian perspective on communicative and cognitive development. In F. D. Minifie and L. L. Lloyd (eds.), *Communicative and cognitive abilities—early behavioral assessment* (pp. 151–184). Baltimore: University Park Press.

Morton, J., and Johnson, M. H. (1991). CONSPEC and CONLERN: a two-process theory of infant face recognition. *Psychological Review* 98 : 164–181.

Munakata, Y., McClelland, J., Johnson, M., and Siegler, R. (1994). Rethinking object permanence: do the ends justify means-ends? Paper presented at the Ninth International Conference on Infant Studies, Paris, June.

Murphy, G. L., and Medin, D. L. (1985). The role of theories in conceptual coherence. *Psychological Review* 92 : 289–316.

Murray, L., and Trevarthen, C. (1985). Emotional regulation of interactions between two-month-olds and their mothers. In T. M. Field and N. A. Fox (eds.), *Social perception in infants* (pp. 177–197). Norwood, N.J.: Ablex.

Nagel, E. (1961). *The structure of science.* New York: Harcourt, Brace, and World.

Nelson, K. (1973). *Structure and strategy in learning to talk.* Monographs of the Society for Research in Child Development, vol. 38, no. 1–2 (serial no. 149). Chicago: Society for Research in Child Development.

Nelson, K. (1975). The nominal shift in semantic-syntactic development. *Cognitive Psychology* 7 : 461–479.

Nelson, K. (1986). *Event knowledge: structure and function in development.* Hillsdale, N.J.: Erlbaum.

Nelson, K. (1988). Constraints on word learning? *Cognitive Development* 3 : 221–246.

Nelson, K., Hampson, J., and Shaw, L. K. (1993). Nouns and early lexicons: evidence, explanations, implications. *Journal of Child Language* 20 : 61–84.

Nelson, K., and Lucariello, J. (1985). The development of meaning in first words. In M. D. Barrett (ed.), *Children's single-word speech* (pp. 59–86). New York: Wiley.

Oakes, L. M., and Cohen, L. B. (1995). Infant causal perception. In L. P. Lipsitt and C. Rovee-Collier (eds.), *Advances in infancy research* (vol. 9, pp. 1–54). Norwood, N.J.: Ablex.

Osherson, D. N., Stob, M., and Weinstein, S. (1986). *Systems that learn: an introduction to learning theory for cognitive and computer scientists.* Cambridge: MIT Press.

Papousek, H. (1969). Individual variability in learned responses in human infants. In R. J. Robinson (ed.), *Brain and early behavior* (pp. 251–266). London: Academic Press.

Perner, J. (1991). *Understanding the representational mind.* Cambridge: MIT Press.

Piaget, J. (1952). *The origins of intelligence in children*. New York: International Universities Press.

Piaget, J. (1954). *The construction of reality in the child*. New York: Basic Books.

Piaget, J. (1962). *Play, dreams, and imitation in childhood*. New York: Norton.

Pinker, S. (1984). *Language learnability and language development*. Cambridge: Harvard University Press.

Pinker, S. (1989). *Learnability and cognition: the acquisition of argument structure*. Cambridge: MIT Press.

Popper, K. R. (1965). *Conjectures and refutations: the growth of scientific knowledge* (2nd ed.). New York: Basic Books.

Putnam, H. (1975). *Philosophical papers*, vol. 2, *Mind, language, and reality*. New York: Cambridge University Press.

Pylyshyn, Z. W. (1984). *Computation and cognition*. Cambridge: MIT Press.

Quine, W. V. O. (1960). *Word and object*. Cambridge: MIT Press.

Quine, W. V. O. (1961). Two dogmas of empiricism. In his *From a logical point of view* (pp. 20–46). New York: Harper and Row.

Quine, W. V. O., and Ullian, J. S. (1970). *The web of belief*. New York: Random House.

Reddy, V. (1991). Playing with others' expectations: teasing and mucking about in the first year. In A. Whiten (ed.), *Natural theories of mind: evolution, development, and simulation of everyday mindreading* (pp. 143–158). Cambridge, Mass.: Basil Blackwell.

Repacholi, B. (1996). Components of children's early emotion understanding: evidence from 14- and 18-month-olds. Ph.D. dissertation, University of California at Berkeley.

Repacholi, B., and Gopnik, A. (in press). Early understanding of desires: evidence from 14 and 18 month olds. *Developmental Psychology*.

Reznick, J. S., and Goldfield, B. A. (1992). Rapid change in lexical development in comprehension and production. *Developmental Psychology* 28 : 406–413.

Ricciuti, H. N. (1965). Object grouping and selective ordering behaviors in infants 12 to 24 months old. *Merrill-Palmer Quarterly* 11 : 129–148.

Rips, L. (1989). Similarity, typicality, and categorization. In S. Vosniadou and A. Ortony (eds.), *Similarity and analogical reasoning*. New York: Cambridge University Press.

Rispoli, M. (1987). The acquisition of the transitive and intransitive action verb categories in Japanese. *First Language* 7 : 183–200.

Roberts, K. (1988). Retrieval of a basic-level category in prelinguistic infants. *Developmental Psychology* 24 : 21–27.

Roberts, K., and Horowitz, F. D. (1986). Basic level categorization in seven- and nine-month-old infants. *Journal of Child Language* 13 : 191–208.

Roberts, K., and Jacob, M. (1991). Linguistic versus attentional influences on non-linguistic categorization in 15-month-old infants. *Cognitive Development* 6 : 355–375.

Rock, I. (1983). *The logic of perception.* Cambridge: MIT Press.

Rogoff, B. (1990). *Apprenticeship in thinking: cognitive development in social context.* New York: Oxford University Press.

Rosch, E., and Mervis, C. B. (1975). Family resemblances: studies in the internal structure of categories. *Cognitive Psychology* 7 : 573–605.

Rosch, E., Mervis, C. B., Gray, W. D., Johnson, D. M., and Boyes-Braem, P. (1976). Basic objects in natural categories. *Cognitive Psychology* 8 : 382–439.

Rovee-Collier, C. (1984). The ontogeny of learning and memory in human infancy. In R. Kail and N. E. Spear (eds.), *Comparative perspectives on the development of memory* (pp. 103–134). Hillsdale, N.J.: Lawrence Erlbaum.

Rovee-Collier, C. (1990). The "memory system" of prelinguistic infants. In A. Diamond (ed.), *The development and neural bases of higher cognitive functions.* Annals of the New York Academy of Sciences (no. 608, pp. 517–542). New York: New York Academy of Sciences.

Rovee-Collier, C. K., and Gekoski, M. J. (1979). The economics of infancy: a review of conjugate reinforcement. In H. W. Reese and L. P. Lipsitt (eds.), *Advances in child development and behavior* (vol. 13, pp. 195–255). New York: Academic Press.

Rovee-Collier, C. K., Griesler, P. C., and Earley, L. A. (1985). Contextual determinants of retrieval in three-month-old infants. *Learning and Motivation* 16 : 139–157.

Rovee-Collier, C. K., and Lipsitt, L. P. (1982). Learning, adaptation, and memory in the newborn. In P. Stratton (ed.), *Psychobiology of the human newborn* (pp. 147–190). New York: John Wiley and Sons.

Rovee-Collier, C. K., Morrongiello, B. A., Aron, M., and Kupersmidt, J. (1978). Topographical response differentiation and reversal in 3-month-old infants. *Infant Behavior and Development* 1 : 323–333.

Schank, R. C., and Abelson, R. P. (1977). *Scripts, plans, goals, and understanding.* Hillsdale, N.J.: Erlbaum.

Scheffler, I. (1967). *Science and subjectivity.* Indianapolis: Bobbs-Merrill.

Searle, J. R. (1983). *Intentionality: an essay in the philosophy of mind.* New York: Cambridge University Press.

Sera, M. D., Reittinger, E. L., and Castillo-Pintado, J. (1991). Developing definitions of objects and events in English and Spanish speakers. *Cognitive Development* 6 : 119–142.

Shatz, M. (1991). Using cross-cultural research to inform us about the role of language in development. In M. H. Bornstein (ed.), *Cultural approaches to parenting* (pp. 139–153). Hillsdale, N.J.: Erlbaum.

Sherman, T. (1985). Categorization skills in infants. *Child Development* 56 : 1561–1573.

Siegler, R. S. (ed.) (1990). *Children's thinking*. Englewood Cliffs, N.J.: Prentice-Hall.

Sinclair, H. (1970). The transition from sensory-motor behaviour to symbolic activity. *Interchange* 1 : 119–126.

Slater, A., and Morison, V. (1985). Shape constancy and slant perception at birth. *Perception* 14 : 337–344.

Slater, A. M., Mattock, A., and Brown, E. (1990). Size constancy at birth: newborn infants' responses to retinal and real size. *Journal of Experimental Child Psychology* 49 : 314–322.

Slater, A., Morison, V., Somers, M., Mattock, A., Brown, E., and Taylor, D. (1990). Newborn and older infants' perception of partly occluded objects. *Infant Behavior and Development* 13 : 33–49.

Slaughter, V. (1995). Conceptual coherence in the child's theory of mind. Paper presented at the meeting of the Society for Research in Child Development, Indianapolis, Ind, March.

Slaughter, V., and Gopnik, A. (in press). Conceptual coherence in the child's theory of mind. *Child Development*.

Slobin, D. I. (1973). Cognitive prerequisites for the development of grammar. In C. A. Ferguson and D. I. Slobin (eds.), *Studies of child language development* (pp. 175–210). New York: Holt, Rinehart, and Winston.

Slobin, D. I. (1982). Universal and particular in the acquisition of language. In E. Wanner and L. R. Gleitman (eds.), *Language acquisition: the state of the art* (pp. 128–170). New York: Cambridge University Press.

Slobin, D. I. (1985). Cross-linguistic evidence for the language-making capacity. In D. I. Slobin (ed.), *The cross-linguistic study of language acquistion*, vol. 2, *Theoretical issues* (pp. 1157–1256). Hillsdale, N.J.: Erlbaum.

Soja, N., Carey, S., and Spelke, E. S. (1991). Ontological categories guide young children's inductions of word meaning: object terms and substance terms. *Cognition* 38 : 179–211.

Spelke, E. S. (1976). Infants' intermodal perception of events. *Cognitive Psychology* 8 : 553–560.

Spelke, E. S. (1979). Perceiving bimodally specified events in infancy. *Developmental Psychology* 15 : 626–636.

Spelke, E. S. (1987). The development of intermodal perception. In P. Salapatek and L. Cohen (eds.), *Handbook of infant perception*, vol. 2, *From perception to cognition* (pp. 233–273). New York: Academic Press.

Spelke, E. S. (1990). Principles of object perception. *Cognitive Science* 14 : 29–56.

Spelke, E. S. (1991). Physical knowledge on infancy: reflection on Piaget's theory. In S. Carey and R. Gelman (eds.), *The epigenesis of mind: essays on biology and cognition* (pp. 133–169). Hillsdale, N.J.: Erlbaum.

Spelke, E. S. (1994). Initial knowledge: six suggestions. *Cognition* 50 : 431–445.

Spelke, E. S., Breinlinger, K., Macomber, J., and Jacobsen, K. (1992). Origins of knowledge. *Psychological Review* 99 : 605–632.

Spelke, E. S., Katz, G., Purcell, S. E., Ehrlich, S. M., and Breinlinger, K. (1994). Early knowledge of object motion: continuity and inertia. *Cognition* 51 : 131–176.

Spelke, E. S., Kestenbaum, R., Wein, D., and Simons, D. J. (1995). Spatiotemporal continuity, smoothness of motion, and object identity in infancy. *British Journal of Developmental Psychology* 13 : 113–142.

Spelke, E. S., and Van de Walle, G. A. (1993). Perceiving and reasoning about objects: insights from infants. In N. Eilan, R. McCarthy, and B. Brewer (eds.), *Spatial representation: problems in philosophy and psychology* (pp. 132–161). Cambridge, Mass.: Blackwell.

Starkey, D. (1981). The origins of concept formation: object sorting and object preference in early infancy. *Child Development* 52 : 489–497.

Stich, S. P. (1983). *From folk psychology to cognitive science: the case against belief.* Cambridge: MIT Press.

Strauss, M. S. (1979). Abstraction of prototypical information by adults and 10-month-old infants. *Journal of Experimental Psychology: Human Learning and Memory* 5 : 618–632.

Streri, A. (1987). Tactile discrimination of shape and intermodal transfer in 2- to 3-month-old infants. *British Journal of Developmental Psychology* 5 : 213–220.

Sugarman, S. (1983). *Children's early thought: developments in classification.* New York: Cambridge University Press.

Talmy, L. (1985). Lexicalization patterns: semantic structure in lexical forms. In T. Shopen (ed.), *Language typology and syntactic description* (pp. 57–149). New York: Cambridge University Press.

Tanouye, E. K. (1979). The acquisition of verbs in Japanese children. *Papers and Reports on Child Language Development* 17 : 49–56.

Tedlock, B. (1992). *The beautiful and the dangerous: conversations with the Zuni Indians.* New York: Viking.

Thelen, E., and Smith, L. B. (1994). *A dynamic systems approach to the development of cognition and action.* Cambridge: MIT Press.

Tomasello, M. (1992). *First verbs: a case study of early grammatical development.* New York: Cambridge University Press.

Tomasello, M., and Farrar, M. J. (1984). Cognitive bases of lexical development: object permanence and relational words. *Journal of Child Language* 11 : 477–493.

Tomasello, M., and Farrar, M. J. (1986). Object permanence and relational words: a lexical training study. *Journal of Child Language* 13 : 495–505.

Tomasello, M., Kruger, A. C., and Ratner, H. H. (1993). Cultural learning. *Behavioral and Brain Sciences* 16 : 495–552.

Trevarthen, C. (1979). Communication and cooperation in early infancy: a description of primary intersubjectivity. In M. Bullowa (ed.), *Before speech* (pp. 321–347). New York: Cambridge University Press.

Trevarthen, C., and Hubley, P. (1978). Secondary intersubjectivity: confidence, confiding, and acts of meaning in the first year. In A. Lock (ed.), *Action, gesture, and symbol: the emergence of language* (pp. 183–229). New York: Academic Press.

Tronick, E., Als, H., Adamson, L., Wise, S., and Brazelton, T. B. (1978). The infant's response to entrapment between contradictory messages in face-to-face interaction. *Journal of the American Academy of Child and Adolescent Psychiatry* 17 : 1–13.

Tronick, E., Als, H., and Brazelton, T. B. (1980). Monadic phases: a structural descriptive analysis of infant-mother face to face interaction. *Merrill-Palmer Quarterly* 26 : 3–24.

Uzgiris, I. C., and Hunt, J. M. (1975). *Assessment in infancy: ordinal scales of psychological development.* Urbana: University of Illinois Press.

Uzgiris, I. C., and Hunt, J. M. (1987). *Infant performance and experience: new findings with the ordinal scales.* Urbana: University of Illinois Press.

Van Fraassen, B. C. (1980). *The scientific image.* New York: Oxford University Press.

Vihman, M. M. (1993). The construction of a phonological system. In B. de Boysson-Bardies, S. de Schonen, P. Jusczyk, P. McNeilage, and J. Morton (eds.), *Developmental neurocognition: speech and face processing in the first year of life* (pp. 411–419). Dordrecht, Netherlands: Kluwer Academic Publishers.

Vygotsky, L. S. (1962). *Thought and language.* Cambridge: MIT Press.

Warhaft, S. (ed.) (1965). *Francis Bacon: a selection* of his works. Dover, N.H.: Odyssey Press.

Watson, J. S. (1967). Memory and "contingency analysis" in infant learning. *Merrill-Palmer Quarterly* 13 : 55–76.

Watson, J. S. (1972). Smiling, cooing, and the "game." *Merrill-Palmer Quarterly* 18: 323–339.

Watson, J. S. (1979). Perception of contingency as a determinant of social responsiveness. In E. Tohman (ed.), *The origins of social responsiveness* (pp. 33–64). Hillsdale, N.J.: Erlbaum.

Waxman, S. (1991). Convergences between semantic and conceptual organization in the preschool years. In J. Byrnes and S. Gelman (eds.), *Perspectives on language and thought: interrelations in development.* New York: Cambridge University Press.

Weist, R. M., Wysocka, H., and Lyytinen, P. (1991). A cross-linguistic perspective on the development of temporal systems. *Journal of Child Language* 18 : 67–92.

Wellman, H. M. (1985). The child's theory of mind: the development of conceptions of cognition. In S. R. Yussen (ed.), *The growth of reflection in children.* Orlando: Academic Press.

Wellman, H. M. (1990). *The child's theory of mind.* Cambridge: MIT Press.

Wellman, H. M., Cross, D., and Bartsch, K. (1987). *Infant search and object permanence: a meta-analysis of the A-not-B error.* Monographs of the Society for Research in Child Development, vol. 51, no. 3. Chicago: Society for Research in Child Development.

Wellman, H. M., and Gelman, S. A. (1992). Cognitive development: foundational theories of core domains. *Annual Review of Psychology* 43 : 337–375.

Wellman, H. M., and Woolley, J. D. (1990). From simple desires to ordinary beliefs: the early development of everyday psychology. *Cognition* 35 : 245–275.

Whorf, B. L. (1956). *Language, thought, and reality.* Cambridge: MIT Press.

Willatts, P. (1984). The stage-IV infant's solution of problems requiring the use of supports. *Infant Behavior and Development* 7 : 125–134.

Willatts, P. (1985). Adjustment of means-ends coordination and the representation of spatial relations in the production of search errors by infants. *British Journal of Developmental Psychology* 3 : 259–272.

Wimmer, H., and Perner, J. (1983). Beliefs about beliefs: representation and constraining function of wrong beliefs in young children's understanding of deception. *Cognition* 13 : 103–128.

Xu, F., and Carey, S. (in press). Infants' metaphysics: the case of numerical identity. *Cognitive Psychology.*

Yaniv, I., and Shatz, M. (1988). Children's understanding of perceptibility. In J. W. Astington, P. L. Harris, and D. R. Olson (eds.), *Developing theories of mind* (pp. 93–108). New York: Cambridge University Press.

Yonas, A., and Granrud, C. E. (1985). Development of visual space perception in young infants. In J. Mehler and R. Fox (eds.), *Neonate cognition: beyond the blooming, buzzing, confusion* (pp. 45–67). Hillsdale, N.J.: Erlbaum.

Younger, B. (1985). The segregation of items into categories by ten-month-old infants. *Child Development* 56 : 1574–1583.

Younger, B. (1990). Infants' detection of correlations among feature categories. *Child Development* 61 : 614–620.

Younger, B. (1992). Developmental change in infant categorization: the perception of correlations among facial features. *Child Development* 63 : 1526–1535.

Younger, B., and Cohen, L. B. (1983). Infant perception of correlations among attributes. *Child Development* 54 : 858–869.

Younger, B., and Cohen, L. B. (1986). Developmental change in infants' perception of correlations among attributes. *Child Development* 57 : 803–815.

Yuill, N. (1984). Young children's coordination of motive and outcome in judgments of satisfaction and morality. *British Journal of Developmental Psychology* 2 : 73–81.

Zajonc, R. B., Murphy, S. T., and Inglehart, M. (1989). Feeling and facial efference: implications of the vascular theory of emotion. *Psychological Review* 96 : 395–416.

Index